Praise for *Saving Journalism*

"A brilliant and unexpected study of how journalism came to be the enfant terrible of the modern world, and what it would mean to lose it."

– **Tom Holland, historian, and multiple prize-winning author of** *Dominion, Dynasty, Millennium,* **and** *Persian Fire.*

"'Saving Journalism' is an important book and Dr Jenny Taylor is eminently equipped to write it. The fourth estate is a vital part of a healthy democracy but, alas, ill fares the land! Jenny excavates afresh the roots of journalism, gives poignant examples of her own and others' experience, and lays the groundwork for a renewal of healthy journalism."

– **Revd Professor Craig Bartholomew, Kirby Laing Institute, Cambridge, U.K.**

"Over a distinguished career, Jenny Taylor has reported from some of the most dangerous places in the world, studied the post-Reformation origins of journalism, and analyzed its current woes, especially the pernicious effects of secularism. She brings these experiences together in a lively overview of what ails news and what can be done about it. All journalists should read it, as should many others. There is nothing else quite like it."

– **Paul Marshall, Senior Fellow, Hudson Institute, Washington DC; and Distinguished Professor, holding the Jerry & Susie Wilson Chair, at Baylor University, USA**

SAVING JOURNALISM

SAVING JOURNALISM

The Rise, Demise and SURVIVAL of the NEWS

Dr Jenny M Taylor

Pippa Rann
books & media

Pippa Rann books & media

An imprint of
Salt Desert Media Group Limited,
7 Mulgrave Chambers, 26 Mulgrave Rd,
Sutton SM2 6LE, England, UK.
Email: publisher@pipparannbooks.com
Website: www.pipparannbooks.com

Copyright © Dr Jenny M Taylor 2025

The moral right of the author has been asserted. The views and opinions expressed in this book are the author's own and the facts are as reported by her, which have been verified to the extent possible, but the publishers are not in any way liable for the same.

All rights reserved. No part of this book may be reproduced by any mechanical, photographic, or electronic process, or in the form of a phonographic recording; nor may it be stored in a retrieval system, transmitted or otherwise be copied for public or private use – other than for 'fair use' as brief quotations embodied in articles and reviews, without prior written permission of the publisher.

ISBN 978-1-913738-33-4

Printed and bound at Replika Press

This book is dedicated posthumously, and with her permission, to Fleur de Villiers, former political editor of *The Sunday Times*, Johannesburg, and foreign correspondent and leader writer at *The Times*, London.

Contents

Acknowledgements 11

PART ONE: THE FOURTH ESTATE 13

STORY—The children's story they could not tell:
Northern Uganda's war 14
Preface 19
STORY—Vicars rhymes with knickers 22
Chapter 1: A Licence to Harm 33
Chapter 2: Prophecy, Discourse and Reality 43
Chapter 3: The Representation of Reality 57

**PART TWO: PROTEST AND
MASS COMMUNICATION** 77

Chapter 4: Putting Down the Mighty 79
Chapter 5: The Nightingale Sings 99
Chapter 6: Pamphlet Revolution: Content Is King 119
Chapter 7: The Religious Matrix of English News 137
Chapter 8: "Mainly a Matter of Spiritual Energy" 163
Chapter 9: First Newspapers in New England,
India and China 179
STORY—Healing the broken:
The Marine Surgeon's tale 203

**PART THREE: SECULARIZATION AND
THE UNDOING OF THOUGHT** 207

Chapter 10: Losing the Plot 209
STORY—"Truth is what we say it is" 223
Chapter 11: Neutrality or Truth?
Knowing What to Report 229
Chapter 12: The Fourth Estate: Recovery of a Mission ... 247
STORY—The people that don't exist 254
STORY—Building out of the ruins 256
Chapter 13: Conclusion and a Call to Action 259

Epilogue: Lapido Media—religious literacy
in world affairs 263
Appendix 1: "Taking spirituality seriously: Northern
Uganda and Britain's 'Break the Silence' Campaign" 273
Appendix 2: Definitions of journalism 299
Endnotes 301
Bibliography 327
Index 337

Acknowledgements

There are many people I have to thank for the part they played in the realization of this project, not least being my staff, contractors and interns at Lapido Media. Carmen Schultz, Jenny Mattey, Richard Porritt, Hmangaiha Renthlei (in India), Sophie Willis and Greg Webb were heaven-sent. As were Revd Dr Arne Fjeldstad, Ann Warren, Revd John Ray, Peter Penfold, Dan Damon and Dr Nick Isbister who were on the boards over the years. Tom Holland gamely agreed to be our Patron. All gaily and with skill and passion supported a pioneering experiment in religiously literate reportage, wherever it might lead. Tony Collins at Lion Hudson originally commissioned my story before the company folded. Vishal Mangalwadi gave me the idea of reflecting on my career as part of the long stream of prophetic journalism. The first attempt at this appeared as a contribution in his *This Book Changed Your World*. Revd Professor Craig Bartholomew, Director of the Kirby Laing Centre for Theology in Public Life at Cambridge, created a post for me from which to take a longer, more academic view of the important but largely hidden back story of journalism. Professor John Wyatt, eminent neo-natologist at University College, London, whose son is a journalist, gave the book intensive care in the incubator of lockdown, with long Zoom calls that kept the baby alive. Fleur de Villiers, to whom the book is dedicated; Revd Professor Charles Elliott, and Ian Cooper all read early versions of the book with such enthusiasm and helpfulness that I began to believe in it myself. Lastly thanks to Prabhu Guptara who also believed.

PART ONE
THE FOURTH ESTATE

STORY—The children's story they could not tell: Northern Uganda's war[1]

"They come for you at 5am. If you're still alive at 6, you'll be alright." With those words, I was ushered to my room for the night: a concrete shed without window glass, deep in the heart of rebel territory in Kitgum, Northern Uganda. This was a story the media was barely covering, and the consequences were too terrible to believe.

The Lord's Resistance Army (LRA), led by the mad witch, Major General Joseph Kony, was at the height of its killing campaign. In this very place, the wife of a former bishop, an award-winning peacebuilder, had been blown up and killed in her jeep. Her daughter was later abducted and raped by Kony's men and committed suicide. Some fifteen months afterwards, my host was taken alive; an ordeal from which he never recovered his sanity.

Twenty-five thousand children had been abducted, many tortured or killed for minor infractions, while a million people were herded into camps at the mercy of Kony's LRA or equally iniquitous government troops supposed to be protecting them. The world had mostly forgotten—or never knew.

I was travelling with the Church Mission Society, which had largely pulled out of the area after nearly a hundred years, leaving only two traumatized workers travelling in and out. The war in Northern Uganda had ground on for seventeen years, largely unnoticed by the world. But something had to be done urgently.

"Far worse than Iraq"
In 2002, BBC's East Africa correspondent Hilary Andersson reported with a desperation that woke

international agencies from their stupor. I was available to respond, and nothing seemed more important to me. I asked to go up to Kitgum on a routine missionary visit to the Anglican bishop. But the consequences were anything but routine.

After three searing days in this remote town, reachable only by plane or military convoy, and a further week on the frontline of the Sudanese civil war, which had provided cover for Kony's raids into Uganda (a result of US bombing raids codenamed Operation Infinite Reach), I returned home in shock. I promised the bishop in faith (not hope) that I would try everything within my power as a journalist to draw attention to the horror.

My hunch was that this war was not being taken seriously because its army had a religious name, and its leader was demanding a return to the Ten Commandments, plus one: thou shalt have more than one testicle. Western journalists lacked a spiritual belief system, so could not understand what paralysed the people in fearfulness. But at CMS we did take spirituality seriously. This, combined with unique historic networks, prayer and religiously wide-awake journalism, enabled the team to drill down to what mattered.

Northern Uganda consumed our lives for the next two years. With a small team of colleagues in London, I threw myself into the cause, initiating and launching the "Break the Silence" campaign.

We brought Bishop Benjamin Ojwang to London. We secured media coverage and government meetings for this former shepherd boy, including an interview on BBC Radio 4's *Today* programme. His voice was strained, the voice of a man facing a firing squad, as he pleaded with the world to help.

James Naughtie, struggling to comprehend, likened the situation to Waco, the US cult led by David Koresh. The enormity of the problem defied normal categories of secular reportage. How could it be that we had given Waco saturation coverage but barely featured this—after seventeen years of continuous horror?

Ojwang's story reached the UN Under-Secretary for Humanitarian Affairs, Jan Egeland, who flew to Kitgum to see the situation for himself. Then he held a press conference in Kampala, promising to triple the aid budget to Northern Uganda.

Egeland's actions set off a ripple effect, and we found ourselves convening round-table meetings with all the major aid agencies: aid agencies like Oxfam and Christian Aid increased their efforts, and Amnesty International incorporated Kitgum into their Small Arms Campaign. In the week before Christmas 2004, the German deputy head of mission in Kampala, Holger Seubert, said that the European Union had stepped up consultations with the Ugandan government to find a solution. At the same time, Bob Geldof's team contacted me and decided to make one of his six films for Tony Blair's Commission on Africa in Kitgum. Geldof was later pictured weeping in his hotel.

Within a little over a year, we had woken up the world. It was religiously literate journalism that made the difference—public-interest journalism that took seriously the spirituality of the people. The 200-year-old Anglican mission, with its deep ties to Acholi life, became the conduit for change. Working within that spiritual network made Northern Uganda less invisible, less "strange."

This whole experience taught me a big lesson. What had stunned Egeland and Geldof was the political and media silence, on an international scale, about the invisibility of those traumatized children.

They had become "night commuters"—trekking every night into the regional capital, Gulu, from their villages. They slept under the buses, a prey to whatever might befall them.

And prey they were. Real horror became normalized, as the consequence of neglect caused by secular journalism. Just one story, etched forever in my mind, makes this point.

John, a 16-year-old abductee rescued by the army, told me he had a small brother with whom he had been taken: a frightened child, who wanted to run home to his mother and get on with his schooling.

Joseph Kony got wind of the lad's misery and decided to make an example of it.

He made the boy dig a small hole in the sandy ground and lie face down in it. Then he ordered John to take a club and bash his little brother on the back of the head until he was dead. The twist was that, just before his little brother died in unspeakable terror and pain, John was ordered to whisper in his bloody ear who had done this to him.

The world had just left children like John in their thousands at the mercy of the LRA for nearly two decades, because to the secular mind it just seemed too bizarre, too remote.

But not to a Christian journalist. This journalism, grounded in the soil of religious literacy, took seriously the social and spiritual forces underpinning people's reality. Before the campaign, a Whitehall desk officer had to consult a map to find out where the war was, despite British aid making up fifty percent of Uganda's budget. After the campaign, a Whitehall spokesman admitted we had changed things—by "considerably increasing international political activity."

Caesar Poblicks Nyeko, Project Coordinator for Kacoke Madit, summarized the impact: "When I saw Bishop Ojwang of Kitgum in front of Downing Street ... this to me felt like humanity has the same language now." Language is the key to change. When people hear their story in their own language, they recognize themselves and are recognized by the world.

Despite still evading capture, Kony has never returned to Northern Uganda to terrorize its children.[2] Prophetic public interest journalism made that possible.

Preface

This book is about journalism; how it began, what it has contributed, and what happens when it fails.

It is specifically about *public-interest* journalism. Not journalism that is interesting to the public, though of course one hopes it is that. But journalism that is *in* the public interest.

"Public-interest news informs and empowers the public about issues of shared concern, from community initiatives to international relations. Without public-interest news, people wouldn't know what was going on around them, wouldn't be able to hold power to account and wouldn't be able to contribute to public debate. Communities would be infected by misinformation and polarisation and, ultimately, democracy would fail."

This summary by Jeremy Clifford appears in the Final Report of the News Futures 2035 project, of which he is a steering board member.

The project is a response to the demise of public-interest news. Public-interest news is dying. It is dying for many reasons, to do with finance, digital adaptation, a universal switch-off from bad news and more. But it is also dying I believe because of a lack of understanding about why we have news at all, where it came from and why it matters.

News is the objective, journalism is the process. This book attempts to make a contribution to the debate about the sector's sustainability, but from an unusual perspective: secularization. I believe that the loss of meaning and the loss of knowledge of our history as media people have a lot to do with what's gone wrong.

What you believe matters and has outcomes. It is not just a matter of private opinion, hermetically sealed from action.

Realizing that lead me, as a secular newspaper hack who became a Christian, into a new journalism.

It led me to Northern Uganda and a campaign that opened my eyes. If journalists were generally so ignorant about the world's faiths, and yet we depended on them to mobilize change, real change was never going to come. Those desperate children were simply going to remain ignored.

Journalists are caught in a frantic news cycle that ends up simply *recycling* a secularist view where nothing much matters *enough* except money.

And yet they have such titanic achievements to their credit, as I have discovered in researching this book.

If they covered AIDS in Africa, they left out what caused most of it: religious blood ritual.

If they covered the war in Northern Uganda at all, they did so without understanding spiritual fear, and it dragged on.

So this book is written out of a lifetime of conviction not just that seeing means believing—and of course it is always vital to go to where the action is—but more importantly, believing means seeing.

STORY—Vicars rhymes with knickers

The voice at the end of the line was friendly but purposeful: "Hello. This is Mr Levin's assistant. He wants you to know he is very impressed with the material you sent him and that he will be following up with an article on it."

This was the mighty *Times* columnist Bernard Levin's office. It was early 1993, and he had written an unusually uninformed piece about religion.

I'd been working as a magazine journalist, travelling particularly to Muslim countries, learning a lot that I had never read in the press.

Now here was the Fourth Estate at its finest, ringing my office because I'd got a story the world had missed: the persecution of the Church.

I'd spent a lot of time on my travels listening as I was told about the way Christians were being shut out of schools and jobs in Egypt or killed in Pakistan for being baptized.

I learned of a Muslim woman who murdered her own husband for shame at his conversion.

Of whole villages being razed to the ground because their inhabitants had the wrong faith.

My first commission for the magazine was a piece of research into the law in Egypt that forbade the building of churches, or even their repair.

Christians were even being crucified in the Sudan; a form of execution that shimmered in the cultural memory but that was unthinkable in the 1990s.

I could sense the groundswell of outrage across the world at these horrors that were getting no coverage, even as they became more widespread. The Islamic resurgence was gathering pace, unnoticed.

Then a delegation of church pastors, some of whom I'd met in Pakistan, arrived in our offices in Kennington, and left us with a huge sheaf of papers recording all the incidents of atrocity and injustice in just that one country.

It was then that Levin wrote the piece that changed my life. It was a penetrating piece about the persecution of Jews in Russia, and why the Jews were so often uniquely targeted as scapegoats. "The Christians, of course, were persecuted at the beginning, but haven't been since then; still, it would be a nasty shock for them if they were told they were going back to the days when Domitian ruled the roost."[3]

This represented a peculiar blind spot. To add insult to injury, Levin joked in a subsequent piece that perhaps because vicars rhymed with knickers, the Church would always fail to be taken too seriously.

I sent Levin that stack of documents.

He followed up with a series of pieces on the persecuted church, starting with one entitled "Islam's Fearful Blood-letting".[4]

He also reproduced verbatim the courageous testimony of an Iranian Protestant pastor at his trial on a charge of apostasy—for which the penalty is death.

Mehdi Dibaj's crime was to have become a Christian.

He had been incarcerated for nine years for changing his religion, two of them in solitary confinement, during which his wife left him.

An Amnesty campaign in which I took part won him his freedom, but he never lived to enjoy it. He was found shot in the back in an alley in Tehran.

What has stayed with me ever since is how Levin, perhaps the greatest of all newspaper columnists, who had been the scourge of Communist Russia, helping no doubt to stiffen the sinews of Thatcher and Reagan, could have been so ignorant.

And not just ignorant, but blindly prejudiced. A sensitive and serious religious seeker, he was willing to change, as a good journalist does, on presentation of good evidence.

But I realized there must be something deeply wrong with our journalism if one of its most eloquent practitioners could get away with such religious illiteracy.

More Christians died for their faith in the twentieth century than the whole two thousand years of their existence. Not only did he not see, but when he learned about it, he denied it.

I started joining more dots. What else were we in the West not seeing because journalists did not believe it?

If we believed religions were "great", but without serious issue—whether for us as citizens or journalists—we would not hesitate to assume that mass immigration was a simple matter of importing a million-strong workforce from Mirpur, say, just to work in factories, and increase the tax take.[5]

Or that all religions were equally irrelevant before the great tide of secular materialism that was apparently sweeping all before it.

But I was not convinced that the government understood what they were doing. Religions have their own agendas and trajectories.

As anthropologists have noted, religious migrants have far more agency than is ever acknowledged in the mainstream discourse.[6]

Muslims' specific demands not just for welfare provision but for status was dominating government business and affecting regional and local government.

I contributed to a book about it called *Faith and Power: Christianity and Islam in 'Secular' Britain*, which sold out.

I then went on to do a Ph.D. on the subject. I had a hunch that in order to administer the inner cities, where religious migrants mainly congregated for cheap housing and ethnic solidarity, the government was "stretching" its own vaunted secularist credentials.

They were finding themselves having to use Anglican gathering points and convening power to accommodate the needs of these new citizens. They were having to use long-latent religious language and identity markers at conferences. Secularization is deemed the inevitable withdrawal of the transcendent from different sectors of society, including government, law, and so on. But it seemed, where the inner cities were concerned, secularization was not so inevitable after all. Christianity was in fact proving very useful.

I produced a study of one government department, the Inner Cities Religious Council, to make the case that the government was "de-secularizing" according to four of the rubrics of David Martin's *A General Theory of Secularization*.

That meant the nation was ceasing to be governed coherently or consistently. It meant one law for one group and another for a different group. While Catholic childcare projects in deprived East London boroughs were being refused state funds "because they were religious", mosques were being built with public funds, so long as they could be classed as community centres.

At least one project for rehabilitating newly released prisoners from Wormwood Scrubs Prison in South London was forced to close because prayer was offered for the ex-cons.

Yet libraries of specifically religious books in Hindi were being resourced out of council tax.

It seemed that religion did not matter so long as it was not "our religion".[7]

Then 9/11 happened.

I discuss the reaction to this elsewhere in the book. But, to a give personal context, I had just finished my Ph.D. My oral examination (viva) was coming up in two months, examined by Professor Martin himself.

It was a timely acknowledgement that the secularization he had studied did not take enough account of polities affected by the mass in-migration of people of "other faiths". He had only studied Christian countries.

Globalization, the mass movement of peoples from everywhere to everywhere, which was now happening apace, meant that secularization was not necessarily an inevitable process, and was arguably going into reverse so that parts of Britain could be governed at all.

"Secularization" was a myth, therefore. But its power as an idea hung around. Pervasive, it was now creating dilemmas for "secular" civil servants trained merely to resolve problems.

Problems can be solved. Dilemmas require judgement and there was little of it around.

Secularization, which could not provide answers to dilemmas, was still what sociologists were calling "the dominant discourse". I say more about this in chapter 11.

Yet journalists were still subscribing to it, as was evident when sometime in the 2000s, a PR executive at the BBC told me solemnly that "journalists leave their religion at the door when they come to work."

I was increasingly alarmed by such an attitude, and worried about the effects of it on reportage. As I recount in later chapters, if you do not see right, you fail to see much at all.

Religious illiteracy, combined with a dominant view that secularization was inevitable, was in fact stopping journalists doing their jobs.

And if they could not incorporate the visceral things that make life tick for the world's majority, we were in trouble.

There would be not just a mismatch, between what was actually going on and what they believed was going on, but eventually a great switch-off of readers and viewers.

In trying to coerce readers to see the world through a lens of secular neutrality, newspapers were putting themselves out of business by producing nothing much that people cared about, despite often gargantuan efforts.

And so it has proved. In the United States, the newspaper industry lost $1.3 billion worth of editors' and reporters' jobs in the decade to 2018—or 60 per cent of its workforce.[8]

In the UK, in the years between 2005 and 2018, as reported by the BBC, more than 200 local newspapers closed, the number of regional journalists halved, and 58 per cent of the country did not have a dedicated local newspaper any longer.[9]

As I write this, the famous London newspaper, the *Evening Standard*—which under its Russian oligarch owners, the Lebedevs, became a flimsy freebie in 2009—has announced it is to become a weekly, its editor Dylan Jones having declared he "never reads print newspapers."[10]

I am not trying to make the case that this shattering attrition can be attributed to secularism.

What I am arguing is that the seemingly unstoppable loss of advertising revenues to social media companies, which is now almost universal, has been possible *because of the lack of ideological conviction necessary to resist it.*

This is unlikely to be the end of the story. New news sources are springing up, sometimes the vision of just one journalist working alone.[11] I worked successfully with mainstream journalists for more than twelve years on a niche approach to news and with an innovatory charitable funding model. "The press"—be it online or not—does have a future.

But that may depend on young writers recovering a hunger for truth that is prepared to do the hard yards sacrificially as of old; a hunger that charities and readers are prepared to nurture and pay for. But to get there, I believe we must know where we've come from.

Going back to go forward
In order to find the path forward, this book goes back in history. This is in part because of a specific piece in the jigsaw of survival: the link between public-interest journalism (PIJ) and prophecy.[12]

PIJ is discussed in detail in chapter 2, but its link to prophecy came as a surprise to me, when I was asked to write a chapter in a book about it.[13]

Prophecy is a specifically *religious* calling to speak up, particularly on behalf of those who are powerless and marginalized.

But if journalists don't get religion, what happens to that dimension of their task?

PIJ does not simply impart information that might be useful to people. It scans the horizon, bringing other somewhat intangible attributes to the task. These are foresight, a passion for justice, a perennial realism about the dark side of human motivation, a refusal to remain sanguine in the face of comfortable complacency, and a restlessness in the search for answers to dilemmas that gum up the machinery of business and government.

I wanted to know whether prophecy is in fact journalism at its best and whether prophecy's recovery is inherent to the survival of the journalism that is real news, not just infotainment.

Journalists should be first responders to what is *not* immediately apparent, not just the first to follow the fire engines.

My target readers

I have written this book for several reasons, and several audiences.

As a practitioner, I want to put the record straight about the public gift that characterizes journalism at its best. And I want to give back to an industry that I loved, warts and all, and from which I benefited.

It was an immense privilege to be identified fully with, and be allowed to serve, several quite disparate communities with my campaigns and reports.

I want to inspire a new generation to learn and believe—and serve likewise.

I can hardly claim to be an expert on media studies. There is simply too vast a literature to canvass, and anyway, I find much of it dull.[14] It is also changing far too fast to catch it comprehensively.

I want to share the questions my own career raised, as it dawned on me what had been cancelled from the work we do.

The book is in three parts. Part One is a dive into the murky waters of the present day, the corruption of the press without an overt moral compass, the lazy reportage, the news deserts, and the plagiaristic resort to robotic news cycling that is fixing on the vacuum like a succubus. The light shines brighter against such a backdrop.

Part Two explores the steps that constitute the always revolutionary journey to the making of the Fourth Estate we recognize today. They lie among the medieval swamps and riptides of ideological change and chicanery surprisingly like our own.

Religious dissenters, working against massive cultural pressures that cost their lives and livelihoods still hold up a mirror to our own apathetic quest for truth worth telling.

I agree with Jonathan Heawood, until recently Executive Director of the Public Interest News Foundation, that we can "take the best from the past and present, and shape the media of the future".[15]

The philosophical undercurrents may, it is true, be set against the depredations of the digital revolution emanating from Big Tech's bases in the US.

But the apparently glittering offer of its distribution models is still dependent upon the flesh and blood effort of human beings out on the news beat.

For sure, what's changing is possibly an immense threat to the news industry. But Generative AI could be the dog that eats its own tail. If it develops in the way it currently is, where developers appropriate all content without any compensation at all—"they will destroy the very news content on which their models are trained."[16]

News organizations, therefore, still have massive leverage they can monetize. And that means that the moral dilemmas, and human orientations of journalists, will always continue to matter.

So I believe we will continue to need to understand how the acids of secularization have eaten into our "lifeworld" as producers and consumers of hard news and repair the damage.

As Rob Corbidge wrote on his Substack on 7 June 2024 regarding AI-generated search results, "the user experience is still one looking for a user case." This is also true much more broadly. Readers do not like what they're getting and are switching off. Just as they did with Google's much vaunted new method of information retrieval. Google reduced the presence of its GenAI "Overviews" feature barely days after going live with it.[17]

Part Three then goes on to look broadly at the confused matrix of ideas in which journalism happens today and suggests ten action points to unscramble it. A world with no clue to its origin and purpose is like a narrative with no plot, going nowhere. It does not deliver for journalism, or for its consumers. But that's not how it was. Political theology and religious "knowing" are the unlikely contenders once again in the recovery stakes. The future is always to play for.

Chapter 1
A Licence to Harm

Journalism, the process of reporting news that its writer deems to be *in the public interest*, can be said to have begun after the Reformation of the Church in Germany. It began with pamphlets about religious issues, and was made possible by the invention a hundred years earlier of the printing press and by the availability of paper, ink and a distribution network. I will cover the technical elements of this as we go on. But this is not a history of journalism. It is an attempt to look at a unique element of the long process: the peculiar gelling of technique with motive or vision.

There are clearly discernible moments when change gripped Europe that may tell us what is missing now, as news deserts leave our rulers unaccountable once more—and as corruption on a vast scale is resulting in the media becoming the enemy of the people.

For something went terribly wrong at the beginning of this century with the Fourth Estate, a term still current to describe the watchdog role of the press.

George Orwell had perhaps too much currency in attempts to define the sector. "Journalism is printing what someone somewhere does not want printed. Everything else is public relations," he wrote. For Orwell, real journalism was a defence against the encroachments of tyranny, specifically the Stalinism he had witnessed in the Spanish Civil War and which his "beast fable" *Animal Farm*, published in 1945, set out to expose.

But journalistic licence, so essential to the watchdog role, becomes itself tyrannous without checks. The *Guardian*'s Nick Davies, in *Hack Attack*, used *Animal Farm* imagery to lambast contemporary journalism itself in 2014. His work courageously exposed in granular detail the News Corps' phone-hacking scandal, exposing just how ubiquitous was the corruption that has done so much to destroy the public's trust in its watchdogs. He writes:

> They [Rupert Murdoch's staff] hid the emerging scandal from their readers like a Victorian nanny covering the children's eyes from an accident in the street—"you don't want to see this". Some did this because they were linked to the crime by common ownership or by their own guilty secrets about the lawbreaking in their own newsrooms; some turned away for fear of upsetting their political allies. Too many journalists had simply ceased to function as independent truth-tellers, separate from and critical of the people they were writing about. The crime reporter made common cause with the police, and also with criminals. The political correspondent developed a loyalty to one party or faction. The media reporter became a tool for his or her owner. The news executive turned into a preening power-monger, puffed with wealth and self-importance, happy to join the élite and

not to expose it—all rather like the final moment of *Animal Farm*, when the pigs who have led the revolt against the humans have come to adopt the behaviour of the rulers they were supposed to challenge: "The creatures outside looked from pig to man, and from man to pig, and from pig to man again; but already it was impossible to say which was which."[18]

The hacking scandal was of an altogether different magnitude of corruption from the "blagging" that is regarded as legitimate in the journalistic pursuit of crime.

Rupert Murdoch's *News of the World* weekly national UK tabloid *depended financially* on stories acquired from the illicit tapping of voice messages.

Murdoch himself built an infrastructure of dishonesty, in cahoots with bent policemen that kept his empire ahead of the game. Instead of being the watchdog of the people, the media became the wolf.

For sure, getting a story can require the breaking of social taboo; sailing close to the wind of what is acceptable behaviour. From doorstepping the grief-struck, to writing lurid pieces from the frontlines of crime and war, journalists have always had to risk the law.

That may be a good thing if it challenges "group think". But at the end of the twentieth century, it had wrought its own destruction.

Far from being a model of accountability worth fighting for, the press became the enemy.

As someone with a licence to harm, a hack came to be seen as little better than a crook.

A journalist himself, the human rights and public interest journalism advocate Jonathan Heawood (whom

I've already mentioned), founder of the first independent press regulator, Impress, even describes "press freedom" as a myth, a cover for a licence to make money by lying.

"Was this principle really being used to protect the public from an overmighty state? Or had it been co-opted by powerful businessmen to protect themselves from scrutiny?"[19]

Now senior journalists are writing of the current state of journalism in almost apocalyptic terms.

"A vast engine for harm" was *UnHerd* founder Tim Montgomerie's verdict before he set up the online opinion platform.

"The most prodigious capability for spreading lies the world has ever seen", said *Guardian* former editor Alan Rusbridger.[20]

It was Rusbridger's newspaper that alienated other editors with its dog-eat-dog investigation of journalistic skulduggery over phone hacking. The campaign even risked bringing the *Guardian* down. It stood alone against threats—shamingly—from its peers.

Davies' first book, *Flat Earth News*, was his first attack on his own profession.

"The more I looked, the more I found falsehood, distortion and propaganda running through the outlets of an industry which is supposed to be dedicated to the very opposite, i.e. to telling the truth," he wrote.[21]

The more he searched for an explanation, the more alarmed he became by the scale of the problem and by its complexity. Until he worked his way into the project, he had no idea of just how weakened it had become, and just how prone it was to fail to tell the truth.

"I was forced to admit that I work in a corrupted profession," he wrote.[22]

Rusbridger, who backed Davies throughout his campaigns concludes. "The stakes for truth have never been higher."[23]

American media academic Clay Shirkey, who writes about the social and political effects of the internet and social media, predicts a long trough of decline in accountability journalism.

"The old models are breaking faster than the new models can be put into place."[24] The digital revolution is a "real revolution".[25] "I think a bad thing is going to happen, right?" he adds.

The missing dimension
Against such a depressing picture of Fourth Estate journalism of modern times, I want to pit two different exemplars from an earlier epoch.

Welshman Gareth Jones had secured an interview with Hitler and tried, unsuccessfully, to warn Lloyd George of the Fuhrer's build-up for war.

He travelled under a false identity to Russia and got the story, denied at the time, of the famine in Soviet Ukraine, known as the Holodomor.

The *New York Times* was happily publishing their Moscow Bureau Chief Walter Duranty's pro-Stalin lies about it, even though famished Ukrainians were said to be eating their dead children.

Jones persevered. He saw the starving villages with his own eyes, and followed his hunch that the farmers' grain was being trucked secretly to Moscow to show off Stalin's revolution.

He got the story out by sheer good luck after discovering that newspaper magnate William Randolph Hearst was visiting Wales.

He crashed Hearst's meeting. Hearst listened and went on to publish the story in the *New York Journal* in March 1933.

Jones however did not live to see his thirtieth birthday. He is believed to have been shot in Japanese-occupied Mongolia by Soviet agents.

But his work lives on in the film *Mr Jones*, made in 2019: a vital reminder of the suffering of the Ukrainian people at the hands of Russia long before Putin.

<u>The stigmata of truth</u>
Gareth Jones was not the only journalist to get the story about Stalin's Russia. A year earlier, in 1932, Malcolm Muggeridge, writing for the UK *Guardian*, was on a USSR propaganda trip with a group of foreign correspondents, under the eye of the state censor.

Through the window of his train carriage, he saw something that changed his life.

"For the most part the small stations we rattled through were cleared of people, but sometimes there were some bedraggled looking peasants clustered together on the platform. Noticing one such cluster, a large German correspondent carelessly threw out of the window a leg of chicken he had been gnawing at. There was a concerted move to pick it up. The gesture and the response have stayed with me through the intervening years like stigmata."[26]

By the simple expedient of getting off the train to look, giving the censor the slip, he discovered Ukraine was being ruthlessly starved for political ends.

By slipping out into the countryside unmonitored, he saw for himself the horrors that luminaries like George Bernard Shaw, Anglican divines, and the *New York Times* had somehow managed to justify.

He sent home an unvarnished account of famine, forced labour and mass executions.

Muggeridge's personal exodus had taken him from a suburban upbringing in Surrey in the 1920s to Stalin's Moscow by way of the *Manchester Guardian*.

His socialist credentials were impeccable: his father was a Labour MP; and his wife Kitty was Socialist royalty, niece of Beatrice Webb who co-founded the London School of Economics.

Muggeridge at first idolized his editor, Ted Scott, son of the famous CP Scott, who established the trust company that funds the paper to this day.

Yet he grew disillusioned and deeply cynical, accusing Scott of not wanting to know "what's going on in Russia, or to letting his readers know."

Indeed, he parted from the newspaper he had initially joined with such exultation.

"An honest mind was as out of place there as a virgin in the pages of Casanova or a pregnancy in DH Lawrence's", he later wrote.[27]

Worst of all for Muggeridge—and George Orwell—was the collusion of the US and UK press. Indeed, the BBC was George Orwell's model for the Ministry of Truth in his book *Nineteen Eighty-Four*.

Meanwhile, colleague Walter Duranty of the *New York Times* "put his money on Stalin", not—believed Muggeridge—for reasons of humankind, but of power.

The *New York Times* for years gave great prominence to Duranty's message. They built up him and his message when "they were so evidently nonsensically untrue".

He came to be accepted as the great Russian expert in America, playing a major part in shaping President Roosevelt's policies on the USSR, which lasted for a generation.

Muggeridge was convinced this was not because the *Times* was deceived. "Rather, because it wanted to be so deceived, and Duranty provided the requisite deception material."[28]

It was at Duranty's door that Muggeridge lays many of the global scandals of misrepresentation that have continued to this day.

He lists them: Cuba, Vietnam, Latin America [Nick Davies adds the Iraq War, the rise of global Islamist terror, the unreported build-up of the Ukrainian invasion by Russia and many more].

This fixation with power, evident still in the way some conflicts get 24/7 coverage, when worse scenarios accrue barely a paragraph, was addictive for all who came near it.

Muggeridge reflects deeply on how, until his revelations, "truth could be co-opted by politics to become a lie affecting the whole world", and how journalists at the very highest level had colluded in that lie.[29]

Truth was, he decided, an early casualty of the twentieth century. To Nietzsche, "God is dead". Muggeridge retorted: "It is truth that has died, not God."

Muggeridge sought redress for his battered soul as a biographer of Mother Teresa.

But his experiences in Russia had left him bleak about all world endeavour, and particularly disillusioned about journalism. In India he came to see what mattered: that "suffering is the sacrament of love".

For this latter-day prophet, telling the truth had a cost. It was not about what was left out, but what is left in.

It took him to a new world, and surprisingly to the first Lausanne Congress on World Evangelization in 1974, set up by the British Anglican John Stott and the US evangelist

Billy Graham!

Alan Rusbridger, confronting the power and responsibility of the press, also saw the terrible consequences of its corruptibility.

Jones and Muggeridge prompt us to believe that journalism needs to be prophetic to protect itself—and us—from its own worst inclinations. We need therefore to look for the root of prophecy to see what clues if any it offers for the survival of journalism.

Chapter 2
Prophecy, Discourse and Reality

Nick Davies, like Muggeridge before him, identified the vast power of journalism to create a narrative, whether true or false.

This is one of the most radical functions of the press: the creation of discourse or "talk about talk". Discourse provides the background to our lives and shapes our minds and world.

Discourse has been defined as the conversation a nation has with itself. It talks situations, nations, cultures, into existence.

Without discourse there could be only the most vestigial communication: and very little administration, law, history, culture. And that was once the case.

Culture production relies on *written* speech and the public's "people power" that writing creates.

But, like everything else, even discourse did not "just happen".

The evidence is limited, but it is possible still to see how vernacular discourse originated. It is a story with which we should be more familiar, if we are to "get" the impulse behind public interest journalism.

Inventing the vernacular

Vernacular writing—writing that speaks to and for ordinary people—was invented; it is not inherent to human nature. This should come as a surprise since we take it so for granted.[30]

Hebrew was the first widely written vernacular in the ancient Near East.

A summary only will have to suffice for the argument of this book, but it is the case that for two thousand years, people in the Semitic Near East did not write, or even particularly identify with the language they spoke. The scribes and rulers shared cuneiform, a script, but it was not based on a language anyone spoke.

Then something changed.

Somewhere between 1200 and 550 BC—the Iron Age—language spoken by West Semitic people got written down.

This was Hebrew, and it appears to have been quite literally invented.

It was written down in the form of history, law and prophecy to form the one extant text of that period that there is for us to consult—and that is the Hebrew Bible, or what Christians call the Old Testament.

Says Seth Sanders: "The Bible's impact requires us to consider the deliberate writing down of Hebrew was a deliberate historical event."[31]

Israelite writers in the Iron Age did not have a national language handed to them; they inherited no similar communication from their cultural ancestors.

History was not supposed to be about a people; it was

only the king who mattered.

Then suddenly, and uniquely among the region's cultures, Hebrew began being about the people instead. Contemporaneous inscriptions tell us this, since they specifically addressed seers and craftsmen.

In so doing, the Hebrew language, says Sanders, created a sense of being a people: a people conscious of itself.

The text that formed this people was the Bible, but evidence for that must come from *outside* the Bible to corroborate it. But there is a problem, since there are no manuscripts of edited Hebrew literary texts remaining from before about 250 BC. (This is the only clearly dated biblical material.) There is much more after that date.[32]

Sanders has to use something else therefore, and all there is that he can use is evidence from archaeology.

Newly discovered marks on stones in Hebrew—known as epigraphy—are what serve to corroborate his point. These he believes demonstrate that a politics based on communication was playing a role a thousand years earlier than 250 BC, the stage at which the Bible was likely to have been begun.

The evidence is now available to show that something cataclysmic did indeed happen then.

The evidence of inscriptions from the time of ancient Israel supports the supposition that extant biblical material must be based on something else that happened.

Both types of writings, the epigraphs on stones and the biblical text, address people in the same but very specific new way: as communication not about the king and his divinity, but about God and the people.

Hebrew, it is Sanders' conclusion, must have been invented for a different purpose than the royal inscriptions in surrounding cultures.

Its invention seems to have been a *response* to something overwhelming; what you might call a supreme collective brainstorm, a deliberate choice to communicate an overwhelmingly massive apprehension of being politically and theologically different from the surrounding cultures.

Seeing it this way sheds light on what the Bible was: communication believed to be from a god (God) to a specific group of people, by means of intermediaries—known as prophets—for a specific purpose.

He says: "Embodied in the Bible, this ancient invention endures as a productive model for political community."[33] But who did the work?

The crucial role of prophets

It was a group of men called prophets, we now know, who created for the very first time in history a form of political communication that could address this group called Israel. They told its story, and let the audience see itself as part of that group and that history.

Vitally for our purposes, "the Bible is the first text to address people as a public."[34]

We shall go on to see this pattern repeated right through this book, as it is, of course, what journalism continues to do: addressing people directly as a group, taking it for granted that they matter.[35]

Problems with reinstating God

What was it that caused this momentous decision to communicate? It was a response to something that happened that gave sustained new value to the receivers of it. It changed and galvanized them.

The problem for us—as secularists—is, of course, God. Where Sanders is elliptical about the divine action in history, biblical scholar Craig Bartholomew faces head-on the challenge here.

Many scholars, he says, both Jews and Christians, affirm the centrality of the Mount Sinai event when the Commandments were given to the nation's leader, Moses, sometime between the sixteenth and thirteenth centuries BC.

And yet at the same time they are unsure as to whether to suggest it really happened.

"For many it is the generative 'event' and yet [they] assert that it] may be entirely imaginary."[36]

Bartholomew however, backed up by Sanders' work, states unequivocally that "Sinai should be understood as an epochal, historical event".[37] It happened.

It is, he and others say, an example of "special divine action". God clearly did speak—or something like it—with Moses on Mount Sinai.

Whatever it was that happened there, we can be sure it was so seismic that it laid the foundations for a text that has been with us, informing and sustaining public discourse ever since.

This was not just the revelation of the Commandments, in Hebrew writing, which up to that point did not exist.

The giving of what became known as the Covenant was straightforwardly epochal.

"Whatever it was that happened on Mount Sinai, it caused a massive revolution in how the Israelites saw themselves, their role and the way they communicated."[38]

What Bartholomew argues is that without the god's (God's) desire to be answerable to his creation, there would be no communication at all.

That seems a huge claim, yet aspects of it are not without illustration elsewhere.

The decision to form writing out of a local spoken language happened at other times in history, setting up comparable reverberations.

Sanders uses examples from much later in history to bolster his argument.

Sanskritist Sheldon Pollock for instance was the first to show that there had been a vernacular revolution around 1000 AD not only in Europe but also in South Asia.

Where languages for sacred texts had been the norm, springing from and creating a religious universalization, something changed. Instead of Latin in France and England, scribes began writing in demotic French and English.

Sanskrit was similarly "retooled" to write Tamil and Javanese at around the same time.

Says Pollock: "Vernacular literary cultures were initiated by the conscious decisions of writers to reshape the boundaries of their cultural universe by renouncing the larger world for the smaller place, and they did so in full awareness of the significance of their decision …

"Using a new language for communicating literarily to a community of readers and listeners can consolidate if not create that very community."[39]

This is exactly what it did to the Hebrews. Up to that time, script had been used in the surrounding nations merely for administration of ritual, or to legitimize the power of the ruler.

The Old Babylonian laws of Hammurabi for instance, the endlessly copied centerpiece of the scribal curriculum, were never cited by name, or treated as foundational for a community: "They did not make anyone who they were."[40]

The laws of the Torah in the Pentateuch—the first five books of the Hebrew Bible—on the other hand communicate differently.

"They speak to someone imagined as capable of hearing and responding" writes Sanders:

> Deuteronomy addresses a "you," Israel, which is also part of a "we" that includes the laws' speaker, Moses. The audience member who "hears" the call of "Hear, O Israel" in Deuteronomy 6 joins a group for whom "the Lord is our god, the Lord alone."[41]

When you hear your story in your own language and understand that that history and those laws are for your participation, then you recognize and are recognized; you exist as both object and subject.

You exist as a people.

This is a vital clue as to what really underpins the momentousness of the gift and power of journalism, as we shall see later.

Language creates a people.

I need to anchor all this now in the contemporary world to bring it to life, and it is so foundational for this book and for the survival of journalism, that it bears repetition, and stressing:

Vernacular literatures go hand in hand with vernacular polities. Language creates a people and on the back of it, a political entity.

It was the Bible that molded Europe. Gottfried Herder is still controversial for arguing this: that "only through language can a people exist".[42] Benedict Anderson even described European nations as "imagined communities" that arose out of the Reformation and printing.[43]

And, on the basis of archaeological research, Seth Sanders takes this argument all the way back to the roots of Western civilization itself.

A standard written Hebrew must have been circulating for well over a century, judging by graffiti and inscriptions that have been discovered on walls and bits of pot and on monuments all over Israel and Judah.

These had suddenly been repurposed for other contexts. Texts had begun to mean something new for people, whether inscribed on marker posts or in the biblical text.

Taken together, this becomes the oldest body of evidence not just about the past but about the present.

That is because it rehabilitates "a vital contemporary debate about language, culture and power", a debate that has been as it were "cancelled".

That's because Nazism, which first surfaced in the 1920s, cut us off from our own historical cultural hinterland.

National socialism's seemingly appalling debt to the potency of scripture in the formation of Europe's nations, distorted for its own needs, has paralysed academic analysis of Bible translation and all discourse since.

This potency seemed to be nothing less than the cause of Europe's divisions: the fascist destruction of its peoples.

Sanders' work goes right back behind this academic impasse, however—to a possible rehabilitation of the generative function and history of scripture—as a means to reconnect language to people authentically. This is of immense significance also for the history of journalism, I want to argue.

The germ of democracy
The creators of this discourse were prophets, seers, visionaries. There are five books of law in the Hebrew Bible and twelve of history, but more important even than these are the eighteen books of prophecy, which frame the rest.

To repeat: prophecy comes to be the most decisive of the three discourses because it provides the frame for the other two.

What makes the Bible so powerful is that all three genres of discourse are produced specifically *as* prophecy. In other words, the prophet was the one who spoke of the purposes assigned to both past and present through law.

In all other cultures of the era, it was the king who had the right to speak for a people. But for the Israelites "the ideal interlocutor for a people is a prophet."[44] Certainly, "oracular messages"—direct quotes from a god—had a long history in the ancient Near East. But literary prophecy, a message circulated to and for a public in writing, and for their benefit, did not exist.[45]

Prophecy as writing had before this always been a state secret, written in tunnels or royal courtyards, away from the public gaze. There had been no narrative with prophets acting at the centre. And whereas sovereignty had been vested in the military power of the assembled kin groups, or the state (the king), now "the people are addressed through the circulation of texts, as a public."

As Sanders puts it neatly, "text trumps king".[46]

The ability of the Bible to create a "people" and become its very power is an extraordinary phenomenon that one sees repeated whenever and wherever it is first translated.[47]

And it has to go on being translated, otherwise it loses its power to "speak".

Orthodox Hebrews still insist today that the Torah be studied only in Hebrew. Yet at Pentecost, according to Acts 2, everyone heard the Gospel in their *own* contemporary tongue:

All of them were filled with the Holy Spirit and began to speak in other tongues as the Spirit enabled them.

⁵Now there were staying in Jerusalem God-fearing Jews from every nation under heaven. ⁶When they heard this sound, a crowd came together in bewilderment, because each one heard their own language being spoken. ⁷Utterly amazed, they asked: "Aren't all these who are speaking Galileans? ⁸Then how is it that each of us hears them in our native language? ⁹Parthians, Medes and Elamites; residents of Mesopotamia, Judea and Cappadocia, Pontus and Asia, ¹⁰Phrygia and Pamphylia, Egypt and the parts of Libya near Cyrene; visitors from Rome ¹¹(both Jews and converts to Judaism); Cretans and Arabs—we hear them declaring the wonders of God in our own tongues!"[48]

The biblical writers believed "the Holy Spirit" was the first and archetypal translator of "good news", the electric shock treatment of global communication.

To reiterate the argument: Bible translation, the writing down of vernacular speech was motivated by a peculiar religious and prophetic impulse. It both signified and gave rise to the development of public discourse.

Prophecy, a response to a divine fiat, creates consciousness. It invokes an identity, a calling, a mandate. It was the prophets who used language to invoke justice and order.

Sanders concludes:

What emerges as remarkable about the Hebrew Bible is not only that it speaks in the voice of God, but how this voice at once directly addresses its audience and represents that audience's responses as both determinative and unpredictable. It speaks in the voice of a God who can inflict terrible punishment, but not coerce obedience. Instead, it circulates through and by means of the people it addresses.[49]

In the Old Testament we find a theological and political call articulated by prophets to participate in a distinctive order where none like it existed; a calling to pursue truth and justice in a way that created discourse, and a people wedded to it.

These people were to be nothing less than a light to the nations.

Prophecy
What then do I mean by prophecy? It is an idea with which the pioneers of journalism themselves identified, as we shall see, but since it is one that has fallen out of use, we must make a very short detour at least.

The English word "prophet" is the transliteration of a compound Greek word derived from *pro* (before/toward) and *phesein* (to tell); thus, a προφήτης (prophētēs) is someone who conveys messages from the divine to humans.

Originally it meant a person in touch with or speaking for a god to a king.

Increasingly in the Old Testament, this is reversed in a cataclysmic *bouleversement*: it carried the idea of advocacy *on behalf of* the people—a calling from God to speak up for the downtrodden *to* the King.

So, as an example, Isaiah in the Hebrew Bible (Old

Testament) is told to tell the rulers of Sodom to "listen to the law of our God" for the sake of the people: to "Seek justice, encourage the oppressed, defend the cause of the fatherless, plead the case of the widow".[50] This is revolutionary in Near-Eastern governance.

Prophets came to be characterized as visionaries, poets, theologians or religious philosophers, and when they were authentic (which was often not the case) especially as social reformers or radicals, they were upholders of holiness: seers and intermediaries.[51]

They paid close attention to, and did not operate detached from, the social, political and religious events occurring during their time.[52] Their preaching and writing declared the reign of God among men, and particularly as with Jeremiah, called the whole nation to account.

The prophets perceived history as an interaction of Yahweh with humanity. Events and the consequences of human action manifested God—and we shall read of that again. "Stuff mattered".

The Philippine public theologian Annelle Sabanal says of the prophets: "With their persistent criticism of abuses of power, opposition to official or royal policy, and call for reform and changes, one may think of them as God's watchdogs in the world of politics and in the exercise of power."[53]

It was what's more, the adversarial prophets who were regarded as the ones who had spoken truthfully and were most often killed for it.

But what did this development in communication—the emergence of a "you" valued so highly as to cut out the king—signal in the bigger scheme of communication history?

We must move now to the first of two developments

in classical thought without which journalism could not have arisen. The first concerns reality—subject matter—and its representation; the second the possibility of the transformed self.

Chapter 3
The Representation of Reality

The representation of reality—the object of journalism—has important antecedents which we must now investigate in some detail.

In classical times, the existence of ordinary people did not generally count in literature. Their lives had little or no significance. They did not count either as observers, or as fit subjects about whom to write. In Roman law, a witness was not someone called to testify according to facts, but someone "drawn in" to give an opinion.

The testimony of women still does not count as much as men in some jurisdictions, such as Pakistan. In biblical times, Mary Magdalene's evidence to the other disciples that "Christ was no longer in the tomb that Easter morning, but that she had seen him in the garden outside" was simply dismissed by the men. They thought she and her companions (Joanna and another Mary according to Matthew's Gospel) were "talking nonsense",[54] and went off to see for themselves. Yet, it was precisely to such implausible witnesses that the most important message of all time had been given, according to the relevant reports: the Gospels.

This was not just significant, it was revolutionary.

The shame of entrusting an important message to a woman (not least, a prostitute) would have caused the record to be expunged. Yet here were lowly people being entrusted with what they regarded as the greatest truth of all, to make a point: the truth came from beyond themselves, short-circuiting custom.

Had it not been the case, it would and could not have made it into the historical record.

Modern thinking ignores this. For example, the Sea of Faith movement in Britain holds that truth is a fabrication, not contingent on history. "The Sea of Faith is an informal network of men and women—some attached to places of worship, some not—who accept the modern view that all the religious faith traditions are wholly human creations, not the product of 'revelation' from some extra-human source."[55]

But this position is a logical and historical impossibility: Mary's witness was revolutionary in act and impact. It came as so powerful a conviction—the testimony of her own eyes under the compulsion of a realization so comprehensively convincing—that it did in fact overturn history and tradition.

This is certainly what the early Fathers of the Church taught. In the Greek tradition, particularly as expounded by St Basil (329-379), "Perfection is from without." Man was far more than the possibilities he carried within himself. This was good news: the good news that s/he was only a little lower than the angels, purely by virtue of being a subject of the Creator whose purposes were eternal.

This fact opened up the concept that human creative potential, Basil believed, was way beyond what our inherent capacity seemed to dictate.

Human beings could be message-bearers and world changers *only* because perfection was not something they could simply think, merit or attain. "Man's destiny goes beyond all that is comprehensible within the immanent possibilities of his being," O'Donovan sums up.[56]

Human potentiality is unthinkable—literally more than one can think—and unpredictable therefore.[57] Unfashionable, even suicidal, though it is to say it in the modern context, it has been *given*—as revelation. Allowing revelation elbow room in the present culture would dramatically change who we seem to be, and what we can aim to do. It would change reality. It did change how reality has been represented in the past.

Representation received what is believed to be its finest exploration in Erich Auerbach's magisterial work *Mimesis: The Representation of Reality in Western Literature*. Written in exile, this made him one of the most celebrated of all literary critics of the last century.

Auerbach fled Nazi Germany for Turkey (despite there being Nazi sympathizers in the country) where he taught literature at Istanbul University. He was separated from most primary sources, but he used the texts to which he did have access to make a case for the unique development of literary character in the Old Testament *and* for the reasons why that should be so.

So I want to turn to three heroes who, for Auerbach, exemplify intersections of momentous literary change.

Our first hero is Abraham. Auerbach compares the way the Hebrew Bible's authors handle the call of Abraham to take his only son up Mount Moriah and sacrifice him there with the way Homer handles the epic story of Odysseus' return home to the island of Ithaca after two decades of wanderings.

The fact that Mount Moriah is the mountain where Solomon's immense temple was later to be built (completed in 957 BC) indicates for us the vast significance of Abraham's encounter there for the whole of succeeding Jewish—and world—history.

Abraham—and subsequent patriarchs—underwent a profound metamorphosis on Mount Moriah, a formation brought about "because God [had] chosen them to be examples".

Odysseus, on the other hand, upon his return remains exactly the same character as he was when he left Ithaca two decades earlier.[58]

The narrative of Abraham is not a tale purely about his circumstances, as was the *Odyssey*, but it was about how Abraham changes *because of* the way he responds to those circumstances.

In the Old Testament stories, there is more to politics than the events themselves, unlike the *Odyssey*. Beliefs, or doctrine, and the promises of God are carried by, realized through or incarnated in those circumstances. They are "fraught with background":

> The Bible's claim to truth is not only far more urgent than Homer's; it is tyrannical—it excludes all other claims. The world of the Scripture stories is not satisfied with claiming to be a historically true reality—it insists that it is the only real world, is destined for autocracy. All other scenes, issues, and ordinances have no right to appear independently of it, and it is promised that all of them, the history of all mankind, will be given their due place within its frame, will be subordinated to it. The Scripture stories do not, like Homer's, court

our favour, they do not flatter us that they may please us and enchant us—they seek to subject us, and if we refuse to be subjected, we are rebels.[59]

To stress again, this idea of personal development is entirely foreign to Homer, or the other writers of antiquity. Such a concept sets up an overwhelming suspense that is not merely stylistic, the artifice of a teller of great legends, but is the very story itself. God is working His purposes out in the *very stuff of life* of those who attempt to respond to Him. The absoluteness of this belief gives rise to certain specific literary possibilities, unknown before. Most crucial of these is the belief that ordinariness is full of personal and narrative potential. To put it more simply, life—your life— is a story: and it is one in which you can change, depending on what you are led to believe. You can see how vital this is for journalism.

Reporting the ordinary
Our second literary hero is a "mere" serving-maid in the story that three Gospels tell of Peter's denial of Christ during Christ's trial.

In the story, as it is told in Matthew, Mark and Luke— in John the gender of the slave is not given—this girl recognizes Peter in the courtyard outside the court.

A serving maid would up to this point have figured in literature, if at all, only as a comic figure in a play about an aristocrat in disguise. Here, she features in the story of another lowly character, a fisherman, whose denial proved to be the foundation experience for an institution that is still with us today.

The story has it that this maidservant recognizes "the Galilean" as he tries to warm himself in the Temple forecourt. He has sidled in to be close to where his friend Jesus is standing before the Roman Governor Pontius Pilate, on trial for his life.

The maid cries out: "And thou also wast with Jesus of Nazareth ... This is one of them." Peter denies it again and again, and then—hugely shamed—goes out and weeps bitterly.[60]

Yet, from such a tragically mortifying nadir in the life of one insignificant man, there emerges—transformed by the love of his Lord—a leader of such conviction that the whole world knows his story.

A scene like Peter's denial fits into no antique genre: "too serious for comedy, too contemporary and everyday for tragedy, politically too insignificant for history".

"The form, which was given it, was one of such immediacy that it's like does not exist anywhere else in ancient literature."[61] Auerbach believed that there was no single passage like it in an antique history that employed speech like this "in a brief, direct dialogue".[62]

In short, Peter exists in the literature at all because he is shown to have been loved by Christ, the second Person of the Trinity, whose Passion changed the world.

This tiny event, sparked by a female slave, is a literary event of such moment that it has echoed down through the centuries.

Christ's "memory" has come down to us because of the slow unfolding of a story carried and embodied through time by first an oral, then a literary, community that it has shaped. The drama of Peter's shame at being recognized by a female slave, and the ensuing sense of his own failure (which was even predicted by Christ), both is *and* is not catastrophic. A sudden awareness of who Christ is, and who *he* is as a result, transforms him completely, and presumably those to whom he tells the story, which—despite his lowly status—gets passed on and on.

All subsequent history hangs upon Peter's very *ordinariness*.

The far deeper moral forces at work guarantee it. Peter's story emerges from antiquity to power, a narrative that is with us *still*. His moral squalor is capable of momentous transformation—the force of it being that it could presumably apply to absolutely anybody. He suddenly knows far more than he could ever have imagined, *because* he sees he is loved. It is an epistemological truism that to love (and be loved) is to know—I explore this in the next chapter—and forever after, as a result, we ourselves can peer at the very stuff of life and find it charged with world-changing potential, meaning and significance: with development in other words. It is *as a result*, a journalist's privilege to peer at the world.

Non-people made real: a story from Sheffield
How do these ideas—about the value of reality and witness-bearing—impact what an authentic journalist looks for when searching for a "story"? Maybe the following vignette helps towards an answer.

When I was training in Sheffield to be a reporter, I was sent out for an hour into the streets to "find a story". It was understood that the streets were teeming with stories, and all I had to do was get out there, get my mind into gear, and get scribbling. And what did I do? I went into a local café for a coffee to get out of the cold! And as I sat there, someone who had been seated at the Formica-top table in front of me suddenly got up and left. I was alerted by the waitress behind the counter shouting "Oi, come back!" and yelling to anyone within earshot that the bloke had left without paying. I chatted to her and learned that her little business (and others like it) was losing money hand over fist because of such cheats … and I wrote up the story—with quotes from the waitress, the manager, the local councillor and the police—until the tiny incident had become a "story": a local scandal requiring changes in urban policy on security and police monitoring.

My role as witness, reporter and mediator of change to bring about justice in this small instance relied on my taking seriously the experience and words of a woman who would have been deemed by the ancients to be not just insignificant, but *beyond reality*. As we've seen recently in America, the ability of journalists to take seriously those who are "not part of their élite circles" is no longer as innate as it once was. The *Guardian* reports a very telling comment from a Trump supporter, as to why Trump won the first election:

> "I'm so tired of the media and Democrats bellyaching about Trump getting voted in. It's what the people wanted! It's pretty sad when all you hear is gloom and doom on the news, which I thought was supposed to be a balanced representation of the two sides. Surprise! There is a whole other part to this country outside of your newsroom walls that actually thinks differently from the mostly liberal ideas that most news outlets put out there."[63]

But, back to my Sheffield café and its pilferers. This could never have been a story before the Christian era. I could not have written it in the first place, as my testimony would not have been valid. So, the minute events of that lunchtime would have carried no weight, no portentousness at all.

Likewise, in the classical era, that waitress would have been a slave; a non-person. Just such a "non-person"—in the form of the serving-maid who recognizes Peter—blazes into history for the first time in the pages of St Luke's Gospel.

More to us than we think
Our third literary "hero of the self" is Augustine of Hippo (354–430), who was deeply influenced by Greek thought and, of course, by the Gospel and the biblical writings of St Paul.

Augustine continued the literary and social revolution begun in that firelit temple forecourt with Peter and the serving wench. His impact on the world (and, ultimately, journalism) began with his work *Confessions*, one of the most important books of all time, in 397; and, according to some, finished it only in 403. Prior to that, there was no work of literature like it: for example, the opening passage has no parallel in either classical or Christian literature:

> Great are you Lord, and greatly to be praised; great is your power, and your wisdom is infinite. And yet we lowly creatures desire to praise you, for we are a part of your creation; we carry with us the fact that we will die as evidence of our sin and proof that you resist the proud.[64]

No other work begins with a direct address to God. Augustine invented a form and style unique in his own oeuvre and, what's more, in the traditions he inherited.[65]

For sure, Ovid wrote three anguished poems in elegiac couplets from exile in Pontus on the southern coast of the Black Sea (in what is now Romania), banished by the

Emperor Augustus for an undisclosed misdemeanour, but they never rise above his circumstances to become part of some over-arching narrative. They are a long series of complaints to anyone who will read them, full of wounded *amour propre*.

"The author himself is his own theme," he writes unapologetically in *Tristia* Book VI. "As the swans of Cayster, they say, along its banks, mourn their own death with a fading cry, so I, exiled far off on the Sarmatian shore, take care my funeral will not pass in silence ... I've turned people's thoughts now to public verse, and instructed them to remember my name."[66]

Ovid's lament is sometimes couched as a prayer to whichever god may hear: his muse Thalia, the muses in general, the Emperor Augustus, the gods in general ... His pleas beg them to remember and help him, couched in the same terms as appeals to his wife, and to his friends, but without much more conviction than that.

Augustine, on the contrary, even with the threat of barbarians at the gates, celebrates rather than laments his weakness. His weakness serves only to enhance the disgrace his God suffered because it was endured *to raise him up.*

> I was not humble enough to conceive of the humble Jesus Christ as my God, nor had I learnt what lesson his human weakness was meant to teach. The lesson is that your Word, the eternal Truth, which far surpasses even the higher parts of your creation, raises up to himself all who subject themselves to him ... He would cure them of the pride that swelled up in their hearts and would nurture love in its place, so that they should no

longer stride ahead confident in themselves, but might realize their own weakness when at their feet they saw God himself, enfeebled by sharing this garment of our mortality. And at last, from weariness, they would cast themselves down upon his humanity, and when it rose they too would rise.[67]

Reflecting so clearly that sense that "perfection is from without" noted earlier, Augustine's long, complex animadversions were addressed as a *response* to his Creator in praise, not as anguished self-analysis: God already knew him, intimately.

What we must understand, in terms of the journalistic self, is that Augustine was reading himself and his life, whatever befell or had befallen him, in the light of a presence that, he believed without a doubt, *loved* him. This love was constant, predictable and purposeful. Such a context inevitably changed his view of himself and hence his "take" on the world around him. And that shaped what he felt he could and should do. It engendered a response.

We may love another; we rarely love ourselves. And if we do, we are generally insufferable, as Ovid shows. That self—*the* self—emerges fully for Augustine only through what he experienced as the gracious love of one who knew him well enough to accept him; and, knowing all, forgive all. That is the suffering, restored self that surges out of antiquity and into the following millennium, barely understood, traduced and squandered often, but in the long view of the world, triumphant. It is the self that views life humbly, above all gratefully, hungry for goodness and justice, knowing its own weakness, but not crippled by that knowledge because such knowledge is not the last word. It is eager to join itself to its Saviour. As James O'Donnell's commentary says:

> [Augustine] gestures in our direction and mentions us from time to time, but he *never addresses his readers*. As literary text, *Confessions* resembles a one-sided, non-fiction epistolary novel, in the presence of the silence (and darkness) of God. What he attempts is a radical turn away from the self, enacted from common sense—seen as tragically flawed by mad self-love—towards the wholly other, and thus toward the *true* self—for to him, we are not who we think we are (2.0).[68]

The self is not truly itself, and hence interested in more than itself, until it is a *transformed* self; transformed, that is, not by the espousal of some fashionable conceit, some ideology, but *loved into being what it was made to become*. Taking interest in other people and the world outside the self is a prerequisite of journalism.

This is a transformation made possible only by the spiritual apprehension and confirmation of what was reported in Scripture: the sacrifice of a God who Himself wished to be seen as getting Himself out of the way of our fear of Him. Fear of the divine—unbelievable as it is to our secular hearts—crippled the psyches of men and women for millennia, leading to all kinds of behavioural absurdities, distortions, oppression and cruelties, human sacrifice being not the least of them.[69]

"The testimony to my past sins—which you have forgiven and hidden away to give me happiness in you, *transforming my soul by faith and by baptism into you*— may that testimony stir the heart in those who read or hear it", Augustine writes (10.4). And it did stir the heart—many hearts. Indeed, this one book influenced the world more profoundly for the next one thousand years, than any other than the Bible itself—and still does, albeit distorted now by modern psychoanalysis and philosophy.

The pilgrimage of a soul to God, or rather, to its true self—which is a story of hope, humility, realism and actual change—was in the words of Roland Bainton, "more important than the conquest of a province",[70] the only precedents for Augustine's uniquely engaging and vivifying work.

In describing his own tortuous course, he analysed all mankind.[71]

His work had and gave relevance to everyone who read it. He was himself an illustration of man's corruption, redemption and continuing imperfection. This is not autobiography but spiritual psychodrama.

Hard for us to see it now, but the proverbial man in the street has his significance and reality for a journalist, in large measure because of the supercharged impetus given to his individuality by Augustine's exposition of the Gospel's relevance. *People matter. Ordinary people matter.* Without this, there could be no journalism.

For a sense of the scale of Augustine's achievement, we must turn back again to Erich Auerbach. Augustine, he says, feels and directly presents human life, and "it lives before our eyes."[72] Before the Bible writers and their inheritor Augustine, it was not reality that was described. Reality simply was not considered significant enough. True, reality was inferred, but only stylistically. And there were just two styles: an élite style, which conveyed the correct opinion of the subject matter, and a low style, separate from it, suitable only for comedy. The rule of the separation of styles remained inviolate. "Everything commonly realistic, everything pertaining to everyday life, must not be treated on any level except the comic, which admits no problematic probing."[73]

There could therefore be no serious literary treatment of everyday occupations and social classes, of everyday scenes and places, customs or institutions—in short: of the people and their lives. And without any treatment of the social forces that underlay the facts, there could be no social history, no exploration of culture, no critique, and (most importantly for us), no reportage. This was because, as we saw with Ovid, the ancients' way of viewing things did not see forces; it saw vices and virtues, successes and mistakes.

Yet it is precisely in the intellectual and economic conditions of everyday life that forces are revealed which underlie historical movements; these, whether military, diplomatic, or related to the inner constitution of the state, are only the product—the final result—of variations in the depths of everyday life. Yet aristocrats were reluctant to become involved with growth processes in the depths. They attributed to them the feeling that these were "vulgar and orgiastically lawless"...[74]

With Augustine, on the other hand, everyday life is what he uses to illustrate the forces arising from the depths of the constitution of his times. One is exhilaratingly sharing his experiences directly: his theft of a pear; his meeting with Alypius in the marketplace giving rise to a dismayed reflection on the gladiatorial spectacle whose bloodlust so corrupts his friend; his love for and repudiation of his concubine.

He is *reporting* these things, as it were, because the One to whom he speaks created him. "He" (as observer) and "they" (as actions) are rendered thereby as of more than surface significance.

Such ordinariness was possible of expression only because Augustine believed that "in the ordinary" is revealed the workings of God. This is mind-blowingly new: a revolution, a self-consciousness that arises from a sense that history itself is being called into being by an outside yet inner force, and a force moreover that calls him into fuller and fuller being by its loving knowledge of him.

That leaves us as journalists with the novel thought: that despite the centuries that have elapsed (trending towards a secular view of the world), our heritage means we can express ourselves in the context of momentous social change, we can endeavour to report at all, by dint of developments in thought that rested on *love*.

Where, therefore, love is not present in our writing, we fail our origins. Our very stylistic tools, the level of language with which we write—whether tabloid, broadsheet, and perhaps supremely X (Twitter)—also owe their origins to this levelling of aesthetics in the two styles.

That the King of Kings was treated as a low criminal, that he was mocked, spat upon, whipped, and nailed to the cross—that story no sooner comes to dominate the consciousness of the people, than it destroys completely the aesthetics of the separation of styles. It engenders a new elevated style that does not scorn everyday life and that is ready to absorb the sensorily realistic, even the ugly, the undignified, the physically base. It is clothed in eternal significance, which ultimately ennobles all things and makes them worthy of reporting.

Just to emphasize what has happened: "a new *sermo humilis* is born, a low style, such as would properly only be applicable to comedy, but which now reaches out far beyond its original domain, and encroaches upon the deepest and the highest, the sublime and the eternal."[75]

Unless this revolution had happened (thanks to Augustine), journalism—which deals most often in the lowly, the dark and the sordid in order to bring it up and out into the light—could not possibly have happened. A belief in perfectibility through the existence of a loving Other, which makes the self itself purposeful and safe in that purpose, also makes for a change it is hard to imagine happening in any other way.

Self-in-relation, and the value of opinion

The unmistakable echoes of this thinking sound again and again in Western history.

Indeed, the very word "person" itself began to develop with the Christian understanding of the "Word". The word was God, according to St John. The idea of a person therefore came to be charged with divine potential; as one through whom the Word sounds (*per-sonare*, meaning 'through, to sound').

Even in the second century AD, the jurist Gaius still recognized Roman law assumptions about distinctions of persons, giving three tests as to one's status. This meant that the word "person" was still purely physical and descriptive. It had no significance beyond that.

Yet, by the 12th century, this had developed to the belief that no individual could be discounted, if all were *logos*-bearers. So, according to Pope Innocent III (1160–1216): "You shall judge the great as well as the little and there shall be no difference of persons."[76]

Not only this, but canon lawyers had individuals in their sights when, in the eleventh century—in response to Cluniac reforms, necessitated by the indiscipline and corruption in the Church—they hammered out a Europe-wide moral order based on the firm belief that the secular authority could not govern souls.

This was finally embedded in the DNA of European thinking with Gratian. A teacher of Canon Law at Bologna around 1140, Gratian became Bishop of Tuscany. His most famous declaration is in his *Decretum:* "Natural law [*jus*] is what is contained in the Law and the Gospel, by which each is to do to another what he wants done to himself and forbidden to do to another what he does not want done to himself."[77] This was foreign to the ancient world, with its fixed hierarchy of human value and "everything in its place" idea of natural law.

Larry Siedentop describes this as a "bouleversement" in the structure of society itself, imposing the biblical "golden rule" on the ancient theory of natural law so that equality and reciprocity are made the mainsprings of justice,[78] and foreshadowing a freeing of the mind to give a far wider scope and a more critical edge to the role of analysis.[79] This was because society—and the world—ceased in theory to be compartmentalized. If laws should be applied to all equally, universal theory could be discussed. "*Is* as opposed to *ought*" could be distinguished, since laws applied to all.

Ironic indeed, then, that journalists and academics often condemn Christianity, as I did, in the belief that it may cost them their freedom to think.

What the canon lawyers of the twelfth century won ultimately for journalists was the primary role of the "person": a role shared equally by all, no longer secondary or subordinate to their social role. Social roles no longer exhausted the subject's identity. Being a "seigneur", "serf" or burgher might be added to or subtracted from an individual's identity, but the individual or "soul" remained.[80]

In the ancient world, by contrast, your civic rights inhered only in your status as citizen, as the master of a household, or *oikos*. Loss of your household through exile or cataclysm, as happened to the eminent poet Ovid, ended your civic status, and there were no rights outside it. Slaves, women and refugees had been simply non-persons in law.

From the insight that the person was an individual self—valuable in relation to, and respondable to, its Creator, Christ the King—there emerged over the next six hundred years the legitimacy of individual witness and the legitimacy therefore of individual opinion.

Conclusion

The idea of narrative, the idea of the transformed self and the idea of reality as being worthy of representation, all owe their origins to seismic developments in ancient Hebrew religious thought.

The Bible[81] was the first text to address people as a public.[82] And Peter the fisherman and the serving wench were the first lowly characters to play a major role in any drama.

Then Augustine elaborated a theory of self, that could be transformed into more than itself, through love.

Now we must find out what links all this with the early Reformers. For it was their energetic pamphleteering that ultimately brought European nations with their own languages into being as discernible entities.

This is what gave journalism its practitioners, its subject matter, its audience and its role.

The soul was engaged in a drama with its Creator. The Jewish response, to a sense of God's purposes for them and for creation, created not just a language but a hugely dynamic narrative thrust. This in turn gave value and meaning to ordinary mortals, once considered beneath notice: once again including Peter the fisherman and the serving girl in the courtyard, his accuser.

These ideas take tangible form at the dawn of mass communication, to which we turn in Part Two.

PART TWO
PROTEST AND MASS COMMUNICATION

Chapter 4
Putting Down the Mighty

We have had a glimpse of how prophecy seems to have led to the creation of ordinary talk, forming and reforming a people as they came to see themselves as part of a bigger story of freedom. We saw how it led to a revolution in realism, reality being something suddenly worth representing. And finally we saw the supreme value placed on the individual. Now we move on many centuries to where the pattern seems to recur in such a way that some conclusions can be ventured.

The story repeats what for some readers will be familiar. For others it will be new, perhaps unwelcome—and anyway irrelevant—depending on your view of historical causality. I believe however that this history bears revisiting. The connection—between the Reformation's impetus to translate and share the Bible and modern newspapers—came as a revelation to me. It accounts for the inchoate sense of honour deep within what remains of the press. The chain of connection between the renewal of individual conscience and the validity of popular opinion bears restating, even in sketch form. For the sermon was the first form of mass communication—and it could topple empires. The fifteenth century, with the print revolution and religious reformation, is foundational in the long tale of journalism.

1. Conscience—the individual right to think and speak

We pick up the narrative in Languedoc and Provence in the 1100s with the persecution of a group noted for its anti-clericalism, harbingers of the Reformation, whose valour proved irrepressible through tortures and martyrdoms.

The Waldenses were rebels and thinkers named after their leader Peter Waldo (1140–1218), a Lyons merchant who took to the streets to preach to anyone who would listen, that the Catholic Church was a sinful example of gluttony. He took his inspiration from the earlier *reformatio* of martyred Arnold of Brescia (1090–1155), a monk from Lombardy in northern Italy. This Arnold was a man of deep learning who had studied the scriptures and particularly the early days of the Church. What struck him was the simplicity and integrity of the proto-Church, when the disciples met together in their homes, without clergy, and holding everything in common. But it led him into very dangerous waters indeed. He was quickly captured and hanged at Rome as a schismatic on 18 June 1155.[83]

His disciple Waldo pressed on. He commissioned monks to translate the Latin New Testament into the language spoken by the people (*romance* or Franco-Provençal). Such a move was well-designed to upset the apple cart of religious authority. And this was well before Wycliffe translated the New Testament into the newly formed language of English in 1382. Waldo gave up his wealth, renounced many Catholic doctrines and rituals, and (most shockingly of all) advocated that any layman or woman had a legitimate voice, and could preach without the say-so of the bishops. The Waldenses, or *Vaudois* in French, went on to challenge all authority in the church, relying instead on direct biblical learning.

Their protest was doomed, alienating the élites and tearing at the fabric of a society whose sympathy would have helped them. Forced to flee, they ended up in the valleys of the Italian south, living in limbo, open to questioning and unafraid to speak out. Free thinkers who fell afoul of the Church there were aplenty in the early centuries of the second millennium. The Waldenses were only one such group, but they have endured to this day, migrating eventually to North Carolina in the US, where they remain to this day.

It was after Brescia's death, and in the relative safety of Calabria, that Waldensian literature revived in the early part of the fourteenth century, the first gleam of light of the Renaissance.[84] From out of religious persecution came the energy and resolve for social transformation. One of their number, Barlaam—a Greek-speaking French monk, perhaps the first French protestant (1290–1348)—was said to have been the first to revive, beyond the Alps, the memory of Homer. This rediscovery of classical, principally Greek, learning and attitudes took seriously the rounded development of the whole person. Barlaam influenced the two fathers of humanism: the poets Petrarch and Boccaccio.[85]

Notwithstanding, the Waldenses were excommunicated in 1184 by Pope Lucius III, enduring further centuries of persecution, being depicted as witches and burned at the stake in the Vatican's attempt to exterminate them.

They endured terrible tortures right up to the seventeenth century, tortures that are memorialized not just in the caves they had sometimes to hide in, but in John Milton's sonnet "On the Late Massacre in Piedmont". One man had his penis cut off and stuffed into his mouth, and then he was put on public display like that.

They were even said to have been cooked alive and eaten.

The Waldenses have come to be regarded as a significant forerunner of the Protestant Reformers. So significant in fact that Reuters reported how Pope Francis asked the forgiveness of the remaining 45,000-strong membership at a ceremony in Turin in 2015.

The battle for the right to think and speak freely had commenced in earnest.

Man the measure of all

The Renaissance—or Rebirth—emerged out of these very pogroms. Renaissance is shorthand for that revival in letters that from the twelfth century onwards gave rise to a more human-centred way of looking at God's world: "Man the measure of all things", in the words of the Florentine Giovanni Pico della Mirandola (1463–1494). It went some way to undermining or at least rebalancing the searing, life-denying asceticism of much medieval spirituality.

The recovery of the thought of Aristotle brought a focus back on this world, a desire to understand how the world worked. Realism regained its appeal—a theme that crops up again and again in this narrative. Aristotle appealed to Christians concerned with God's purposes for the *world*. Where Plato's idealism had confounded church spirituality for a millennium—diverting attention away from reality, into prayer and abstruse conjecture—Thomas Aquinas

(1225–1274) brought the focus back.

By synthesizing Aristotle and biblical learning, Aquinas earthed theology back into the real world where—because of the Incarnation, the "enfleshing" of God in Jesus Christ—he felt it surely belonged. This had profound implications for science and experimentation—and ultimately reportage. Why? Because medieval humanism was not like modern humanism, which is a rejection of Christianity. In its fascination with the created order, it was its realization. And without the long gestation of a sense that *what is there can be known and discussed*, reportage could not possibly have gained traction.

Perhaps we might put this into sharper focus by reference to the fact that much of Hinduism, for example, regards what is there as illusion, as *maya*. On the contrary, early Renaissance luminaries Petrarch (1304–1374) and Dante (1265–1321) took Christian-infused literature to altogether and—for some—new heights unsurpassed to this very day. They did this by drawing from the idea that God's most sublime creation, whom he gifted with reason, was mankind itself.

Humankind, made in God's image—so the Renaissance jubilantly had it—was created to embody and bring about God's purposes, and to act in his name, as his vicegerents. This is perhaps best conveyed in one of Petrarch's most well-known aphorisms: "While life is in your body, you have the rein of all thoughts in your hands." The body was not something to be mortified, starved and subdued—as in Tantric Buddhism—or ignored and treated with contempt as in ascetic and Ignatian monasticism, for it was the very seat of cultivation.

Printing and prophets

This brilliant gift might never have been fanned into the flame it became had it not been for the invention of printing. Printing made the dissemination of ideas an everyday fact of life.

Learning had (up until then) been acquired from manuscripts, inked laboriously by hand onto parchment—goat or sheep skin—or the more expensive calf skin, vellum.

However, there just were not enough goats or calves to supply the presses. It was fortuitous then that a method of making paper using pulped linen rags had just emerged in Europe, arriving probably from China via the Muslim Levant. As with so much inventiveness, paper originated at court in China, as early as the second century. But it was kept secret for hundreds of years by those who could control its use and the power it gave. It emerged in the Arab world in 751, when the governor-general of the Caliphate of Baghdad accidentally captured two Chinese papermakers in Samarkand in Uzbekistan and, with their help, founded a paper mill there.

This paper was made from macerating rags in water, pressing and drying them, and finally covering them in rice starch, to make a less permeable surface suitable for writing on.[86] From here, aided by an abundance of hemp and linen—two raw materials perfect for making paper—production spread to other cities in Asia, particularly Baghdad and Damascus.

War proved to be the engine of change: paper arrived in Europe with the Arab conquest of Sicily and Spain in the eleventh century. However, it was considered inferior to parchment, and (in 1221) Holy Roman Emperor Frederick II prohibited its use for public documents for a while. That was because, most inconveniently, rice starch also proved attractive to insects which ate it, shortening its shelf life.

Nonetheless, the arrival of paper—coinciding with the growing awareness of a lost world of literature that put the person back into focus as the subject of God's concern—had primed the Renaissance. The fuse was lit by seemingly ubiquitous outbreaks of protest by brave individuals against Church authoritarianism. Chief among them were John Wycliffe and Jan Hus. Their respective vision and courage paved the way for the Reformation, but they lived too soon to bring it to pass. They deserve mention in passing, to reinforce the fact that the price of freedom of speech and conscience was bloody.

Morning star, weak goose

John Wycliffe (1328-1384), perhaps the greatest of these writer-prophets, is known as the "Morning Star" of the Reformation, in part because he emerged against an apocalyptic backdrop of plague and the Black Death of 1347-8.

The plague killed between 30 and 60 per cent of Europe's population—perhaps two hundred million people, a number and an impact too colossal for the contemporary mind to compute.

Wycliffe was an Oxford don (Master of Balliol), a Catholic philosopher and theologian. He believed that the Church had fallen into sin and should be divested of all its property, its clergy to live in complete poverty.

His compassion for those who suffered and his indignation at the "shepherds" who had turned into "wolves" led him to protest indulgences and superstition in forthright terms. He particularly loathed the "magical" idea of transubstantiation (the belief that the bread and wine at Communion changed into the real body and blood of Christ).

Above all, he protested the use of a Latin Bible incomprehensible to ordinary people. Two hundred years before Tyndale, he advocated vernacular translation of the Vulgate, the then standard Latin Bible, into Middle English. And he set up an order of Poor Preachers who would take Bible truth to the people.

For this, he ran into such trouble with the authorities; although he died of a stroke, he was posthumously excommunicated, his works were destroyed, and his bones were dug up and burned.

Life turned out worse for Jan Hus (1369–1415), that other pioneer, who publicly defended the teachings of Wycliffe after he arrived at Charles University in Prague. One of Hus' principal protests was the view that the people were the Church, not the clergy. The Gospel was for their salvation, not for the Pope's power. For his advocacy of reform, he too was first excommunicated and then burned. He could be heard singing psalms as he was dying, tied to a post.

Before his execution Hus declared: "You may kill a weak goose, but more powerful birds, eagles and falcons, will come after me." The statement was a pun, as *Hus* is Czech for goose. Martin Luther took this personally, as prophecy.

It sparked a militant reaction: Hus' followers, known as "Hussites", defeated no less than five Papal crusades against them between 1420 and 1431. The world changed as a result of their resistance.

The writings in ink and parchment of these forerunners lacked printing's immediacy and effect, however. And their lives were snuffed out too soon to permeate the consciousness of all Europe, although they influenced Savonarola and Luther, who both went on to exploit printing.

It was just at this point in history that Johannes Gutenberg's invention emerged—and we now turn to look at what happened in more detail, noting as we do the similar contours to our own communications revolution. Its significance for us is that (eventually) anyone could launch their own ideas, thoughts, and reports onto a world agog for information.

Here, now, was a portable machine that could be set up almost anywhere, using flexible metal type that could disseminate new thoughts, on a daily basis.

Gutenberg's genius was not to invent a press itself—the Chinese had been doing that with woodblocks for centuries to print Buddhist texts—but he combined ideas from workaday functions in his Mainz locality: the wine press; metallurgy; and paper. And geography was on his side: Mainz, on the Rhine and Main rivers—the former imperial capital—provided for good distribution opportunities. It all made possible the replication and spread of a vast amount of learning. Everyone could become their own priest, their own prophet, and at last—just as with X (Twitter)—their own journalist. Let us look closer at this invention to appreciate what lies at the basis of our wordy world.

Piety the print driver

What is thought to be the first dated piece of print that we have from Gutenberg's printshop was, ironically enough, the very thing that Reformer Martin Luther "protested" against nearly eighty years later: indulgences, or pardons.

Gutenberg built up his business first on the printing

of such small items, which—like the production of pilgrim mirrors with which he launched his business, initially—were a major part of the so-called "economy of mercy". Merit, like money, could be earned.[87] As Neil McGregor points out: "At every stage of the process, from prayers for the dead to the remission of sins, late-medieval piety was the financial driver of Gutenberg's technological innovation."[88]

Modern readers generally have little idea of the desperate spiritual need of an illiterate religious people, who had little if any sense of the hope taught in a text to which they had no access. Even the clergy in Gutenberg's time were often illiterate, teaching that forgiveness of sins had to be earned through "satisfactions". If you could not fulfil the requirements of the Church to satisfy the need for pardon by the time you died, you went to so-called "purgatory" until you could.

The merit process was a long and desolate business. An even worse fate awaited you depending on the amount you had sinned, and the amount of satisfaction you could pay.

The production—and, later, outright purchase—of pardons was so widespread and ubiquitous, over so long a period of European history, that it comprised much of the economy, and with it a vast market for print.

Pardoners and purgatory

A short detour is in order here for our secular times, to explain what an indulgence is—for they are still produced. An indulgence was a "spiritual commodity",[89] an act of forgiveness on a piece of paper with a space where the signature of a bishop (usually) or other "pardoner" and the date could go. It afforded relaxation of the pains of purgatory.

Purgatory was an invention of the Church, weakly justified by just one apocryphal verse of scripture.[90] Only God could forgive sin, but the Church believed it could impose and administer "satisfactions" or penalties, which they could also reduce or remit altogether.

Sin, in its religious sense, has become a largely obsolete word. If you Google the term, you get pages of learned articles about trigonometry. Supplement writers use it to mean "being naughty", a peccadillo. The Cambridge Dictionary gives as examples "wasting food" and "For my sins, I'm organizing the office party …". Originally it meant to ignore the Creator, which was deemed to be catastrophic.

Therefore, indulgences were arguably the only form of social insurance there was. As such, their efficacy— wedded to the mechanization of their production— form the driving force of a viable business model that underwrote the ecclesial economy and, with it, the communications of Europe.

By the late fifteenth century they had become a form of currency by which the Church could exert its influence not just locally but internationally with a degree of calculability. The pope could "declare an indulgence" for some purpose and raise money for a pressing project. The need for pardons had cleverly become a form of Europe-wide lottery to raise money for public works.

One of the first to roll off Gutenberg's printing press was to raise funds for the relief of Cyprus against a threatened Turkish siege. Indeed, one theory has it that the whole system of indulgences had its roots in the mid- to late-eleventh-century need to defend the faith against Islam. Salvation in the shadow of easy death, invasion and religious slaughter was part of the psychological reward system in a highly realized and tangible way.[91] Salvation becomes, as we shall see in the next chapter, the nub of our story.

Salvation the crux
Gutenberg is known for the very first printed Bible in history—and he financed it from indulgences and other single-sheet productions, such as church notices, publishing blurbs, and schoolbooks. Over time, 180 identical copies of the Vulgate in Latin eventually rolled off his presses, in a typeface as close to the style of familiar written manuscripts as could be conceived.

What is rarely appreciated nowadays is just how colossal an undertaking printing a whole Bible would have been for a small print shop.

> " ... the printing of the 1,282 pages of an edition of 180 copies would have taken roughly two years—a very considerable time for capital to be tied up before sales allowed the partners to recoup their investment. The work required constant injection of new funds. The logistical requirements were beyond anything previously experienced in a book world accustomed to manuscript books emerging from the copyist one at a time."[92]

Customers paid around 20 gulden (gold penny) for a paper copy of the Gutenberg Bible and 50 for a copy on vellum. This was at a time when a stone-built house in Mainz would have cost between 80 and 100 gulden and the annual pay of a senior craftsman was between 20 and 30 gulden a year.[93]

Reformation scholar Andrew Pettegree well conveys the enormity of the risks entailed. Indeed, they eventually destroyed Gutenberg when his partner Johann Fust sued him for what he alleged was "theft" of the original loan.

Gutenberg was also thrusting out into a world of superstition, a frightened world that viewed as witchcraft what printing made possible. This is evident from several sources, including the following description of a sales trip to Paris, by Fust, who took with him some early copies of the Bible:

> Fust undertook the sale of them in Paris, where the art of printing was then unknown. As he sold his printed copies for 60 crowns while the scribes [who produced manuscripts] demanded 500, this created universal astonishment: but when he produced copies as fast as they were wanted and lowered the price to 30 crowns, all Paris was agitated. The uniformity of the copies increased the wonder; informations were given in to the police against him as a magician; ... a great number of copies being found [in his lodgings], they were seized; the red ink with which they were embellished was said to be his blood; it was seriously adjudged that he was in league with the devil; and if he had not fled, most probably he would have shared the fate of those whom ignorant and superstitious judges condemned ... for witchcraft.[94]

Why then, to our cynical minds, would it be natural for Gutenberg to undertake such a project? Purely for prestige? But he risked stigma as the devil's apprentice, and possible calumny as a subverter of the existing and highly élitist manuscript culture.

Why would anyone want a printed Bible, since manuscript Bibles were viewed as precious enough already by noblemen–collectors, for whom a well-stocked library was a mark of social standing? But such reticence is overplayed, given the reception his Bible in fact received.

Perhaps Gutenberg took on the assignment for gain? But he stood to lose everything in such a risky venture, as indeed he did when Fust sued him. To meet demand, then? Yes, more likely.

There was a palpable sense of wonder associated with his Bible. Elizabeth Eisenstein states that on the Continent, Gutenberg's German compatriots were acknowledged and lauded for being the first to set up printing shops in Italy, France and Spain. The colophon[95] to the famous Bible of 1460 asserts that "this noble book" was born in "the bounteous city of Mainz of the renowned German nation, which the clemency of God has deigned, with so lofty a light of genius and free gift to prefer and render illustrious above all other nations of the earth."[96]

Wherever the craftsmen went, they "publicized the local history and special virtues of the towns in which they worked ..." thus enhancing the reputations of the local rulers across Europe who invited them to set up shop and, so to underwrite civic pride, contribute to local prosperity and enhance that personal sense of significance that the spiritual reality of the era conveyed.[97]

This would seem to justify the conjecture that Gutenberg risked everything partly for *religious* and not just pecuniary reasons. This was an age of religious belief. Even scepticism was expressed in religious terms. It is not fanciful to think that Gutenberg may well have believed that what he was doing was for eternity, inherently meritorious; a sacred undertaking that would benefit not just his own soul, but civilization itself. And of course, in the end, even make him rich.

Consequences for journalism
Replicability is a key attribute of a newspaper, along with contemporaneity, periodicity and public distribution. The first of these essential attributes became possible only with Gutenberg's invention.

But it was not until fourteen years after the invention of his press that Gutenberg and Fust were able to exhibit the trial pages of his masterpiece at the Frankfurt Fair in 1454—where Pope Pius II saw the first printed sheets—and so cause the sensation.

The Bible was to make Gutenberg's name, and so draw greater attention to the revolution he had made possible than any number of short, printed works. Because it was printed in Christendom's lingua franca of Latin, its use could spread around the whole of the world that mattered.

For our purposes, however, its significance lay in the spur it gave through replicability to universal literacy. Ordinary people started to want to know what it said. Now, within reason, they could. They no longer had to rely on erroneous priestly interpretation; they could read for themselves. And what they read astonished them. Indeed, it astonished the most learned of clerical scholars, Martin Luther, as we shall see, and changed the course of history. But reading was beginning to take off for ordinary people, too, like a whisper of freedom.

It is oddly synchronous that printing was invented and being developed for only a decade before there was a huge subject for its industry: the Fall of Constantinople in 1453. By far the greatest stimulus to the growth of a European news industry was the relentless encroachment of the

Ottoman Empire.[98]

Constantinople was the apogée of Eastern Christian civilization: a place so glorious that Vladimir I, the first Christian Emperor of Russia, converted his entire nation to the Orthodox version of the faith in 970 overnight, upon hearing tell of Constantinople's marvels.

The shock, then, of Constantinople's catastrophic fall must have reverberated with force and horror across the world, giving huge impetus to the generation of news, for which the print revolution seemed made.

Although the sack of Constantinople by the Turks under Mehmed II shattered any lingering illusion of continental safety, paradoxically it fomented the intellectual revolution that became known as *the* Reformation. Fleeing Christian asylum seekers salvaged and brought with them from Constantinople's fabulous scriptoria and libraries precious manuscript copies of the New Testament in Greek. This was the language in which it had originally been authored by the Evangelists.

This brought with it to the West, which had only the crude but official Vulgate or Jerome translation, a quite new awareness of Scripture. The Latin Church had grievously declined from the standard of truth and purity upheld in Scripture.[99] A spectacular printed Greek New Testament based on these manuscripts was prepared for wide dissemination by Desiderius Erasmus (1466–1536), in 1516, and printed by Johann Froben (1460–1527) of Basel. It was an instant sensation. As the Renaissance master Dante Alighieri, looking back, wrote in *Divina Comedia* in 1555:

> "E'en they whose office is
> To preach the gospel, let the gospel sleep,

And pass their own invention off instead."[100]

Now the Gospel was awake, and with it, Europe.

<u>The divine art</u>
It was not surprising, then, after these public and agonizingly protracted struggles that for the first generation of printers, the Church would be the new industry's most significant customer.[101]

God had quite clearly provided a tool for the conversion and neutralization of Europe's greatest foe, Islam. "Printing was dedicated by the special grace of God to the redemption of the faithful," wrote the author of a student manual illustrated with the first printed regional map of Palestine.

By creating the possibility of replicability, God had also dealt a winning hand to the Church itself. Printing made possible the wide availability of the writings of the Church fathers, fanning the flames of the Renaissance. Not only that, but the demands of liturgical conformity across the whole continent could be met in a breath-taking affirmation—or so it seemed—of divine approval.

2. Individual conscience and the political system
The Borgia papacy, however, was not so gleeful. We come now to the second major consequence of Bible translation and accessibility: the influence of the printed sermon.

The apocalyptic preacher Fra Girolamo Savonarola (1452–98)—the Frate as he was known—relied on print to disseminate his incendiary sermons against the incestuous Alexander VI.

It was Savonarola who prepared the Europe-wide theatre of religious dissent onto which Luther then strode.

Despite holding no formal, secular office, this strange little friar, with a haggish face framed in the shadow of the monastic hood of his Dominican order, is key to our story. For, with as mesmerizing a voice as could be remembered, he captivated the humanist intelligentsia of Florence simply by his uncompromising clarity. His insistence on content rather than form reinforced a "stress on the primacy of truth".[102]

But whereas Luther later had the protection of Frederick the Wise, Elector of Saxony—and survived— Savonarola was on his own. He regarded himself as a prophet. So he did not set out to endear himself with the authorities. Indeed, he publicly and repeatedly urged the French to march on Rome and destroy it, to save the corrupted Christendom project.

He went so far as to claim divine insight into Rome's downfall and all Europe unless his prophecies were heeded. He had his sermons about King Charles VIII of France returning to reform the Church by the sword printed and put on sale.

He rapidly became a sensation, the best-selling author in Florence; between 1495 and 1498, editions of his sermons came out at the rate of one every fortnight.[103] They were printed in a Latin that everybody with any clout across the whole continent could read.

Savonarola's searing sermons against Papal corruption, élitist profligacy and sexual immorality proved the dawn of an electrifying new idea: that personal conscience disseminated by means of print, could change the political system. And it did.

It is said that Savonarola's congregations often numbered up to 14,000 worshippers, standing on stone floors, often in the cold. Yet they flocked day after day to hear him. If they couldn't hear, or fell asleep on their feet, they could fall back on the printed version.

His passionate denunciations of corruption led, as he suspected it would, to his death. But not before he was subjected to a horrendous period of prolonged torture in the Palazzo Vecchio. His hands tied behind his back, he was hoist by a rope hanging from the ceiling, so that his arms came out of their sockets, breaking one of his limbs. His tormentors did this several times until he recanted, changed his mind, then recanted again.

Shame at his weakness led him to write even more, despite being barely able by now to hold a pen. His two beautiful *Meditationes* on Psalms 31 and 51, written during the period of his torture, were later reprinted by the Protestant founder, Martin Luther.

The Pope panicked. On 23 May 1498, without justification, the Frate was executed by strangling. He was then burned at the stake in Florence's main square before his beloved Duomo. It sparked, not surprisingly, a huge and morbid wave of puritan zeal. In a penitential tsunami, of which we have only the barest inklings from campaigns to tear down statues and memorials that offend our modern sense of virtue, the residents built bonfires and burned their own musical instruments. They destroyed their playing cards, gaudy clothes, profane works of art, "and other vanities".[104] The Humanist philosopher Pico della Mirandola went to live in a monastery. Botticelli, famed for his fleshly ladies evoking classical Humanist themes, began painting profoundly religious canvases instead. The Florentines even proclaimed Jesus Christ the ruler of their city.

Preachers were now able to send their messages from beyond the grave, as editions of their collected sermons continued to be published long after their deaths. Daniel Defoe, who had the same reforming zeal as Savonarola, got the point 200 years later, when he wrote: "The preaching of sermons is speaking to a few of mankind; printing books is talking to the whole world."[105]

The most vigorous impetus given to popularization before printing came from the felt need of preachers to keep their congregations awake. Sermons therefore proved to be an investment of manageable size for a printer, and they were affordable for readers. Pettegree notes that this early print surge prefigured the later experience of Germany during the fury over Martin Luther. It sent a powerful signal to a city élite that had turned its back on book production. The ruling class had paid a heavy price for their disdain of print based, as it surely was, on spiritual blindness: they misread the people. They lost their peerless cultural ascendancy, which went instead to Germany. The lessons of the Savonarolan success in Florence would be well-learned by Europe's other ruling power, Germany.[106]

So, we now turn to Germany, specifically to Eisleben (in what is today Eastern Germany), where Martin Luther, the lynchpin in the history of journalism was born. A heretic to the Roman Church, he became popularly known as the "Wittenberg Nightingale" for the winsomeness of his utterance. Before he sang, "the full potential of print as a news medium was only just beginning to be recognized."[107] But when he did sing—also, like Savonarola, against institutionalized spiritual abuse—the effect was electrifying, both on print and journalism, as we go on to see.

Chapter 5
The Nightingale Sings

Luther's life of protest acted as the fulcrum between the medieval world of widespread illiteracy and religious fantasy, with its intellectual dependence on a Church of diktat, and the modern world of inquiry, communication and public debate. For his protest came as the whole of Europe was undergoing a shift from script to print in a relatively short span of time. Eisenstein concludes categorically that the revolution was complete, "By 1500, one may say with some assurance that the age of scribes had ended, and the age of printers had begun."[108]

Wherever one went, across all sorts of European frontiers—from Mount Etna to regions north of Stockholm, from Atlantic coasts to the mountains of eastern Montenegro—during the last half of the fifteenth century one would find the same sorts of new workshops in major urban centres. They produced books in almost all Western European languages.[109]

Luther was born just as all sorts of barriers in knowledge and in social and political life were falling, made possible by the "period of decompartmentalization" that was the Renaissance.[110] By this is meant that all forms of knowledge were able to begin to cross-fertilize each other. Theory could begin to interact with practice—and Luther not only helped more than any other to turn the tide, he rode it as it came in.

Theology needed to be real for Luther. He bet his life on what he read in the Bible. His was a "permanent achievement" with huge implications for empiricism and the dissemination of knowledge.[111] We turn therefore to encounter the great man, with his legs astride the two epochs.

Beginnings
Luther (1483–1546) was, like Savonarola, an earnest and conscientious young man. He was born in Eisleben, a mining town in Thuringia. His father came from peasant stock but was forced to try his hand as a miner, rising to own and manage a copper mine in nearby Mansfeld.

Luther was devout in the Catholic way, assiduous for his salvation, anxious and prone to depression about his sins, oppressed by the terror of death and the possibility of hell: the pervasive and ever-menacing reality of judgement in the Europe of his day.

After university at Erfurt, he eschewed the career in law his father had wanted for him, after a near-death experience. A later incident in which he was felled by a lightning strike—it is unclear if he was struck, or just fell through fear—while walking back to university from a trip home, convinced him. In great spiritual distress, he cried out from where he lay to the patron saint of mining:

"Blessed St Ann! I will become a monk!"

He kept his vow, despite some disapproval especially from his father, and in 1505 joined the Order of Augustinian Friars in Erfurt.[112] It was no picnic; he fasted sometimes up to six hours a day and prayed to three saints every day. The scrupulous 22-year-old was setting out to assuage his anxious fears about hell by earning his salvation the hardest way possible. It was a time when night vigils interrupted sleep, money for food had to be found by begging, and even to speak with a woman was forbidden. He learned the whole Bible by heart. The hardships gave him, for a time, peace.

He was then invited to do his doctorate and teach at the new, only partially constructed Augustinian university, established by the ambitious elector of Saxony, Frederick the Wise, at Wittenberg in 1502. This had the very first printing press in the capital, producing its first books that year. Wittenberg was still small, the unprepossessing but nonetheless politically significant capital of Electoral Saxony. To be an "Elector" meant you were one of the seven most important princes in the Holy Roman Empire, one who could elect the Emperor—and Luther was to have a lot for which to thank Frederick in due course. However mean your province, your power as Elector was undeniable. Under Frederick's aegis, Luther continued through penance, suffering and self-denial to try to appease what he had been taught about Christ, and so win for himself a state of grace.

Luther's 95 Theses: Europe's first mass media event
Luther certainly never intended to spark a revolution. It was true, however, that he was being remoulded by the fresh winds of Humanism, and powerful movements in

theology that were sloughing off the futile conjectures of medieval scholastic learning. He drank deeply of the works of Augustine of Hippo, the African bishop whose sense of dependence on God's grace alone for his being and salvation prefigured Luther's own sense of moral helplessness.

But it simply did not occur to Luther that by following his powerful conscience he would clash with the powers that be, nor was it his intention. His protest—against indulgences—when it came, was a concern to protect the papacy from what he found out was happening locally in its name. His target was the indulgence preachers, who—more like tax collectors—were doing the bidding of blatantly unscrupulous middlemen like the young and ambitious Archbishop Albrecht of Brandenburg (1490–1545), and his sidekick, the unpleasant Dominican, Johann Tetzel (1465–1519).

Albrecht had been allowed by Pope Leo X to amass two other powerful offices at the same time in return for a fee of 20,000 gulden, which he raised in a deal with Fuggers, the great medieval banking family. The pope allowed him to repay this debt by the sale of a papal indulgence in the archiepiscopal lands under his oversight.

We saw in the previous chapter that the average annual pay of a senior craftsman in Germany at that time was around 100 gulden. Therefore, 20,000 was a vast sum, and Albrecht had to devise a smart way to pay it off and so maintain his status. The weaselly Tetzel was it. Tetzel started preaching just outside Wittenberg, near enough for Wittenbergers to slip out to hear him, even though technically he was not permitted to go outside the Archbishopric territory.

Luther knew nothing of the political shenanigans, but did notice the locals returning from hearing Tetzel, lighter in pocket, and clutching their indulgence certificates. He learned also that other preachers were being cancelled so that worshippers could go and hear Tetzel, who clearly had form. Luther was worried.

He got hold of the document justifying the indulgence, Albrecht's *Instructio Summaria*. For the appropriate fee paid, it seemed to promise much more than remission of the penalties the Church was then entitled to apply after confession: remission from guilt itself. In fact it promised to remit all guilt forever, not just for them but for their relatives in purgatory too! Albrecht was clearly desperate to "win big". Or as Graham Tomlin tactfully puts it "in the most charitable terms, the *Instructio* failed to make it clear that it only applied to satisfactions, not forgiveness."[113]

Luther, as a theologian and therefore guardian of the Church, had to do something. He wrote to the 27-year-old Albrecht alerting him to the presence of Tetzel, and decided there should be a debate. He publicized this event by posting 95 Theses on a *Disputation on the Power and Efficacy of Indulgences* on the university's bulletin board—the great West door of Wittenberg Castle Church—on 31 October 1517. It was perfectly normal to post such adverts on the church door. But in posting this one, Luther unintentionally put his life on the line, and the whole world's destiny with it.[114]

Although this is an apparently bland action to our modern interpretation, this document struck at the very heart of religious power. Originating in a substantial need for psychological and spiritual relief, the enormity of indulgences is almost impossible for us to imagine today yet, if we cannot imagine the scale of this, we can have little idea of the tremendous moral cataclysm that underpins the modern era.

The spiritual context in which we live is so vastly removed from what it was then. We hardly think about the afterlife as being a consequence of this life, if we think about it at all. Sin barely registers with us, or so we think, even as we feel vaguely ill at ease over so much in life. And yet we do have a sense of rightness, particularly in public dealings. When we discover MPs have been selling access to Parliament, or that the Queen's hearse when leaving Balmoral, conveying her body to her own funeral, displays on its window an advert for the undertakers driving it, we are disgruntled.[115] Luther was appalled. For ordinary people, the monetization of religion, and the exploitation of what was their birthright, is corruption, and Luther felt it should be outed.

But not just that. Luther was not actually against pardons: they were as much a part of the medieval life as say, supermarkets are today—the means of securing sustenance at a time when access to spiritual goods was deemed even more of a necessity for survival than food. Luther was a monk. He practised everything required of him to an obsessive degree. If he missed prayers, he would catch up with them in his own very limited time. None of it eased his sense of failure; his suspicion that he did not make the spiritual grade. He spent sometimes up to six hours in confession, ransacking every last corner of his conscience for "hidden faults" in order to find the peace he was so sure should be his. When required to say Mass for the first time, directly addressing—without mediation—the great high King, he was nearly physically sick with nerves. Terror overwhelmed him. His sense of unworthiness proved almost crippling.

Luther's despair saved him, for it goaded his questing intellect. If God was love, why was he so afraid? If the truth set you free, why was he forever captive to a panoply of Church-mediated prescriptions dependent on the Pope? Luther could only see that God was all Judge and no love, his righteousness being all about punishing sinners, his "gospel" just the promise of judgement. "Here was a God he could only ever cower before."[116]

The very town architecture reinforced fear. Above the entrance to the cemetery surrounding the church in Wittenberg, which Luther would see every time he entered it, was carved into the mandorla or almond-shaped aureole, a stone relief of Christ seated on the rainbow judging the world. So angry did it look, the veins standing out, menacing and swollen, on his forehead[117] that it provoked hatred in Luther.

"I hated the righteous God who punishes sinners, and secretly, if not blasphemously ... I was angry with God." It seemed to him that God hated his creatures and made impossible burdens for them.

But Luther had discovered something shattering. He was not reading about fear in scripture. Scripture was full of the love and action towards his creatures of a God who wanted them safe; wanted them to love Him back. If that was so, then the forgiveness pronounced by the priest after confession must mean something.

It was only in 1519 when Luther, according to his memoir written nearly thirty years later, alighted during his studies at the monastery upon one particular biblical verse. It was Romans 1:17: "He who through faith is righteous shall live." What Luther realized in his shattering moment was that all he had to offer God *was* his sin. In exchange, God would not only *not* punish him but would give him his *own* righteousness: quite a gift.

This was not what the Church was teaching. The Church taught personal effort, the exhausting, pointless hamster-wheel of penance. Yet to question the Church—the Pope, the supreme power on earth who alone could interpret scripture—was to be guilty of heresy, and that was punishable, not with a slap on the wrist, but by death.

What Luther had been expecting from God was in fact man-made. The Bible was being misinterpreted, wholesale. "It was this good news that reformed Luther's heart, and this message that he would proclaim to bring reformation to others."[118]

This epiphany, despite the political danger of it, broke into his dungeon of despair, gave him the joy and peace he had been seeking, and in rapid succession, a quite superhuman burst of energy to make all this known.

Like a good journalist who has discovered a huge story, he began to write—feverishly. He wrote faster than three printers could print, expounding and consolidating his earlier misgivings about the whole papal and pardon system—and, inevitably, fomenting a direct confrontation with Rome. We will find that similar "bursts of energy", flowing from a similar impulse, impacted the rise and course of journalism.

Harnessing social media

The modern West has largely jettisoned the possibility of religious faith. But without it, Luther could not have penetrated the labyrinth of ecclesiastical reasoning with different thinking; he could never have entered the system at all. He needed Greek to understand St Paul, Latin to read Augustine and Aquinas. He needed to be au fait with the Chaldean and Hebrew languages. He needed a vast amount of theological and classical scholarship. And he never would have bothered had he had no faith or fear of God in the first place.

The import of Luther's *Theses* is hard to make resonate in modern discourse, but we have to try. Here are three that embody the key to the door of the past, with their preamble:

> "Out of love and zeal for truth and the desire to bring it to light, the following theses will be publicly discussed at Wittenberg under the chairmanship of the reverend father Martin Luther, Master of Arts and sacred Theology and regularly appointed Lecturer on these subjects at that place. He requests that those who cannot be present to debate orally with us will do so by letter.[119]
>
> 19. When our Lord and Master Jesus Christ said, "Repent," he willed the entire life of believers to be one of repentance ....
>
> 20. Therefore the pope, when he uses the words "plenary remission of all penalties", does not actually mean "all penalties", but only those imposed by himself.
>
> 21. Thus those indulgence preachers are in error who say that a man is absolved from every penalty and saved by papal indulgence ...

Luther wanted a debate, in the normal way. He did not want and, least of all, expect a violent revolution. The consequences of this invitation to a debate need not be rehearsed here, as the story is long and detailed and deserves a proper treatment that can be found elsewhere.[120]

For our purposes, it is enough to note (as I have said already), that the escalation of Luther's pamphleteering on the back of the reaction he provoked was, after Savonarola, Europe's—and arguably therefore the world's—first mass media event.[121] The torrent of publicity that accompanied each step of the drama he unleashed was unprecedented, taking even him by surprise: "It is a mystery to me how my theses, more so than my other writings ... were spread to so many places. They were meant exclusively for our academic circle here ... They were written in such a language that the common people could hardly understand them."[122]

Yet, within forty years no part of Western Christendom remained altogether unaffected by it.[123] Luther with his trenchant, excoriating and principled writing, was unputdownable. His writing and its force seemed unbelievable in the cramped confines of Catholic authoritarian society. He created an avid readership and hence a huge market.

It is estimated that between 1517 and 1519, Luther's thirty major publications sold well over 300,000 copies, making "Lutheranism" "the first child of the printed book".[124] People wanted to be free—but with God's permission; and they evidently wanted to read what Luther was saying.

The Lutheran archivist Josef Benzing gives a stupendous tally of 3,692 separate editions of works by Luther that went into print.[125] Even his printers could not keep up with him, so new was this kind of thing, and he had to slow down. His assault on the confessional alone had, by 1521, run into fourteen editions and put paid forever to the idea that the individual conscience could be externally controlled, by priests or anyone else—let alone bought.

The brouhaha could have cost him his life. For refusing to renounce what he had written, he was finally declared a heretic on 3 January 1521 by Pope Leo X. For this he should have been burned at the stake, but there was no popular consensus against him and, anyway, there were mistakes in the charges made against him. He was excommunicated at the Diet of Worms in April 1521 and formerly condemned as an outlaw by Emperor Charles V.

But publicity—and Frederick the Elector—saved him. Luther gave everyone the slip after his hearing, and en route by wagon for Wittenberg, he was daringly kidnapped incognito by Frederick's men for safe keeping and taken to the Castle of Wartburg. There he grew a beard, dressed as "Sir George", a knight, and kept his newly hirsute head down.

In hiding in the castle from the Pope for ten months, it was there that he produced a rough, vernacular translation of the Bible, "the first German book to be a book of the people."[126] One of Luther's opponents, Cochlaeus, grumbled that "the common people loved it, and cobblers and old women studied it and argued about its texts."[127]

Luther generates a "public"

Luther was able to garner widespread interest—even before there was recognizably such a thing as a "public" audience.

Nonetheless, the public started to come into its own from this time in large part because of the ferment of opinion his writing generated, coinciding as it did with the development of perspective or viewpoint in Renaissance art. Human beings became aware of themselves over against their perceived world.

Marshall McLuhan defines the public as "a great consensus of separate and distinct viewpoints".[128] This concept was itself increasingly attributable to new self-awareness. It was brought about by access to contemporary literature. Contemporary, as opposed to the already available classical literature, also impressed on the newly literate classes a sense of otherness: that the present was distinctly different from the past.

The continuum of learning reinforced by the slow laborious products of the scriptorium had ruptured.[129] Print fragmented the body politic into thinking units, even as it decompartmentalized broader habits of conceptualizing and transmitting knowledge about the world, and the self.

People's minds started to work differently, or in differentiated fashion. And for perhaps only the second time in human history, a great reading public was to judge the validity of revolutionary ideas through a mass medium that used the vernacular language. The first time this had happened was with the invention of Hebrew and the writing down of scripture. This time, that medium combined the arts of the journalist and the cartoonist.[130]

"The public" had reached a stage of incipient development in time to protect Luther. Other reformers—like Arnold of Breschia, John Wycliffe, Jan Huss and Savonarola—were too early to benefit, and fell afoul of the dominance of Rome.

The availability of technological mechanisms and distribution channels for Luther's writing meant that protest could no longer be snuffed out on the whim of a pope but rather it could be carried to every corner of the empire. And, anyway, the empire was expanding with the discoveries of Christopher Columbus under the extraordinary rule of Ferdinand and Isabella of Spain. This, and the news of it, further consolidated the changing perspective that Europeans had of themselves. Expanding horizons, both psychologically and geographically, gave Europeans self-consciousness in a quite new way.

Additionally, the social media of Luther's day—print—was harnessed not just to the readiness of populations for what he had to say, but to the existing civic structures of Europe—the magistracy—which slowly rallied to his cause.

Printing's revolutionary capacity for multiplication, and the faith that motivated its exploitation generated a "new learning". The presses were working, the printers were multiplying, the press made possible methods of study that were only in embryo in the days of manuscripts and, though libraries were still tiny by later standards, knowledge was increasing.

The Renaissance (and the Reformation that came on the back of it) was not only powered by new information: this was a movement of the spirit: "... more a movement of faith than of reason", notes an eminent scholar.[131] It had echoes of Pentecost. Indeed, the Reformation effected a great transformation of popular religion whereby the agelong medieval sense of contrast between ideal and real was beginning to merge into an educated sense of contrast between what the Bible taught, and the largely fantasy religion popularly practised in the Church.[132]

Printing made possible popular reading and the appropriation of a more authentic truth, and with it a dissolving of old ways of seeing and being.

Freedom through print: embarrassing Reformation?
For fashionable scholars of our own day, the Reformation has been something of an embarrassment. Luther's huge awareness of the grace of God sets him today against his peer Erasmus's faith in human reason. His religious fervour has been judged contrary to tolerance and to intellectual advance, undermining contemporary inquiry.

The writer of the Cambridge History of the era says that no one would today be willing to list the causes of the Reformation.[133] Christopher Marsh has coined the expression "the compliance conundrum":[134] the curious fact that people accepted the changes wrought by the Reformation.

Eamon Duffy purports to be equally puzzled. Why was the Reformation accepted at all, given Europe's ubiquitous loyalty to ritualized religion? "The jury is still out on that complex question," Duffy says.[135] The Reformation, he contends, was a violent disruption, not the natural fulfilment of most of what was vigorous in late medieval piety and religious practice.

But this seems to deny the essential Catholic formation of the Reformers and betrays a curiously bifurcated mindset. Late medieval Catholicism, despite papal corruption, exerted an enormously strong, diverse and vigorous hold over the loyalties and imagination of the people, up to the very moment of the Reformation.[136]

Yet it created a huge hunger it evidently could not satisfy. It merely fed the beast. Luther and his closest colleagues were Catholic monks, famished for God and for peace, who pursued the logic of their faith as they found it afresh in newly available and far better translated Scripture.

Far from being hollowed out by authoritarianism, paganism and superstition, the religious world—both clerical and lay—was a highly productive and spiritually vigorous continuum.

For this very reason people were ready for a deeper, more bracing truth than the often-ignorant clergy had allowed them. Indeed, according to Erasmus (1466–1536) the clergy were "so universally loathed that even a chance meeting is said to be ill-omened ... they believe it's the highest form of piety to be so uneducated that they can't even read."[137]

Was it not that Luther's dazzling liberties, attested by newly available copies of the biblical text, seemed to afford them a guilt-free new access to a God they had only vaguely heard about, and longed to know more of?

Did not the simultaneous social impact of printing, and the rapid and exhilarating contamination of ideas that it caused, serve precisely to reinforce the effect?

For the American writer Steven Ozment there can be no puzzle as to the appeal of the Reformation: it was freedom to know, promoted through print.[138] He builds up from primary sources—pamphlets, vernacular confessional manuals and fifteenth-century lay catechisms—an awesome picture of what normal religious life had exacted from participating laymen and women.

In a sense, journalism was powered by the awfulness about which the Reformation protested: another detour is in order to convey the strength of it.

From fear to love

Children from the age of seven were expected to be confessed.

Adults were grilled in the confessional about not just their sex lives but even their thoughts and fantasies. Priests were undoubtedly avid for vicarious thrills that clerical celibacy denied them.[139]

The confessees simply wanted inner peace, which the whole futile process undermined.

Picture catechisms conveyed dramatic messages by woodcuts depicting the gruesome suffering of sinners in purgatory and hell. One such manual pictures people in hell feeding on their own flesh, with the caption: "The pain caused by one spark of hellfire is greater than that caused by a thousand years of a woman's labour in childbirth".[140]

The confessional had become "a workshop for priestly mischief". The fright and shame generated by religious art on the eve of the Reformation must be considered among the motives behind the liturgical simplification and iconoclasm of the early Protestant movement.

Images were no longer the "layman's Bible" but had become impediments to the spiritual growth of the laity,[141] and turned the confessional into "a veritable tyranny".[142]

Instead, the Lutherans put into the hands of the laity detailed guides, doctrine by doctrine and practice by practice, to reformed religion.

One of the most important early examples of this is Guillaume Farel's *Summary and Brief Description of All that is Necessary for Every Christian to Have Confidence in God and Help his Neighbour.* In it, he exhorts, "Christians, leave the cruel tyranny of those who have placed unbearable burdens on your backs while lifting not a finger in your behalf, and come to him who has taken and bears our burdens upon his shoulders."[143] If it wasn't liberating, it wasn't Christian.

The revolutionary social and spiritual programme of Luther and his followers was largely carried out on the back of pamphlets like this.

They exhorted Bible reading, a deeper dependence on a loving God, and support in hard times.

One pseudonymous author in 1521 attempted to bridge the old and new religion with such a pamphlet. It went through eleven editions in five years and was translated from Latin into French and five other vernacular European languages besides. It said:

All should diligently learn to read and write so that each may read the Bible frequently, especially the gospel portion, both for himself and to his children, and especially on holidays. For the gospel has such power that the more deeply one reads it, the more one comes to understand God. And the more one understands God, the stronger becomes one's faith. And the stronger one's faith in God, the more one is moved to love his neighbour and heavenly values. Also the Bible is the greatest consolation on earth in time of adversity.[144]

In the wake of such publishing, the religious values and habits of centuries were permanently abandoned by a very large part of Western society.[145]

Where the priest had been a magician—he could after all at the altar perform the miracle of transubstantiation, "who held the key to eternal life in his hand"[146]—such priestly mediation was done away with.

The Lutherans attacked the medieval Church for demanding too much, not too little, from laity and clergymen, and for making religion psychologically and socially burdensome.

Luther's assault on the confessional attacked writings that "try to frighten people into going to confession." "Instead", he wrote in *Sermon on the Sacrament of Penance*:

> [y]ou should not be debating ... whether or not your contrition is sufficient. Rather you should be *assured* that after all your efforts your contrition is not sufficient. This is why you must cast yourself upon the grace of God, hear his sufficiently sure word in the sacrament, accept it in free and joyful

faith, and never doubt that you have come to grace.[147]

He described as "utterly useless and altogether harmful" the entire traditional catalogue of sins according to motive, theology and cardinal virtues, the five senses, the seven deadly sins, the seven sacraments, the seven gifts of the Spirit, the Beatitudes, the alien sins, the twelve articles of faith, and the silent sins.

One gains something of a sense of the force of Luther's conviction with its echoes of Christ's tirade against the Pharisees with the following:[148]

> Who can recount all the tyrannies with which the troubled consciences of confessing and penitent Christians are burdened—the deadly constitutions and customs with which they are daily harassed by silly manikins who bind and place on the shoulders of men very heavy and unbearable burdens which they themselves do not want to touch even with one finger? Thus this most salutary sacrament of penance has become nothing but sheer tyranny ... a disease and a means to increase sins.[149]

Until now, he maintained, penitents leaving the confessional had rejoiced more in their liberation from the torment of getting their confession right than in any absolution they might have felt they had warranted from the priest.

Such writing, now in print, ripped through Europe's growing reading populations.

It handed them a new, spiritually charged intellectual independence. And it reinforced developments in knowledge triggered by the Renaissance. There was an empowering sense of selfhood and of personal responsibility in the Kingdom of Heaven made possible on earth that the Reformers exulted in. But what were the practical consequences for journalism of this extraordinary shift?

Chapter 6
Pamphlet Revolution: Content Is King

News there had always been. Kings and courts, dictators and dealers all over the world needed to disseminate their "news"—edicts (or trends) relevant to trade. From Caesar Augustus to the Chinese emperors, from spies to military planners, news was a commodity people had always needed—and paid for—and it made the world go round. But the Reformation democratized communication itself.

Developments such as Gutenberg's secret formula for a type of ink compatible with the "new" invention of paper and Maximilian's establishment in 1490 of an imperial postal service were crucial to the story. But news now had a focus and a point for everyone: it had *content*.

Any magazine or website editor knows that "content is king". What we see coming together in the early-to-mid sixteenth century is threefold: a pent-up hunger for spiritual truth and growth; freedom of expression, given full rein by the prophetic force of individual preachers; and the seemingly limitless possibilities for pastors to feed their flocks with authorized printed texts.

No longer were the faithful at the mercy of the exploitable "dreams of ignorance". And, as the revolution grew, so its consequences became more important to individual readers who "needed to know". An immense growth in pamphlets that disseminated knowledge to the populace at large took hold, with vast social and political changes consequent upon it. We turn then to the pamphlet revolution.

Popular writing proves pivotal
The German Reformation introduced a new form of book, the *Flugschriften* (or religious pamphlet), and an original business model.[150] These deflected disposable income from the purchase of handwritten manuscript books (mainly from the Italian élites) towards printed pamphlets in those lands most culturally linked to the German Empire. Wittenberg, where Luther lived, protected as it was by the patronage of the Elector Frederick the Wise, formed the new *locus operandi*.

An inauspicious town of just two thousand souls at the beginning of the sixteenth century, Wittenberg was very much in the shadow of bigger neighbours like Leipzig and Lubeck. It now became, by the second half of the century, the largest centre of production of books and pamphlets within the German Empire.[151]

Flugschriften introduced the idea of a shorter, cheaper publication, feeding and being fuelled by people's thirst for news. What mattered were the issues of redemption and salvation that preoccupied all Christians. The search for answers to these troubling questions allowed the market for religious books to grow exponentially.

Indeed, Pettegree makes the point that it was this popular writing, rather than academic discourse in scholarly Latin, that proved pivotal. Just as with the invention of Hebrew, so biblical thought written in the common tongue proved a game-changer: "The decision to pen his *Sermons on Grace and Indulgences* for a vernacular audience was in many respects the decisive moment of the Reformation, far more so than the posting of the theses."[152]

It was such short pastoral works in German that anchored Luther in the affections of his growing German public and secured his reputation as a man of God. Shorter works of consolation and admonition poured from his fluent pen and the Wittenberg presses during these years, cementing Luther in the people's hearts as pastor to the German nation.[153]

It is hard for us to imagine anything to do with religion mattering so much. Those of us who lived through the bombing of the Twin Towers by al-Qaeda zealots in 2001 may have had a glimpse of this scenario. Or those who experienced the coronavirus lockdown as the angel of death seemed to pass over the whole world, may also have sensed the awesome numinous breaking through our secularized shells. These were times when the whole material edifice of a world created by humans seemed to melt and become meaningless; a great abyss opening, to be replaced by nothing for which we had been prepared. And so it was then.

For example, it is believed that London alone suffered forty outbreaks of bubonic plague between 1348 and 1665, raising deep existential questions. On top of the religious convulsions, and partly causing them, death from disease halved Europe's population.

The quest for meaning, and a yearning for something else after so pitiful a life, became very real. This primed even poorer people for reading matter, and literacy rates shot up. There was evidence everywhere of a huge increase in the number of active readers in European society. Education expanded more quickly than almost any other pursuit of the sixteenth century.[154] Reading matter was coming in waterfalls.

Pamphlets foundational for journalism

Printers had begun experimenting with pamphlets between 1450 and 1530 following the invention of printing.

A new type of book took off, far shorter and cheaper than the theological and scholarly texts that had dominated the market in manuscripts. These pamphlets and broadsheets created the opportunity to turn the existing appetite for reading material into a mass market. News could become, for the first time, a part of popular culture.[155]

To us pamphlets are disposable bits of paper that litter our lives; the inserts inside magazines, comprising unsolicited advertising, are about as welcome as train announcements. Pamphlets—on the coffee table at the dentist's or by the till at the supermarket—are mere ephemera today. Hard to imagine that they both signified and, indeed, formed the bedrock of the world's freedoms.

To the reformers they were the clickbait of real religious change. Virtually synonymous with the age of print, they eventually developed into periodicals and, finally, newspapers. They started as the social media of powerful religious men with ideas to disseminate. Pamphlets formed the basis of the news industry, since they provided secure work for pioneer printers throughout the first century of print without too much outlay. What's more, the burgeoning reading public could increasingly afford to buy them.

So what was a pamphlet exactly and how did the industry work? We have in fact lost most of the language to describe exactly what a pamphlet was, so a little work of imagination is necessary. Essentially, it was a very short book, without a cover, printed on a single sheet of paper that had been folded twice and then cut. This was known, for obvious reasons, as "quarto" because it formed four sides: one fold was called "folio"; three folds was "octavo". A pamphlet typically consisted of between one and twelve sheets folded thrice, or between eight and ninety-six pages in quarto.

The word "pamphlet" first appears in Anglo–Latin writing in the fourteenth century, and in English in the fifteenth.[156] The usage derives from *Pamphilus seu de Amora*, a popular twelfth-century Italian love poem. With the diminutive "-et" ending, it became any small book originally handwritten on parchment. Then it became a small stand-alone item. Religious controversialists were bound to see the potential of this new medium.

Pamphlets tended to recount local events, rather than sensations in faraway places. The exhortatory power of such events—murders, executions, battles, hazards and disasters—seems to have been more powerful if the events happened in or close to the reading community.[157] They had a highly personal charge.

Secondly, a cadre of publishers in the major print centres like Antwerp and Augsburg emerged specializing in such literature, which was short and produced to a remarkably high standard. The *Flugschriften* were bound into books, arranged thematically or chronologically.

They described news of battles, treaties of the French Wars of Religion, the conflict with the Turk, the "discovery" of America in 1492, floods and catastrophes, and they were all read semiotically—that is, as signs of divine action.

Much publishing followed the relentless march of Islam over the next one hundred years: across the Balkans, through eastern Europe and the Mediterranean, right up to the ultimate push back in the Gulf of Lepanto on 7 October 1571, when the Spanish and Venetians saw off the Turk for good. It bears repeating that for contemporaries— and quite distinct from our own historical perception— the interest in the Americas was always dwarfed by the incessant, recurrent fear of Muslim conquest: the first Turkish siege of Vienna by Sultan Suleiman with 150,000 men and camp followers (in 1529)—that is as big as the army that invaded the Normandy beaches on 6 June 1944 to repulse the Nazi advance and begin the ending of World War II. The capture of Tunis (1535), and the disasters at Algiers (1541) and Djerba (1560) were all significant news events.[158]

This burgeoning market for news fitted ideally into the expanding market for cheap print, and it swiftly became an important commodity.

Most significantly for us, it "took its tone from the new genre of pamphlets that had preceded it: the passionate advocacy that had accompanied the Reformation."[159] It was very different, therefore, from the standard discreet, dispassionate services of the manuscript newsmen who supplied the merchants and other subscribers.

This trend, by contrast, was committed and engaged, intended to persuade as well as inform. News of catastrophe far away and of grizzly murder nearby was meaningful, entertaining and transformative. And in at least thirty-four places, Reformation controversies were responsible for the first introduction of printing, or the restoration of a previously moribund print tradition.[160]

It was long lasting too, as new Protestant churches began to be established across the empire, requiring a mass of liturgical and pastoral materials in print.

Germany leads the world
From the very beginning, attitudes toward printing were shaped by the fact that it originated as a German invention and was introduced over the Alps and Pyrenees by itinerant German craftsmen.

The English tradition is somewhat anomalous in this respect. Instead of Germans coming to England, an English merchant went to Germany: William Caxton, practically synonymous with the beginning of printing in England, went to Cologne to learn his craft, practised it in Bruges, and then returned home setting up his press in London and entering history thereby.[161]

A German printer from Cologne set up the first Oxford press two years after Caxton. Of those who engaged in the early sixteenth-century English book trade, two-thirds were foreign-born.[162]

Pamphleteering became the principal medium of discourse, generating so significant a means for the creation and dissemination of "public opinion" that in the end the arch persecutor of Protestants, Holy Roman Emperor Charles V himself, was forced to give ground.

Charles' early military success at the battle of Muhlberg against the now Lutheran princes of the Holy Roman Empire, the Shmalkaldic League, was short-lived. The printing press now came once more into its own. Deprived of the princely leadership of Johann Frederick of Saxony that had defined Protestantism in the 1530s, the initiative now fell to a group of ministers determined not to compromise the Lutheran heritage. Printing presses established in the rebel city of Magdeburg poured forth a torrent of defiance and vitriol against the emperor, and against those whom they felt had abandoned the cause. Deprived of the rapid victory that had seemed within his grasp, Charles was forced to give way.[163] The Peace of Augsburg of 1555 would secure the Lutheran heritage and the future of the churches of the German Reformation for the next hundred years. And it was pamphleteering that gained the victory.

Calvin and the importance to journalism of Providence
Luther's call for reform did not succeed everywhere in Europe: Italy, Spain and France being the obvious exceptions. But the fury of publishing activity, for and against his teachings, had demonstrated the extent of popular appetite for short, printed work. Even the Emperor's agent remarked upon it. In a report from Augsburg in 1520, three years after the theses were posted, he noted the "evident popular excitement and the outpouring of printed works."

These were the first "books" the urban reader at the lowlier end bought. And as the Reformation controversies grew, publishers who had benefited from the public appetite looked for new ways to satisfy it. As a result, publishers began to exploit more systematically the evident possibilities for news.

But a further factor must be considered: the mood music coming from Geneva. We need to understand how the hum of another great thinker, Jean Calvin, and his accompanists penetrated the European consciousness. They generated an orientation that made news reading almost a matter of life or death; rather in the same way that

FOMO—fear of missing out—fuels the modern appetite for Instagram and TikTok among teenage users.[164]

The foundation of investigative reporting
Jean Calvin (1509-1564) was born in the Picardy region of France. He studied law in Orleans and biblical languages and classical and Christian antiquity at Paris. From there he was later forced to flee to Basel, after a brush with the Inquisition through association with his friend Nicolas Cop's questionable views on justification by faith.

This connection was controversial indeed, because it was deemed anti-Catholic,[165] being as it was identified with Luther who had dispensed with priestcraft and the whole ritualized economy of mercy.

While in Basel, Calvin wrote his famous *Christianae Religionis Institutio (Institutes of the Christian Religion)* in 1536, aged just 27. This masterpiece concerned the "true Church" as opposed to "the Church under the papacy", which he took to mean the use of legal power buttressed by wealth to raise a claim over consciences. The true Church implied pure preaching of the word and the right administration of the sacraments.

Calvin's vast theological output need not concern us. His anthropology, his views on social responsibility and on providence should do, however; since, together, they meshed a worldview so powerful that what became known, against his will, as Calvinism—he was a shy man, wanting to deflect all glory to God—became one of the forces that shaped the modern world and with it, investigative journalism.

Calvinism is a word with which it seems natural to pair the adjective "hardline". "Puritan" seems to evoke a narrow, joyless and unrelenting religiosity from which we would do well to steer clear. If we think at all, we prefer Irenaeus' "life in all its fulness". We think of dour expressions, alarming headwear, and a theology of predestination that preached that nothing you could do could guarantee your own salvation. God had worked it all out at the beginning of the world and that was that. We perhaps think—and shudder—at the thought of Servetus, whom Calvin denounced and had put to death in Geneva for heresy. We may even think of Max Weber's well-known view that it was simply fear that impelled the growth of Calvinist religion, as the "elect", unable to *prove* their election, were forced to *demonstrate* it, by their worldly activity and evident prosperity.[166] Only the saved were allowed to receive Holy Communion, and the only way to prove that you were saved was to manifest it in your appearance. (This is perhaps a precursor of the atheist Communist persecution of the bourgeoisie.)

But this is all the negative side of a revolution that was more about the universal availability of grace freed from ecclesial hierarchy, even a hierarchy of values, and of its huge system of control. What changed was the very thing that made journalism possible: the new value given to the ordinary—people and events—and a rejection of clerical mediators. This made personal commitment to what you could know for yourself not only possible, but essential—with significant ramifications as much for reportage as for science.

The rejection of mediation was closely connected to the Reformers' rejection of the medieval understanding of the sacred. Salvation, they believed, was exclusively the work of God. No priest, monk, works or novenas could affect it, buy it, or merit it on behalf of others, as had been the case for grim centuries.

And although Calvinism has been caricatured as a heartless—and even psychologically damaging—religion of proscription, this is, in the long view, unworthy. The point of harping on about the helplessness and depravity of mankind, as this form of Protestantism did, was to throw into the starkest relief the power, mercy and agency of God. God alone could bring about a salvation utterly beyond the machinations of human agency, particularly that of the Church. What is more, God *wanted* to rescue his unworthy creatures. And he wanted to do it beyond all considerations of justice or merit. "It was an unaccountable salvation by an almighty and merciful God, against all rational human hope and utterly disregarding our just deserts."[167] It was precisely this that, in the awe and gratitude it evinced in many, became the "tremendously potent motive force behind revolutionary change", from Europe, to America and eventually even China, as sociologist Charles Taylor states.

Reality recovers its meaning
Along with the end of priestly mediation went the mediaeval Catholic understanding of the Church as the locus and vehicle of the sacred. Luther, who had been a monk, even renounced his vows and married a nun. He "sprang" her and eight colleagues from their convent, hidden in empty herring barrels.

No group of religious preachers was needed to accrue merit on behalf of others. They could not, for all believers stood alone before God. No one could mediate grace for another person, nor was it needed.

Neither was anyone nor anywhere more holy than anywhere else. Creation itself was the arena of God's sovereignty; the secular—from the Latin *saeculum*, a religious idea meaning "this world" as opposed to the world to come—was the locus of divine action. Indeed, it made "the local" pregnant with new meaning. It rendered reality itself full of divine possibility. Catholic ideas of the sacred had been characterized by contempt for and renunciation of marriage, sex and work. Now Platonic idealism, celibacy and monasticism were rejected.

This led to an enhanced status for what had been previously demoted as the "profane" life. Now Creation itself was viewed as the place of God's activity and saving love. Everywhere was shot through with the glory of God. Holiness consisted purely in responding to that fact, in works of love and mercy.

There was no hierarchy of caste or values in the new religion. The *contemptus mundi*[168] of preceding centuries had elevated renunciation and a disembodied spirituality of monasticism. Now, instead, scientific inquiry began to take root. After a thousand years of the Vulgate translation of the Bible and St Jerome's misreading of the Book of *Ecclesiastes*—characterized by the despairing refrain "all is vanity"—suddenly hope, joy and the fulness of life in the Providence of God in Creation were within the reach of all.

This new movement must have been profoundly disturbing to believers who had been guided for generations by spiritual manuals of worldly renunciation and physical self-mortification. Thomas à Kempis' tortured *De Imitatione Christi (The Imitation of Christ)*—written between 1418 and 1427—was the bestselling devotional work of all time other than the Bible, even more than Augustine's *Confessions*. Instead of working to improve life here on earth, this publication (and countless other such manuals) had comforted the deprived and sorrowful by promising bliss in the life to come.

Moreover, the Humanists—in casting off a historic subservience to received tradition over scripture—laid the path for the first generations of the Reformed movement's new concern for accuracy in the study of actual texts. They approached learning with a fresh historical sensitivity. They were interested in distinguishing critically and incisively between the authentic sense and import of biblical and other documents, and the accretions of institutionalized interpretation. The new mentality led to an empirical search for undiscovered truth. And it led finally to the rise of natural and experimental science in the seventeenth century.

In a nutshell, empiricism was the study of reality rather than merely the reinforcement of received ideas. Francis Bacon could not have written his *Novum Organon*—the basis for modern science—without Calvin: "a striking witness of the fruitfulness of these impulses" says one commentator.

The Reformation thus saw a marked shift in the goal of science from contemplation to productive efficacy. This was based on a fully biblical understanding of humans as stewards in God's creation, which was affirmed by God in the very first chapter of Genesis in the repeated phrase: "and God saw that it was good". So it must be worth investigating.

Affirmation of ordinary life
Now, back to Calvin himself. Imagine being a 12-year-old boy in the hotbed of life at his father's home in Noyon in Picardy, in the precincts of the cathedral. The atmosphere would be one of fixation with death, and it was beginning to pall. Prayers for the dead; the all-embracing menace of purgatory (mentioned nowhere in the approved canon

of Scripture); chantries endowed by the rich for psalms to be sung all day long, to shorten the purgatorial time spent by the beloved dead; candles lit for the dead; an endless procession of rituals that seemed to fly in the face of Christ's exhortation to "let the dead bury their dead":[169] all of these customs a surreptitious and ignoble means to provide a living for clergy without other income. The Roman Church, many felt, fed on death. Popular sentiment is very evident in a short dramatic poem called "eaters of the dead", *Die Totenfresser*:

> Be quiet about the gospel
> And preach only papal law.
> We will then be lords and the laity servants
> Who bear the burdens we lay upon them.
> All is lost however
> If the gospel gets out
> And things are measured by it.
> For it teaches none to give and sacrifice to us –
> Only that we should live simple, impoverished lives. [170]

The worm was turning. And there were dramas that piled on the attack, helping non-literate lay people to grasp what was wrong. In one such play, various characters bemoan Reformation principles taking root and spoiling their games. A Catholic chaplain worries about laymen reading and so turning the gospel against the priests who are supposed to mediate it.

His special fear is that the celibate priesthood would be forced into marriage, for it would limit their debauchery. A bishop explains how he can be both shepherd and wolf to his flock, granting indulgences that remit sins, and demanding concubinage and cradle fees (terms for the bribes paid for him to overlook clergy whores and their resulting progeny). The holy man laments: "Should priests ever come by legal wives / We would lose the fat in our sausage." A diocesan prior urges the pope never to slacken preaching, singing and protesting his power over heaven and hell. "That's what keeps the poor fools, the laity, under control."[171]

Calvin would have been aware of all this context from a young age. Imagine, then, the sense of freedom and empowerment that washed over impressionable young Christians like Calvin as he got close to the scriptures and realized not just what he had been denied, but what the authentic truth was.

And the truth, with its guarantee of justice, was written into the warp and weft of Creation. "The heavens declare the glory of God" was a favourite Reformist text. Far from needing the protection of priests and bishops, popes and princes, humankind had God Himself as protector and strength.

Calvin's mature thought on this emerges powerfully and decisively in his *Institutes of the Christian Religion*, published when he was just 27 (in 1536, in Latin), then in French five years later:

> For as he justly shudders at the idea of chance, so he can confidently commit himself to God. This, I say, is his comfort, that his heavenly Father so embraces all things under his power—so governs them at will by his nod—so regulates them by his wisdom, that nothing takes place save according to his appointment; that received into his favour, and entrusted to the care of his angels neither fire, nor water, nor sword, can do him harm, except in

so far as God their master is pleased to permit. For thus sings the Psalm, "Surely he shall deliver thee from the snare of the fowler, and from the noisome pestilence. He shall cover thee with his feathers, and under his wings shalt thou trust; his truth shall be thy shield and buckler. Thou shalt not be afraid for the terror by night; nor for the arrow that flieth by day; nor for the pestilence that walketh in darkness; nor for the destruction that wasteth at noonday" (Ps. 91:2-6).[172]

Calvin, a refugee in fear of his life once anti-Protestant pogroms began in France, knew nonetheless where his confidence lay. He even had to lower himself from a window—by means of bedsheets tied together, with the authorities hard on his heels—after he condemned the traditionalists in a speech at the University of Paris.

But his belief that such things happened under the eye of a beneficent Lord, who commanded eternity, the ultimate context of people's lives, strengthened him:

> Always bear in mind that there is no random power, or agency, or motion in the creatures, who are so governed by the secret counsel of God, that nothing happens but what he has knowingly and willingly decreed.[173]

Creation was the proof, for it was the very theater of God's glory. God and the meaning of life could be read in everything that happened. Providence was "the disposing and directing of everything to its proper end by incomprehensible wisdom."[174] Indeed: "… single events are so regulated by God, and all events so proceed from his counsel, that nothing happens fortuitously."[175]

Suddenly we are not dealing with religion, or metaphysics, but the "here and now"; with life as it is lived and breathed. What makes it foundational for the coming of real journalism, was its "affirmation of ordinary life".[176] As another Puritan, John Milton—who is to be pivotal for the freedom of the press—puts it in *Paradise Lost*:

To know
That which before us lies in daily life
Is the prime wisdom.[177]

It was novel and exciting, and people wanted to know about it. Suddenly there was a hunger for news—because "news" was news about what *God* was doing, and not just the Church. And that meant work for news writers and printers.

Conclusion
"God has come to his people and set them free," sang Zecharias in the Temple at the circumcision of his son John, known as the Baptist.[178] And so it was again with Luther's discovery that nothing he could do could merit the spiritual freedom he craved. Only the lovingness of God could—and already had—achieved it for him. All he had to do was take hold of it with his heart.

This discovery was monumental in its consequences for us today. Extraordinary to realize—and too hard for many to grasp any longer—but the truth that Luther hammered out in pamphlet after pamphlet, and that blazed across a continent to change everything, was and is spiritual. Our own sense of reality depends on Luther having got that right. And, however clever and technological we become now, nothing can change that fact. Luther's grasp of all that that meant for those chaffing under the yoke of religious oppression, and his spiritual conviction that risked a horrible death, set the world back on its own two feet. He saw printing as "God's highest and extremest act of grace, whereby the business of the Gospel is driven forward". And it was Pope Leo X who stated in 1515 at the Fifth Lateran Council that printing had been "invented for God's glory, for the exaltation of the faith and the diffusion of art and learning."[179]

A revaluing of the ordinary as the locus of God's action, and the beginnings of empiricism that this entailed were foundational for journalism.

Because of Calvin and the later Reformers, the possibility of reportage—following the facts—had just taken its biggest leap forward yet. And here we briefly leave the story as it was unfolding on the Continent of Europe, to look to England. For it was in England that key developments in printing and the press were about to emerge, impacting the new colonies, and especially America.

Chapter 7
The Religious Matrix of English News

*Knowing is not information
so much as it is transformation.*[180]

God had given Defoe the insight—on such matters as trade, religious strife, and so on—that had been denied to other men, and he must publish the truth as he knew it.[181]

England, cut off as it was by the North Sea from the continent of Europe, had its Reformation late.

Printing itself had been introduced into England in 1476.[182] But it was machinations over Henry VIII's nuptial arrangements from the 1520s that were officially the trigger, borne onward by the zeitgeist of Reformation freedom elsewhere in Europe, which was proving irresistible.

In this chapter we look at how the religious turmoil in Europe, which had laid the foundations of a newspaper-reading culture, infected Britain, and—eventually—New England on the other side of the Atlantic.

Although almost thirty years behind the Continent in its approach to and development of news, the eventual achievement of press freedom in England had huge repercussions on America and the rest of the world, as we shall go on to see.

And it was the development of a vernacular language through the translation of scripture that repeats all over again the story of the creation of Hebrew and—through it—a people. This time however, it happens on the strength of the biggest empire the world had ever seen: Britain's.

Pestiferous protests
Contemporaries initially viewed vernacular printing as the vehicle of a disease—heresy—and it had to be eradicated. Reformation heresy was a poison that menaced the body politic. In a 1530 proclamation, when Henry VIII was still "Defender of the Faith", he warned against the "blasphemous and pestiferous English books printed in other regions and sent into this realm to pervert the people ... to stir and incense them to sedition and disobedience ... to the final subversion and desolation of this noble realm."[183] The state found print technology frightening. It was, according to one commentator "a power unhealthy, infectious, subtly and mysteriously contagious ..."

And what was being printed and circulated? The Bible again, translated from Latin into English by William Tyndale (c. 1494–1536). England was alone in Europe for having no vernacular Bible. The Anglo-Saxons had attempted a translation, and so had Wycliffe—well ahead of continental stirrings—but the impulse had waned for lack of clergy support, and even outright persecution.

In Germany alone, by 1522—when Luther presented his own translation—there had already been fourteen versions since 1466. France, Italy, Spain, the Czechs, the Dutch: the citizens of all these countries had access to Bibles in their own languages.

But just for wanting, from a very early age, to give his countrymen and women the scripture in their own native tongue, Tyndale was betrayed, captured, imprisoned for years, tortured and eventually martyred.

Melvyn Bragg sums up his suffering and his achievement:

> His crime was his unbreakable determination throughout his life, whatever it cost, to give to the English people a Bible in their own language. Against all but crushing odds, over a short adult lifetime spent in constant danger and deprivation and despite unspeakable sadistic cruelties by the English court and clergy, he succeeded.[184]

Bragg, in unusually fulsome praise, marvels at how the English language, based largely on Tyndale's translation, subsequently swept the globe. It liberated thought, seeded Protestantism and inspired books, pamphlets, art, songs, protests and poetry. There has never been anybody to match his achievement. "The quiet English priest and scholar transformed the world of words. He gave his life so that ours could be lived in what he saw as the language of truth."[185]

It was his beautiful translation of the New Testament, with its remarkable cadences and memorable phrasing, that gave Britain not just an old book, but—as with the impulse to democratize Hebrew—a language for ordinary folk. It readied its readers to become the target market for news because it democratized communication itself.

Burned at the stake for heresy in the small Dutch village of Vilvoorde when he was just 42, Tyndale's last words, famously, were "Lord, open the King of England's eyes!" It was not a vain hope. The king could not save him, such was the momentum of anti-Lutheran hysteria Henry had whipped up—then regretted—in his determination to keep the Pope onside his matrimonial machinations.

Nonetheless, by 1535, the first English Bible had indeed been authorized by the King.[186] After his marriage to Protestant Anne (and her subsequent execution in 1536), the King ordered that a copy of Coverdale's Great Bible of 1538—largely Tyndale's work in vernacular English—be deposited in every church in the realm. The King soon regretted this edict too, as the common people were reading it. He tried to limit it to the élite, but with little success.

Tyndale's real legacy however was the King James Version, which did not appear until 1611. Nonetheless, the New Testament and Pentateuch of this version were almost word for word a translation of Tyndale's.

Because of his mastery of the original biblical languages—and ability to harness them to the words, idioms and phrases of folk life—they are still spoken daily today, "proving their quality by their indispensability", says Bragg.[187] Such phrases as "see the writing on the wall", "cast the first stone", "the salt of the earth", "a thorn in the flesh", "fight the good fight", "from strength to strength", "the powers that be" (and many more) are all derived from Tyndale's work. Tyndale worked in the deepest reaches of the rarely tapped reservoir of ordinariness. "From this flood words that give us meaning", says Bragg.[188]

Religious matrix of the first English newsbooks
The intellectual atmosphere in England began to change. Reluctantly, the Tudors saw its potential for their rule. In 1486, Henry VII used print to publish the Bull of Pope Innocent VIII, confirming his title to the throne and his marriage to Elizabeth of York. But, with the spread of Luther's works from 1517—and then William Tyndale's under Luther's influence— they also saw its threat.

Governance (and also war) occasioned the earliest surviving printed news report, in this case the Battle of Flodden in 1513. Henry VIII used print's potential penetration to have his *Defence of the Seven Sacraments* of 1521 printed, for which he received from Pope Leo X the title *Fidei Defensor*, Defender of the Faith.

But, by 1529, the first list of prohibited books was already being promulgated by Henry VIII. He faced a double-pronged menace: the Pope must allow him to divorce Katherine of Aragon, who was inconveniently and dangerously aunt to the most powerful Catholic in Europe, the Holy Roman Emperor Charles V—the very man who had officially outlawed Luther. Lutheranism was therefore a mighty inconvenience in Henry's marital gambit.

Henry's eye had lighted on Anne Boleyn to be his—by now pregnant—new queen. Tyndale was therefore highly threatening to an already fraught enough papal negotiation. As Henry saw it, making the Scriptures accessible even to "ploughboys"—as Tyndale passionately wished—would threaten not just the negotiations, but the entire Catholic clergy power system, which depended on ignorance of what the Bible taught. It would inevitably alienate Rome, with whom the King wished to ingratiate himself, and bring down the house (both ecclesiastic and politic), with a mighty and possibly irreparable crash.

An indication of what was at stake lies in the fact that, from 1521 on (after Luther's excommunication), the Holy Roman Emperor had put in place a draconian array of punishments for publishing, reading or sharing evangelical books. The first executions for Lutheran heresies took place in 1523 of monks at Antwerp, where Tyndale was based. From 1530, the death sentence was passed for even the possession of a Protestant text.[189]

Taking no chances therefore, the King inaugurated, himself, the country's first licensing system in 1530. This system was to be operated by ecclesiastics and applied only to books "concernynge holy scripture", but it was extended by royal proclamation in 1538 to cover all types of printing—and the clerics were made responsible not only for suppressing theological errors, but also for "expellinge and avoydinge the occasion of erroneous and seditious opinions". Despite his reservations, Henry VIII nonetheless had not been able to resist making use of the printing press himself in 1531 in his dispute with Rome.

It was against this fraught background that, not surprisingly, the Tudor era saw the precursors of the newspaper: handwritten newsletters on all kinds of topics, also called diurnals.

But, as printing became more general, newsletters took the form of "London letters" to the provincial presses. Domestic topics remained too dangerous for circulation. Unlike in Germany and in France, because of the Wars of Religion, England's incipient printing industry remained centralized and tightly controlled. There were no regional centres big enough to support printing businesses, and curiously—while printing was deemed essential for the prestige of local civic communities all over the continent—this was not the case in England.[190]

Yet by 1557 the Stationers Company—so-called because of the "stations" that itinerant printers set up in the precincts of St Paul's Cathedral[191]—had been granted their royal charter to exercise wide powers over printing. (We look below at the huge significance for journalism of the relationship between printing, St Paul's and national governance.)

And, in 1586 (under Elizabeth I), the Star Chamber decree set the pattern of regulation for the next hundred years. This required that all books be licensed, with accompanying powers of search and seizure and numbers of printing presses and master printers limited.

The Tudors were forced in their own interests, however, to make increasing use of the printing press: in the last resort, they depended on popular support—or at least the good will—of the governed.

This was a point evidently lost on the Church. The Archbishop of Canterbury John Whitgift was authorized by the Star Chamber in 1586 to license and control all printing equipment in the country. Yet this could not prevent the seven "Martin Marprelate" tracts attacking Anglican bishops from circulating illegally from 1588 for a year. "Full of the language of the streets"—satirical, witty and scurrilous—they caused a tsunami of protest in the Church of England. Their puritan author, provoked by the Archbishop of Canterbury's drive against growing reform, remains anonymous to this day, though his unfortunate and equally zealous Welsh printer John Penry was hanged. The tracts remain an early example of print's religious power and, equally, its threat to Church and State.

A somewhat belated shift in emphasis in worship away from images, objects and corporate ritual, towards words had begun. This was a shift that would have a deep and enduring impact on the Union.[192] And although Luther was the key man in the Reformation, from whom Tyndale learned much by example and works, it was the English—not the German—language that circled the planet. The age of exploration had begun and, as Britain's empire grew, so did the influence of Tyndale's English. Literacy increased and, with it, the commercial capacity within the book trade, provoked by religious tensions from the days of the Elizabethan Church onwards.

The 1580s in Britain, in the middle of Elizabeth I's reign (1558–1603), were a watershed for pamphlet production. But, before we can continue with the story of English pamphlets, and the huge impetus they gave to what emerged as newspapers, we must go back several centuries to take a perhaps surprising detour to the grounds of St Paul's Cathedral. For it was here, at the principal church of England, that the bonds of religion, governance and news were forged.

We may take note of how these bonds made legitimate, deep within the constitution and psyche of the nation, the contextual requisites for the fragile institution of a journalism to come.

St Paul's Cathedral: the "*Times* newspaper for the nation"

The demand for printed works grew in England as Luther's revolution spread.

Cathedrals naturally became the biggest consumers and therefore markets for printed materials, to resource liturgical worship and study. St Paul's in London was already the beating heart of the national polity—and that naturally extended to news, via printing.

St Paul's itself first appears in any historically verifiable way in Bede's note from 730 AD, which records that in

604 "King Ethelbert built a church dedicated to the holy Apostle Paul at Ludgate Hill."

By the time of the coming of print, one thousand years later, the Cathedral was where most books in the country were being sold, either at booksellers' shops or stalls—"stations"—centred around the churchyard.[193]

So, when printing began, St Paul's was already the heart of the English book world. The production of liturgical manuscripts first attracted to the area craftsmen who were at that time itinerant.

And as Margaret Willes, who has done more on this than anyone, notes, "In the various genres [of book and journal development] the Churchyard trade was so often in the vanguard."[194]

St Paul's Cross (on the north-east pavement, close to the bell tower) had been the nation's principle gathering point for centuries. It had summoned the "folkmoot", for freemen of the City, and eventually had a pulpit installed. The focus for national events—and as a stage for grand ceremonial—it was also a centre for political and religious resistance: "the prime site to reinforce the political and religious establishment, and at times to become a theatre of opposition".[195]

News built naturally on this tradition, such that two centuries later, Thomas Carlyle could with hindsight describe Paul's Cross in the seventeenth as having been "the *Times* Newspaper" for the nation, "edited by Heaven itself". The description is even more fitting for the Middle Ages and the Tudor period.[196]

A Parliament to replace the Moot, which had become too huge and unwieldy, met first in St Paul's in 1265. It was then moved to the chapter house and hall at Westminster. Not only were knights summoned to it, but also townsmen, which was a new departure. They were, for example, called to discuss the defeat of the royal army at the Battle of Lewes by Simon de Montfort, Earl of Leicester, who was the focus of leadership for barons unhappy at breaches to the Magna Carta.

Just to underscore the marriage of power and communication—of "the Good News" and news itself, which St Paul's embodied—De Montfort, recognizing the moot site as a customary theatre of opposition, rallied his supporters there. These men were a powerful combination of disaffected magnates and London's principal citizens, summoned by the ringing of what was known as the Jesus Bell. De Montfort was now in control of the capital.[197] King Henry III, Prince Edward and Richard of Cornwall had all been taken prisoner. But Prince Edward escaped from captivity and reassembled the royal forces to defeat De Montfort at the Battle of Evesham that same year.

This sealed the fate of the idea of the folk moot, for when Prince Edward succeeded his father as Edward I, he closed it down as an institution. Even the site disappeared, when the Dean and Chapter of St Paul's enclosed the land on which the moot was held within the walls of the precinct. Henceforward, it was St Paul's Cross that became the prime site to reinforce the political and religious establishment, although still at times a focus for rebellion.[198]

From then on, sermons attracted people in their thousands to Paul's Cross, just as had similar focal points in Florence and Wittenberg. Inevitably, this created a market for printed versions of what was preached for those who either could not hear or who wanted to study for themselves what the "good news" meant.[199] There was no pulpit in the nave of the Cathedral itself from which to speak: the Cross provided the platform, much as Speakers' Corner does now, where points of doctrine could be hammered out by learned men. Or sometimes not.

In 1382, Wycliffe's teachings on the Eucharist were declared heresy at a Council held nearby at Blackfriars. In that same year two *Schedulae* (or articles) of Wycliffe's teachings were pinned onto the doors of the Cathedral—a century and a half before Luther's theses were nailed to the castle church at Wittenberg.

Wycliffe's followers, known as Lollards (which means "mutterers"), fared worse than did Luther. Recantations and penances undertaken in St Paul's Churchyard for preaching Lollardy were replaced by the burning alive of those found to be guilty of the heresy.

One brave victim, found to be a heretic by preaching Lollardy, was John Badby. He had been held in the episcopal prison at the Cathedral and then tried there in 1410, before being burned at Smithfield.

So important and enduring a site was St Paul's Cathedral in setting the national conversation that copies of William Tyndale's Bible translation into English were first burned there, on the orders of the Bishop of London, more than a century later (in 1525).

News fed upon such tumult. Printed news was literally pinned to the walls of the famous building, surrounded as it was by its print stations. It was also sold in the many bookstalls in its shadow, or even in the nave of the Cathedral itself. This was now literally "public" news, sold as openly as on any high street news stand, for personal consumption. Such a context focused minds as to just what news inherently was. Where it had often been mere sensationalist or scurrilous pamphlets sold by hawkers on the street, it was here given credence by its locale.

By the early 1620s, and the continental revolution in empiricism, a vocabulary was developing in order to associate news with facts as a rhetorical or discursive tool.[200] The very lexicon endeavoured to underscore this veracity: a declaration, a brief declaration, a letter, a relation, a discourse, a true discourse, news sent, news from, news out of, a description, a true report and a true recital are all words and phrases used to underscore the momentousness of these early forays into journalism.[201]

The first serial "newsbooks" were not far off now. Journalism and its institutional and social legitimation were gestating, under extreme duress, within the religious heart of the nation, as internecine conflict over religion provided the increasingly gripping subject matter.

Fast-forward to the first newspaper
So, let's return to our main narrative.

There has always been some debate as to what qualifies as England's first newspaper. A newspaper we must remember is formally defined both by sustainable seriality—as well as by precise periodicity, i.e. monthly, weekly and eventually daily—and by consecutive numbering and a stable title.[202]

And the term "periodical" means an offering to readers of *regular* updates of current affairs. This intentionally differed from the one-off accounts of a particular event, supplied by occasional news pamphlets. Joad Raymond claims it was John Wolfe, an imaginative printer who was appointed beadle of the Stationers in 1587, who produced the first proper newspaper thirty years before the *corantos*, which are roughly credited with it.[203] Wolfe's *News out of France and Chiefe Occurrences of Both the Armies* (1592) and *The Continual Following of the French King* (1592) are clearly intended to be serial publications.

These "newspapers" contained only foreign news, however, being less contentious than reportage of events nearer home. Raymond states unequivocally that the concept of serial publication of news was available to and exploited by London stationers from 1592.[204] These fragments of evidence suggest that London may not have been behind the rest of Europe in inventing its newspapers, as it was Wolfe (albeit an Italophile) who took the initiative.

Wolfe's was uncertain work, so much so that Nicholas Brownlees dismisses it as a "pioneer" publication. The first clearly recognizable periodical in English, he says—though irregular—was printed in the colony of Amsterdam on 2 December 1620. Brownlees also states categorically that it was from 1620 [that] periodical print news began in England.[205]

The battles between Crown and Parliament over theological supremacy, and the dissolving of parliament itself by King Charles in 1629, meant that news business in "hot", divisive guise had arrived. It was a going concern in a recognizably modern form.[206] News collators, copyists and vendors could almost make a living at it. But it was to be another century before the first recognizable *daily* newspaper, the *Daily Courant* appeared (in 1702).

At this same time, Amsterdam had become an important hub for news production. The horrendous wars attendant upon the Reformation, which lasted for thirty years from 1618, provided the focus. And it naturally garnered an avid readership. Known as a *coranto*—and also by the generic Italian and German words *avviso* and *newe zeitungen*, respectively—the first periodicals marked the beginning of much more frequent news publication. It was also more recognizable to modern readers as an amalgam of news translated from many different places in the same issue.[207]

Puritan groomers
In our news-saturated world, we may find it difficult to imagine the novelty of regular news like this—and, indeed, to imagine the novelty of knowing how to read it. Editorial "bonding" could not be taken for granted and had to be coaxed. One feature in particular—the paratext (or preamble)—reinforces the impression that it was religious propaganda that lies behind the key developments in journalism: an earnest determination to propel a viewpoint.

The preamble told people how to think. This has been watered down today to the "standfirst", the few words or lines below the headline that orientate the reader and provide a quick overview as to its contents. But the early seventeenth-century paratexts were more significant than this implies. Preambles prepared a readership in how to internalize what they were about to read. Moralisms and commonplaces picked up on the growing sense of providence visible in everyday events that was spreading across Europe from Calvin's Geneva. A new, demystified realism—the bedrock of empiricism—implied not just the action of God in the world, but that what your senses and reason perceived conveyed meaning—and was trustable. The paratexts reflected this. They often concluded with expressions of gratitude to God for some event or situation.

In the late sixteenth and early seventeenth century, such material addressed the perennial question for any writer: "How do I write up my story so as to get people to want to read it?"[208] What these paratexts were doing was socializing readers into a mindset; inducting them for the first time in the correct way to understand and respond to what was happening, leaving them awed, admonished, moved, fearful, hopeful, saved—and wanting more.

One or two random examples of the many available may suffice to give a flavour of the crucial innovation that paratexts were, which is evident for the rest of the century.[209]

In one "black letter"[210]—so-called because of the heavy Gothic typeface that was used—dated 19 February 1599, the news concerns "a strange and Miraculous Accident happened in the Cittie of Purmerent, on New-yeeres euen ... of a young child, which was heard to cry in the Mother's wombe before it was borne ..." The preface is a quarter the length of the story and links up monstrous births with other signs and portents, and the "present troubles in the Netherlands", as a sign of God's wrath.[211]

Or another example, the "black letter" of 11 July 1604: "A true discourse of the practises of Elizabeth Caldwell, Ma: ... in the County of Chester, on the parson of Ma: Thomas Caldwell ... to haue murdered and poysoned him with diuers others ... Lastly, a most excellent exhortorie letter, written by her own selfe out of the prison to her husband, to cause him to falle into consideration of his Sinnes &c. Seruing likewise for the use of every good Christian. Being executed the 18 of June 1603."[212]

The directive nature of the paratexts was a literary innovation of some importance. God's pleasure or displeasure was of immediate and life-threatening concern—and it was right that readers were made aware of it. The political atmosphere was febrile. Religious disenchantment and schism were in the air. Bible knowledge was replacing ritual and religious contest was reaching its regicidal paroxysm, with civil war fought for very religious reasons not far off.

An almost manic intensity was gripping England, comprised equally of fear, desperation and religious optimism. It was borne on wings of adversity, the fright caused by "wrongthink", but carrying far worse perceived sanctions than today. It was terribly important both for their earthly *and* eternal lives that people read the times aright and got right with their God. News texts, therefore, in the formative period 1600–1620, foreground one overriding function of news discourse at that time: reporting the manifestation of God's will. The news paratexts of the day were therefore a matter of life and death.

Another typical example of this is the introductory paragraphs of *A trve relation of two most strange and fearfull accidents, lately happening* (1618):

> The anger and terrible countenance of God, of late shewed in this Land here amongst vs, may awaken vs from the fast sleepes of security, and turne vs to the Lord by true repentance. Therefore least his heauy Judgments in like manner come vpon vs at unawares, and we be taken sodainely sleeping, let vs with the wise Virgins in the Gospell kindle our Lampes, that we may be found ready when our Bridegroome commeth in great glory, to giue euery one as his works shall be.
>
> For we are to acknowledge and consider, that the Lord hath not ceased from time to time, at this good will and pleasure, to send prodigies and wonders in euery age, to forwarne and forearme vs of his Judgements hanging ouer our heads for sin: as appeareth by the late examples declared amongst vs.
>
> In the County of Stafford in the parish of

Burton vpon Trent, dwelled of late a free houlder of good lands & means, named Thomas Henworth, as well stored with money and other household goods, as any of his rancke and calling in Countrey [...][213]

And so, after the religious preamble, the writer's story eventually begins ...

News writers as spiritual guides
A few further examples will reinforce the point. The paratext to *Lamentable newes out of Monmouthshire in Wales* (1607) offers clear advice as to how the story of a flood should be interpreted. The author warns the reader in ominous tones that the account should be read "with that good affection wherewith I doe present it, and I am sure, it both may and will profit thee by putting thee in remembrance why God doth punish others, that so thou maiest thy selfe in time looke unto thine own courses, least he proceed in the same or some more grieuous manner with thee."

Another gripping example is the title of a story that, with a graphic visual so big it leaves no room for more than the imprint details, tells both the story and how to regard it: *A true relation of Go[ds] wonderful mercies, in preseruing one aliue, which hanged fiue days, who was falsely accused* (1605).[214]

The horror of such a story—and the clear attempt to substantiate it as being true—would have commanded widespread excitement at the manifest injustice of man and the saving power of God, exactly as Calvin had taught. The author sees himself as a spiritual guide, declaring that the news, far from being written to excite idle curiosity (as some modern historians suggest), is instead published to provide moral instruction and affirm, or even change a person's life.

Such prefaces were necessary, says Joad Raymond, to "reduce the risk of misreading",[215] risks that were of course grave. "In the vast majority of pamphlets between 1600 and 1620, news stories are not conceived of as being important in themselves, as a stand-alone feature of human existence worthy of expression, but rather as a manifestation of God's will ... news is understood and recounted within a religious framework".[216]

Indeed, there are few examples of simple, straightforward reportage where the reader is simply provided with unmediated facts and information about a certain event. That was to come later. But the compelling power of the innovatory press rested on its being seen as news about society's sinfulness in the eyes of God. The discursive mode of narration is frequently punctuated by an exclamatory, invocatory tone typical of public preaching or even theater.[217]

The reason for this is not clear to modern readers. We believe we arrive at the printed or online page *ex nihilo*, with the capacity for absorbing and filtering news and making sense of it. But do we really "make sense" of the news today? Certainly, we imbibe the facts—with more or less reserve—assiduously "checked" for accuracy, in the wake of "fake news" scandals and AI error. Yet, what sense do we actually make of it? What does it mean, beyond its ability to make us notice it? "What should be laudable in a news organization is not a simple capacity to collect facts, but a skill—honed by intelligent bias— at teasing out their relevance", believes contemporary historian Alain de Botton.[218]

It is hard for us now to reconstruct the felt need for such orientation, used as we are to the daily tide of news washing over us that we think we "get"—as something more or less boring or fanciful or ignorant—here today gone tomorrow and, I have little doubt, even less desirable when we know robots have produced it.

De Botton believes that readers today are "never systematically inducted into the extraordinary capacity of news outlets to influence our sense of reality and to mould the state of what we might as well—with no supernatural associations—call our souls".[219] But that is exactly what the news writers of the early seventeenth century felt they *must* do. Systematic induction, influence, and moulding—with *very* supernatural associations—was exactly how readers were taught, post-Calvin, to perceive reality.

News producers felt there was a lot at stake; nothing less than the reader's eternal future. People read, digested and internalized what was being served up as no less than the acts of God evident in everything that happened—and upon which everything else depended.

Calvin's influence meant a new sense that *everything* that happened "mattered". All news was shot through with the potential to see the glory and the awe-inspiring quality of God—and it conditioned Europe for new forms of communication. It amplified markedly what news was, potentially, in an increasingly troubled political context. It is just not reasonable to think the news industry could have gripped enough readers strongly enough, and for long enough, otherwise.

Building up to a free press: the prophetic trajectory
England's first "newsbooks", developing on the back of news pamphlets, appeared in 1641, a few months ahead of

the outbreak of civil war. They were widely read and highly influential, influencing even today the way seventeenth-century history is perceived.

The reasons for their appearance are rarely fully understood. As we have noted, at first, they contained no English news at all, as it was considered too sensitive and liable to trigger retribution. But their appearance certainly marked a considerable heightening of tension and polarity of religious discourse in the country, which they orchestrated.

Then came John Milton. Without doubt the most important single contribution to freedom of expression in England—and the new colonies of America—after the Reformers was his *Areopagitica*. Written in 1644, it was a passionate defence of unlicensed printing at a time when political paroxysm depended on argument about truth.

Milton (1608–1674) was a Puritan—meaning a supporter of the theology of the French-Swiss Calvin—an anti-Establishment scholar and a supporter of the republican farmer Oliver Cromwell. Milton penned the essay when he was just 36, two years into the English Civil War (1642–51). But his ire was not directed against licensing in general, since he later became Cromwell's censor. He was certainly against the suppression of two of his own tracts written in favour of divorce, considered by the Puritans to be blasphemous and indecent.

"Give me the liberty to know, to utter and to argue freely according to conscience, above all liberties", he wrote, unrepentantly. It was in his *Areopagitica* that he expressed the view that has governed debate about freedom of expression ever since: "Though all winds of doctrine were let loose to play upon the earth, so truth be in the field, we do injuriously by licensing and prohibiting to misdoubt her strength. Let her and falsehood grapple, who ever knew truth put to the worse, in a free and open encounter." It was a sublime expression of faith: that truth was "one" and could be known.

Milton was particularly against "prior restraint"— the licensing by government of work as yet unpublished. Certainly his idea of who should be free to express their ideas might have been limited to those with serious purpose. And, given the struggle of Europe to emerge from under the papal yoke of religious obfuscation, it is understandable that he should deny Roman Catholics rights to publish works in defence of their religion. He would also have opposed today's tabloid press and social media licence.

There need to be restraints, particularly against contemporary media publishers who cite Milton not to promote truth but to prevent accountability.[220] Truth rarely wins in the field against social media when people will believe anything, especially when it confirms their prejudiced views. Unlike Milton's imagined readers, most are not "intellectual pilgrims" says the founder of independent press watchdog, Impress.[221] But that is an argument for a different book.

Within a hundred years, Milton's views proved foundational for an argument, both in England and in the US. This argument emerged later as the First Amendment to the American Constitution.

Just to remind readers of the momentousness of this amendment: it prevents the government from making laws that regulate an establishment of religion, or that prohibit the free exercise of religion, or abridge the freedom of speech, the freedom of the press, the freedom of assembly, or the right to petition the government for redress of grievances. It was adopted in the US on 15 December 1791, as one of the ten amendments that constitute the Bill of Rights. Some say this explains the almost sacred regard in which, until very recently, journalists have been largely held in the US to this day.

Journalism replaces the sermon

Against a backdrop of civil war and religious tumult, Milton saw himself as a prophet. He believed it was his life's purpose "to repair the ruins of our first parents by regaining to know God aright". He did not expect there to be a vast number of such readers, but nonetheless a broader readership was growing, on the back of such conviction.

Many of Milton's antiprelatical works—his diatribes against tithes and taxes, his justification of regicide, and his other work against tyrannical rulers (not kingship as a principle)—became foundational for America's republic, as it sloughed off all vestiges of Europe's ancient enslavement to theocracy. Milton's genius for freedom, and the reformist intensity of his writing, helped to render the intellectual turmoil of mid-seventeenth-century England ripe for developments in communication in both Britain and America.

The Civil War and its regicide made the connection between newsbooks and preaching clear, for both stirred up the people. The 1648 anonymous newsbook *Mercurius Impartialis* admitted:

> That the Pulpit and the Presse are in themselves truly Excellent, no man, (not possessed with a spirit of Madnesse) will deny; but that from thence have issued the ruines both of King and people, and his Majesties Subjects beene Apostacie, Rebellion,

Treason, Sacriledge, Murther, Rapine, Robbery, and all other the enormous Crimes, and detestable Villanies, with which this Kingdome hath of later times swarmed; sad experience hath given us too perfect a sense.[222]

Andrew Marvell brilliantly characterized the sense of a combined loss of a peaceful past and the menacing growth of the power of the press that even now assails the post-digital generation. He wrote:

> 'Twas an happy time when all Learning was in Manuscript, and some little Officer ... did keep the Keys of the Library ... There have been ways found out to banish Ministers, to fine not only the People, but even the Grounds and Fields where they assembled in Conventicles: But no Art yet could prevent these seditious meetings of Letters. Two or three brawny Fellows in a Corner, with meer Ink and Elbow-grease, do more Harm than an *Hundred systematical Divines* with their *sweaty Preaching*.[223]

Journalism had not only been birthed out of sermons; it now replaced them.

More blood and guts: building up to the free press
Things moved on apace. Twenty-one years after Puritan Milton's *Areopagitica* was penned, to add to Britain's woes, plague struck again. It was 1665: the worst outbreak of plague since the Black Death in 1348, which had killed fifteen per cent of the population of London. King Charles II removed himself and his court to Oxford.

Courtiers were afraid even to touch London newspapers for fear of contamination, so it was decided that an Oxford edition should be produced locally. *The Oxford Gazette* emerged from the turmoil. The first official "journal of record" printed in English was to become *The London Gazette* once the court returned home. It began publication on 5 February 1666, taking its name from the Venetian *gazeta*, a small coin, which was the price of a news sheet. Europe was still calling the shots in terms of journalistic developments.

Under the editorship of Henry Muddiman (1629–1692), the *Gazette* produced terse accounts of shipwrecks and events on various European battlefronts, with requests for prayer, on dense, close-printed two-column foolscap spreads, or "papers", which covered a variety of subjects, including commerce, foreign policy and religion. This was an unforced and unselfconscious integration. The very first front-page lead story covered the election of the Bishop of Oxford, Revd Dr Walter Blandford. Samuel Pepys approved. The great diarist wrote: "very pretty, full of news and no folly in it". The first edition of *The London Gazette* also requested prayers following a report of the Consistory in Rome "on how his Holyness had represented to the Cardinalls his great apprehensions that Christendome would break out again into Warrs". Elsewhere the deathbed reconversion of a lapsed Anglican and leader of the [Puritan] "Phanatics" is reported alongside further shipping news.

Authoritative and entertaining though it was, it does not however qualify as a proper newspaper, since it was not printed for sale for a general readership. It was subscription only; the "by Authority", printed under its masthead, meant it had secured—and needed—the King's approval.

Nonetheless, it was a vital part of the build up to a free press. Cromwell had suppressed journalism in the 1650s, as he doubled down to control his new republic. Yet, by the 1660s—and thanks in large part to the hilarious escapades of one Marchamont Nedham (1620–1678)—the public desire for news, as yet haphazard and lurid, was recognized. Nedham was a propagandist and reporter working for both sides during the chaos of the Civil War. He wrote in the first "newspaper", *Mercurius Britannicus* (published by the Parliamentarians in opposition to the Royalists) on 10–17 June 1644: "I have by an excellent and powerful Providence led the people through the labyrinths of the enemies Plots ... I have brought the secrets and sins of the Court abroad, from her Majestie to Mistris Croft her very maid of honour, and from his Majesty to his very Barbour."

Twenty years later, their majesties had seen enough. With the Restoration of the monarchy under Charles II came a brutal return to censorship. In 1663, for example, a printer named John Twyn was convicted of sedition for printing a book arguing that citizens should call to account a king whose decrees violated biblical law. Twyn refused to divulge the name of the author. For so doing, he was publicly castrated and then beheaded. "His privy-members were cut off before his eyes ..."[224] His body was then cut into four pieces, each being nailed to one of the four city gates, as a warning to other printers and writers. The ghastliness of his suffering served merely to reinforce the strength of his cause. Refusing to divulge one's sources remains one of the few points of honour among contemporary journalists.

Despite this, or because of it, newspapers could not be stopped. *The London Gazette* survives with the same name to this day—a permanent institution, and still the bearer of the daily record of government business.[225] As the "newspaper of the Crown" it is also the longest continuously published newspaper.

Conclusion

I have argued that the main innovations in printing and publishing in England, after the Reformation on the continent of Europe, were fuelled by a specifically and peculiarly religious energy. From the theology of justification by faith, which released intellectual captives from the control of Rome, through to the development of a demotic English that made worldwide communication possible, none of it "just happened". It relied on courage, character and conviction, punctuated by horrific martyrdoms. And no doubt as a result, inquiry into the real nature of things moved on apace, bringing popular discourse in its train. We now go on to meet some of the pioneers during what was once called journalism's "golden age".

Chapter 8
"Mainly a Matter of Spiritual Energy"

There began to emerge an extraordinary generation of writers, taking advantage of—and abetting—the slowly evolving public realm. In this chapter we meet some of them and analyse their make-up, for they have something peculiar in common—something that journalists go out of their way to disavow today.

Pillard and Dissenter: Daniel Defoe, father of modern journalism
Chief among the pioneers was Daniel Defoe (1660–1731). Widely regarded as the father of modern journalism, Defoe was a pamphleteer, or advocacy journalist. He loved the street, reporting popular sentiment, covering the nation's industriousness, and events.[226] Journalism was still not an independent craft. But Defoe was absolute in his devotion to the craft of reportage.[227]

He was, says Anthony Burgess, our first great novelist because he was our first great journalist.[228] He was a tireless advocate for social reform, who used his prolific writing and journalistic innovations to influence public opinion for good.

This was an age when English statesmen realized that in order to make their case they needed to have tame outlets. Newspapers were quickly identified as Whig or Tory, with leading writers accepting pensions to write in the party interest. Not Defoe. He was, at different times, in the employ of both; he simply used his positions to do what he felt right. And what was right, he felt, was toning down more extreme sentiment.

Yet to call Defoe a moderate is to fail to understand his motivation: he was a Dissenter until the day he died, which meant he was an outsider. To be a Dissenter—or a Nonconformist, as non-Anglicans were also called—was to court financial and reputational oblivion. It required continued, ardent risk-taking. Son of a highly respected office holder in the Butchers' Company, Defoe was even intended for the Nonconformist ministry, educated at the famous Dissenting academy at Newington Green in London, run by one Charles Morton.

But he turned to commerce instead, always riskily and usually unsuccessfully, possibly to support his writing. Queen Anne was markedly less religiously tolerant than William of Orange, whom she succeeded, and public office was closed to non-Anglicans. A bit of wriggling was possible, however. You could attend a Church of England service once a year in order to qualify for being "Anglican". Useful, if like Sir Thomas Abney (1640–1722)—Defoe's neighbour—you had your eyes set on being Mayor of London. Defoe was withering about such hypocrisy.

Defoe's biographer James Sutherland describes him as one of the great English "masters of journalism".[229]

He spent his whole writing life of nearly half a century advocating causes, persuading men to change their minds, to abandon some established prejudice and to consult their own best interest—and on every occasion he wrote with utter conviction.

Not only did he mean what he said, he believed it was tremendously important that it *should be said*, and that it was his business in life to say it. "It is mainly a matter of spiritual energy," says Sutherland: a natural alertness and liveliness kept him at a high pitch of intensity as he put his thoughts on paper. God, he believed, had given him special insight—on such matters as trade, religious strife, and so on—that he had denied to others, and he must report the truth as he saw it.[230]

Sutherland discerns in all this "the voice of the Puritan": Defoe's Puritan ancestry and Nonconformist upbringing had left a permanent impression on his mind and character.[231] He "never lost the earnestness and the stubborn conviction of having an 'inner light' that are at once the source of the Puritan's strength and of his limitation."[232]

He used his publications as a pulpit. And he retained a keen interest in church affairs for many years, particularly in the general relationship between the Anglican and dissenting communities. Defoe's pamphlet *The Shortest Way with the Dissenters*, published in 1702, parodied the violence of Anglican extremists by taking it to its logical conclusion and advising no less than the extermination of all Nonconformists!

This got him into trouble. High Churchmen, obtuse enough to believe in it at first, were furious when they discovered the hoax. Defoe was charged with seditious libel, sentenced to be pilloried and imprisoned, and his business was ruined—for the second time. But he was hailed as a hero by the crowd, who threw flowers at him instead of the usual stones.

He is regarded as the only "pillard" ever to emerge from the experience with a higher reputation than when he went into it.

And typically, he used the occasion to write, inventing thereby a new form of news.

This was the eye-witness account that could be printed and distributed within hours of its' happening. Written in verse, the first piece was a broadside—a single piece of paper, used normally for proclamations and sold on the street by peddlers. This one was entitled *A Dialogue between the Pillory and Daniel Defoe*. In it he addresses his instrument of torment, the pillory, thus:

> Was it for this you broke my easy rest?
> You know what publick failures I detest.
> How some Grandees are in a Mortal rage
> To See we know the Scandal of the Age;
> And as they are the grievance of the times
> Are most affraid of hearing their own Crimes.

It won him great popular support, expressing what many thought, but few dared to say.

Even so, after three days of humiliation, he was incarcerated in grim Newgate prison.[233] Hardly missing a beat he founded from his prison cell, the *Review of the State of the British Nation*. It ran three times a week from 1704, for an astonishing eight years. Written almost entirely by himself, it carried news, essays on current affairs and gossip, and was the forerunner of both the *Tatler* and the *Spectator*.

Of him, the historian George MacAulay Trevelyan wrote that he was "one of the first who saw the old world through a pair of sharp modern eyes". He was the first master, if not the inventor, of almost every feature of modern newspapers, including the lead article, investigative reporting, foreign news analysis, the agony aunt, the gossip column, and the candid obituary.[234]

He wrote copious enlightened pamphlets about education reform for women and toleration—even asylum—for the mentally ill. And all this activity came before he became well-known for his narrative fiction, with its flair for irony and making people laugh.

Surprisingly, given the apparent "criminality" of its founder, the *Review* was financed by the government.

Primarily political in tone, with much comment and little news, nevertheless—like everything Defoe wrote—it had an independent flavour. His work set down a tradition for the English press via its first-person accounts, underwriting principled advocacy of social reforms.[235]

He was particularly curious about the Christian temper of the people, and marvelled at it, particularly in the context of surviving the plague. Although a child at the time of this scourge, he decided years later that someone should record it as faithfully as possible from eye-witness accounts, even if only in hindsight. He was assiduous in his research for this work, grilling his uncle and others who had lived through the catastrophe for detail.

The result was his *Journal of the Plague Year* (1665), the final page of which is indicative of his method. It comprises a whole page of popular salutations he gleaned had then been extant—and which he purports to have overheard in the street as the plague was ebbing. He felt he detected an openness to the widespread view that this sudden and otherwise inexplicable waning of the pestilence was miraculous:

> "Lord, what an alteration is here! Why, last week I came along here, and hardly anybody was to be seen."
> "'Tis all wonderful, 'tis all a dream."
> "Blessed be God," says a third man, "and let us give thanks to him, for 'tis all his own doing."

Defoe writes: "Human help and human skill were at an end. These were all strangers to one another; but such salutations as these were frequent in the street every day; and in spite of a loose behaviour, the very common people went along the streets, giving God thanks for their deliverance."[236]

The people's religiosity fascinated him. He did not ignore it as superstition, or reinterpret it as being politically incorrect, but simply reported it: for to him it conveyed the people's reality.

To the editor of Blackie's edition of the *Journal*, his was an earnest "religious temper" and because of it, in his opinion "… the convincing clearness of the narrative has never been surpassed."[237]

But this was not propaganda. Where people were religious but deluded, he would say so. He describes a man who, at the onset of the plague, had attracted a crowd at a graveyard in Bishopsgate. This disturbed soul was, he writes, "ranting about a ghost who is said to be pointing to the sepulchral destination of thousands". He also reported on a woman who declared that an angel with a sword in the clouds had appeared to avenge God's wrath. Defoe wrote kindly: "I really did not laugh, but was very seriously reflecting how the poor people were terrified by the force of their own imagination."[238] He saw fit to report what people really believed, rather than rendering it invisible.

He condemns Church ministers who used the plague as an opportunity to preach repentance in a way that "rather sank than lifted up the hearts of their hearers". And he criticized them for failing to imitate "our blessed Lord and Master in this, that his whole gospel is full of declarations from heaven of God's mercy…"[239]

Under the curmudgeonly pseudonym Andrew Moreton, he railed against cruelty and pitilessness. He advocated for care homes—which he called "Protestant Monasteries"—after witnessing the spiteful contempt meted out upon a good friend so reduced in circumstances at the end of his life that he was forced to live in a tiny room with his daughter's family. She deprived him of food, warmth, freedom and love. He self-published this *cri de coeur* as a highly coloured long-form article to avoid "feeing" other journalists and publishers. He begins with the ringing acclamation: "I enquire whether … I can yet do anything for the Service of my Country."

Defoe's Puritanism was as material as it was spiritual. Among his many proposed reforms were: a progressive system of taxation; road-maintenance schemes, involving a community service roster; authorial copyright; and regulation of the press. The eminent nineteenth-century Scottish journalist and philosopher William Minto thought that his *Essay upon Projects* was proof of Defoe's "genius". He commended his powerful advocacy of almost every practicable scheme of social improvement he could think of.[240] His biographer ponders his motivation:

Controversy, argument, the exposure of intellectual folly or moral turpitude were all part of the air that Defoe normally breathed; and so too was his consciousness of himself as a man of moderation, a prophet without honour in his own country, a kind of unreluctant Hamlet born to set things right.[241]

But this prophet has a road named after him in the North London suburb of Stoke Newington where he resided with his wife Mary and numerous offspring. The suburb has to this day become a place peculiarly associated with journalists, as well as cultural non-conformists, religious and otherwise.[242]

The age of the journal begins

The fractious, more recognizable political atmosphere that produced Daniel Defoe also created a crisis of authority for the reporting of news. The search for facts came to be smothered in a fog of opinion, a problem that has never gone away.[243] Politics was poisoning the news. It led to a need for a different product; less noisy and urgent, more nuanced, and leisurely.

The era of the periodical journal had arrived, beginning in France as early as 1665, a country that boasted up to one hundred different titles by the mid-eighteenth century. They largely attempted to avoid direct comment on contemporary events, minimizing the risk of official censure. Articles were longer, the tone more personal and objective: they purported to observe rather than to hector, and they also wanted to amuse. In fact, many of the critical and stylistic features that we regard as integral to journalism were to emerge first in these eighteenth-century journals.[244] They were called "spectators".

Son of an Anglican divine
Joseph Addison (1672–1719), who with Richard Steele founded the *Spectator*, were both what is called "wits"; their journalism was not what would be recognized as such today. Nonetheless, their type of writing, which was popular, proved to be a vital step on the way. The magazine flourishes still today.

Addison was the son of an Anglican divine, who grew up in a religious atmosphere, somewhat removed from the fray. The periodical first appeared in March 1711, and came out daily until the end of 1712. It described itself as "the sober reflections of a detached observer", which was a slightly tongue-in-cheek attitude, since it was always more amusing than that, puncturing pomp and relishing the peccadilloes and foibles of Londoners.

An important aspect of its success was its notion that urbanity and taste were values that transcended political differences. Addison did much to civilize, as well as entertain, thousands of middle-class readers, many of whom were women. He wrote hymns too. His friend and collaborator Sir Richard Steele, also an Irishman from Dublin, had started the *Tatler* in 1709, the aim of the two men being to "civilize public taste", to make the middle class, in particular, more moral and more polite—"to enliven morality with wit, and to temper wit with morality".[245]

Addison famously attacked duelling and, despite his apolitical leanings, nonetheless was given the post of official gazetteer under Prime Minister Harley. He got into trouble in 1714 for a pamphlet titled *The Crisis*, declaring that the Protestant succession was in peril under the Tories. For this he was expelled as an MP, though his fortunes changed on the accession of George I, by whom he was knighted in 1715.

Political journalism creates the public square

So, now we come to perhaps the single most momentous of all journalism's achievements, on the backs of these tireless champions of opinion and reform: the public square itself.

Compared to the press in other European states, the British press by this time was enjoying unique liberties, political expulsion notwithstanding. The leading organs of the time were not oppositional. However, that changed.

Robert Walpole (1676–1745), a Whig and first de facto Prime Minister of England—together with Henry St John Viscount Bolingbroke (1678–1751), a Tory—took to print, paying many thousands of pounds to spirited writers like Defoe to address the public from their own point of view. Pope's *Dunciad*, and Swift's *Gulliver's Travels* took their metier from Addison and Steele's combination of reform-minded literature and journalism in *The Spectator*. Competition from the Whigs erupted under George I, with *The British Merchant*. The Whigs purchased the *London Journal* in 1722—the most important and widely read journal at that time—but it was St John, now in opposition, who can be said to have created political journalism in the grand style.

His journal the *Craftsman*—also known as *The Country Journal* or *The Craftsman: Being a Critique of the Times*—was published at first semi-weekly, then weekly. It was hard-hitting, innovative and successful, running from 1726 to 1752. Liberty could only be safeguarded by a permanent opposition party that used constitutional methods and a legal course of opposition to curb the excesses of legal and ministerial power, as Bolingbroke put it.[246] He advocated a "country party" as opposed to a "court party", which he believed would be less subject to greed. But such oppositional politics were an innovation made possible only by an oppositional press that was constitutionally unfettered.

The innovation that oppositional politics brought about was the creation of popular opinion. Bolingbroke and his friends knew just how to form such a public opinion by using the new press to mobilize the impulses of the like-minded for political use.

Whereas politics had so often been subject to demagoguery and sloganeering, uproars and mob scenes, rather this public opinion was directed by another factor: the establishment of an independent journalism that knew how to assert itself against the government. It made critical commentary and public opposition against the government part of the normal state of affairs.[247] With this journal, and its successor—the monthly *Gentleman's Magazine,* founded in 1731—the press was for the first time established as a critical organ genuinely engaged on behalf of the public in critical debate. It had in fact, become "the Fourth Estate".[248]

Yet Jurgen Habermas' use of the term Fourth Estate here is oddly anachronistic. The Commons continued to try to prevent the reporting of Parliament, for at least another fifty years, and there was no proper gallery until 1803. The Commons gave up the fruitless effort, in fact if not in law, in 1771 when *Evening Post* editor Alderman Wilkes' sentence for breaching parliament privilege, by entering the chamber as a member of the public, was never carried out.

It was not until 1787, sixteen years later, that Edmund Burke allegedly coined the resonant phrase "Fourth Estate" with its European tinge, with one eye on the revolutionary turbulence brewing in France, which worried him greatly. Or at least so Thomas Carlyle has it. It was Carlyle who quoted, posthumously and resonantly, from the opinionated Irish statesman's speech at the State Opening of Parliament. This was the first time the press was able to report from the public gallery, after a long and somewhat half-hearted struggle to keep the parliamentary doors closed to public scrutiny. "Burke said that there were three Estates in Parliament, but in the Reporters' Gallery yonder, there sat a fourth Estate more important far than they all."[249] (Carlyle was also therefore wrong. There was no specific "gallery" for Burke to point to for a while yet.) By this Burke did not mean, as some surmise, that the press—still without their own gallery, but hugger mugger among the public—was the most dangerous; far from it. He meant that it was the most vigilant as to civil rights infractions, rights all too often trespassed upon by the other three Estates: whether the Church (prelates), the Nobility (Lords), or the Commons.

A place for journalists in the public gallery was officially provided by the Speaker only in the year 1803. For a century before that, they had had to gain entry incognito and illegally. And it was only when the Houses of Parliament reopened in newly constructed buildings after the fire of 1834 that purpose-built stands for reporters were installed. This was two years after the first Reform Bill had transformed Parliament—for a long time the target of critical comment by public opinion—into the very organ of that opinion.[250]

With its Dissenting DNA, the Fourth Estate was set to become society's watchdog, outside the other three Estates and therefore (ostensibly) impartial. This is still considered to be a noble thing. Australian media don Julianne Schultz described it in 1998, before the Murdoch phone-hacking scandals, as a "remarkably resilient concept", if, even then, "a somewhat tarnished synonym for the news media".[251]

The free press raised to an institution the ongoing commentary on and criticism of the Crown's actions and Parliament's decisions. By means of the press, public authority was called before the forum of the public. From now on, the degree of the public sphere's development was measured by the state of the confrontation between government and press, as it drew out over the entire eighteenth and nineteenth centuries.

Though moral, it was hardly dull; and it was never merely partisan. Though it drew its finest practitioners from the ranks of the Church—the Dissenting establishment most notably—it was devoted to public causes and social reform. And though funded from the deep pockets of the upper echelons of society, it was making parliamentary democracy possible.

The *Letters of Junius*, anonymous to this day—a collection of private and open letters critical of the government of King George III, written between 1769 and 1772—introduced for the first time a brand of accusatory journalism familiar to us today. They unmasked secret connections of political significance among ministers, the military and jurists, and even the King. Parliament got its own back for a while longer by prohibiting the publication of parliamentary deliberations. But the very public capers of Alderman Wilkes made it impossible to maintain. Anyway, the prohibition proved pointless when "Memory" Woodfall was able to get into the public gallery incognito and reproduce from memory sixteen columns of parliamentary debate for the *Morning Chronicle* and thereby scoop the rest of the press put together.[252] From

1695 censorship lapsed and was not renewed. The growth of oppositional government meant that both sides needed the press in order to put their case forward to the public. Different kinds of law were subsequently introduced in the UK (Copyright Act of 1710) and in 1735 in the US with the extraordinary innovation whereby truth became a defence against libel, which we shall cover in the next chapter.

Lack of partisanship

The peculiar lack of partisanship among some of the leading writers was not self-seeking as we would understand it today. It was founded on a mature sensibility that truth could be written but could not be embodied wholly by one group or another. Writers like Wilkes and Defoe supported causes rather than the parties espousing them—which they joined and repulsed with equanimity—and not entirely because of the pay offered. Historian Andrew Pettegree sniffs somewhat anachronistically at the ease with which writers of the day changed parties seemingly overnight, depending on the pension offered,[253] yet Defoe always claimed to be "a constant follower of moderate principles, a vigorous opposer of hot measures of *all* parties."[254]

Conclusion

Jurgen Habermas speculates only at the very end of his career on the religious origins of England's even-handed public spiritedness, even though he notes much earlier on the unique nature of the context in which things were changing.[255] But his observations go a long way to support the contention of this book: that there was a religious and spiritual dimension to the contexts and characters behind the best innovations in journalism, which tended to set the mercury. It was many centuries in development, but the instincts that characterized it—borne out in the work of Milton, Defoe, Addison and Steele, and the freedom with which they began to operate—suggest a more than ordinary energy and vision emerging out of the Puritanism of an earlier age. That energy was a particular feature of Calvinist religion, which engendered a broad non-denominational respect for the manifestations of what they saw as the divine hand in creation. This was a settled trust in things as they were.

The Calvinists had coined the word "calling". Calling can be defined as a special devotion and dynamism lived out in service as a response to God's summons.[256] Defoe, the father of journalism, embodied this devotion. He incarnated a kind of writing, rooted in observation, that championed work that did not take sides politically, was clear about its moral purpose, was wedded to the truth and pressed urgent cases for reform. This was the "top note" of proper journalistic practice. Without this, it was mere scribbling; a meaner thing, reduced to information at best, noise at worst, even to the point of social harm. Much of the apparent vision and energy of these early "news writers" arose from the protagonists being "outsiders" speaking into the public realm, often heedless of the risk of great personal cost. They regarded themselves as prophets. From their example emerged American journalism—for a time the single most vivid expression of such a vision, as we shall soon discover in the next chapter.

Chapter 9
First Newspapers in New England, India and China

New England on the East coast of America became the new centre of Reformation thought. There the same ideas of religious protest, freedom of expression and print as we have seen elsewhere were all replicated.[257]

What is striking is that more than half a century after the emergence in England of the moralizing Calvinistic paratexts, which schooled readers in how and why they should read news of events, the innovative American "news sermon" seemed to ram home the point. The sermon stood alone, in local New England contexts, as the regular (at least weekly) medium of public communication. It was a compelling channel of information, with combined religious, educational and news functions, and we turn now to explore how it worked in forging what became modern journalism.[258] We then travel even further afield to two other imperial destinations where the same winds of Puritanism were blowing with similar effect.

Sermons and the news in the US

As with the output of the hooded scourge of Rome, Savonarola, New England sermons were first preached in church and then published. Topical, and incendiary, they created a sense of expectancy. More than that, they were regular as clockwork. They were, by definition, a weekly phenomenon, Sunday by Sunday laying the foundational criteria by which newspapers came to be defined.

The possibility of predictability, or precise periodicity, established as custom that all-important bonding with readers. News sermons were therefore powerful in shaping cultural values, meanings and a sense of corporate purpose. Subjects were as riveting as royal births and deaths, military defeats or victories, election results and government decisions, and of course crime. Their popularity provided work for printers, just as in Reformation Germany. And they helped assuage the hunger in readers in uncertain times for a providential reading of events, shaping a receptive news culture.

Puritan theology became admonitory, despite Luther's own revolt against fear towards the loving intentions of God. This theology tended to encourage the reporting of bad news, the staple of all newspapers to come.

The preachers regarded calamities with grim relish as well-deserved; a sign that God reigned and was not at all pleased. The written introduction—or paratext—to one news sermon discussed an explosion aboard a ship in dock in Boston. This had it, snappily, that, "The Times of Men are in the Hands of God. Or a Sermon occasioned by That Awful Providence Which Happened in Boston in New England, the 4th Day of the 3rd Month 1675 (When Part of a Vessel Was Blown Up in the Harbor, and Nine Men Hurt, and Three Mortally Wounded").

As we have noted before, news mattered because it witnessed sometimes to the love and more often to the chastening by God of his people. And while there was business news, it was not broadcast, or widely replicated, being produced exclusively for a closed shop of traders and available only by subscription. The news sermons for Sundays were, on the other hand, open to all.

News, therefore, was developing in America along the same lines as it had in Reformation Europe: as printed reports of providential action, produced with a prophetic impetus and tone. It was anything but leisured or written for entertainment, but news sermons were shot through with a sense of urgency and earnestness. Indeed, in 1681, a general meeting of church ministers in Massachusetts urged careful coverage of "Illustrious Providences" ... which "all showed a glimpse of God's purposes".[259]

The sifting and setting down of Illustrious Providences required a writer/editor. The man for the job proved to be none other than Increase Mather, the best-known preacher in Massachusetts in the late seventeenth-century.

Mather (1639–1723) was an irrepressible communicator, a Puritan clergyman who served in that capacity from the age of 22 until agreeing to become President of America's first and still foremost institute of learning, Harvard College. He remained there from 1685 to 1701. It is no coincidence that it was Harvard that should house the colony's first printing press, shipped from London, England.

Mather wrote about scientific developments and natural phenomena, such as comets, and he would not report without a written, signed statement from his sources!

American journalism began, in short, because the Puritans were obsessed with events. "They could see all around them the providence of God. The great movements of celestial and human history were the prime considerations, but little things carried meaning as well."[260]

Their precarious lives were fraught with expectation. Mather it was who prophesied gloomily that "a day of trouble is at hand." The idea that God was acting in history—history in which the pioneers were actively complicit—gave journalism and journalists their edge. Mather wrote that: "It is proper for the Ministers of God to ingage themselves [in recording] the providentiall Dispensations of God."[261]

Increase's son, Cotton—the same Mather who, to his later chagrin, justified the Salem witch trials of 1692—put it even more daringly:

> To *regard* the illustrious displays of that Providence wherewith our Lord Christ governs the world, is a work, than which there is none more needful or useful for a Christian.[262]

Despite his role in the witch trials, Mather Junior and the other men of New England continued to rail against the limits on freedom and self-determination that the governing British were imposing on their unruly colony. The embittering censorship that accompanied it continued over the next century.

"A great many Providences now recorded"

Cotton Mather was behind the emergence of America's first newspaper, *Publick Occurrences*, on 25 September 1690. But it was an English printer and writer, Benjamin Harris—an ex-convict and exile considered "factious" by the English government during the tumultuous days of the Restoration of the Monarchy (1660-1685)—who is credited with publishing it. Intended as a monthly periodical, its theology proved inconvenient, and earned it official opprobrium.[263] True, it contained "reflections of a very high nature", but his insistence on God's sovereignty was a little too eclectic for comfort.

This was especially so when it concerned the sexual peccadilloes of French allies, and the reliability or otherwise of local Indian tribes. The paper accused Louis XIV of having slept with his own daughter-in-law. And he accused the Mohawk Indians, with whom royal officials were seeking an alliance to defeat the French in Canada, of having mistreated prisoners. Harris, like all journalists, saw a story in hypocrisy in high places, however inconvenient for the colony. The authorities considered such "doubtful and uncertain reports" too prejudicial, and closed the paper down after just four days, on threat of imprisonment.

Its novelty had lain partly in its intended periodical nature. It was, it said, "furnished once a moneth (or if any Glut of Occurrences happen, oftener)". But in style and content it was prophetic—and classically journalistic.

The paper had promised to cover "memorable occurents of divine providence", domestic and foreign public affairs, so "that people everywhere may better understand" them and "assist their Businesses and Negotiations". It would finally do something "towards the Curing, or at least Charming of that Spirit of Lying ..." which was evidently prevalent.[264]

Harris, full of prophetic zeal and an irrepressible desire to see his passions in print, returned to England in 1694 or early 1695, and was promptly imprisoned again briefly for another newspaper venture, *Intelligence Domestick and Foreign*. After his release, he was able to publish in 1699, yet another newspaper, the *London Post* (which ran until

1705), as the political realm edged its way towards an acceptance of the press.

But all this excitement had led Harris to penury and, after all his high-sounding aspirations for truth, he was forced to spend his last years as a quack seller of "Angelical Pills".

Like Defoe, who was also in and out of prison for his faith in journalism, his itch to publish got the better of his need to prosper, and he died intestate. Nonetheless, his memory endures, even if the first American newspaper to last more than one issue was not his own, but another Boston paper, the *News-Letter*, which was published in 1704.

The *Boston News-Letter*'s first editor, John Campbell, had the same religiously inspired intention as the other pioneers: to see "a great many Providences now Recorded, that would otherwise be lost."[265]

Campbell was also a Puritan. He attacked immorality, counterfeiting and profaneness, and stressed accuracy. He wanted to print bad news because it exposed the Devil. It would show that an "awful Providence" was "a warning to all others to watch against the wiles of our Grand Adversary."[266] Campbell recorded what others called "extraordinary judgements". He also covered "mercies"—such as the rapid extinguishing of a fire through "God's good signal Providence"—against a background of moral contextualization in the news sermons of the Mathers, which schooled a readership and created an appetite that nothing else could. The *News-letter* survived for fifteen years.

Campbell's successor as owner of the *News-Letter* (in 1723) was one Bartholomew Green, who presided over the paper for ten years, seeing it as a Christian calling and one recognized as "humble and exemplary" when he died. His emphasis on press responsibility was aimed at helping readers know "how to order their prayers and praises to the Great God."[267] The impetus caught on elsewhere in America, and by 1750 there were fourteen weekly newspapers, and several twice- and thrice-weekly papers too.

Truth the defence against libel
New England had led the way in establishing not just a press, but freedom to publish what the colony's rulers wanted hidden. This received its watershed test with the Peter Zenger trial in 1735, recently memorialized in the hit production *Hamilton*—after the lawyer who won the case. Zenger's story is therefore well-known in some quarters, but perhaps not well-enough in others. As publisher of the *New York Weekly Journal*, he decided to take on the royal governor of New York, the bully William Cosby, who had made enemies. Cosby was cruel, dishonest and corrupt:

> When a farmer's cart slowed down Cosby's coach, the governor had his coachman beat the farmer with a horsewhip and nearly kill him. When Cosby desired some land owned by Indians, he stole their deed and burned it. When Cosby granted new lands to those who applied legally, he demanded and received bribes often amounting to one third of the estates.[268]

Zenger was prepared to publish anonymous stories about Cosby, funded by the governor's enemies, but for which he was prepared to carry the can. He published sermons insisting, scandalously, on the limitation of royal power and freedom of conscience—and was charged with "seditious libel" for his pains. One such article, by Jonathan Dickinson, insisted that, "Every person in the world has an equal right to judge for themselves, in the affairs of conscience and eternal salvation."[269] And he added: "What dreadful work has been made in the world by using methods of force in matters of opinion and conscience."

But, at the trial, Hamilton sensationally and successfully argued that truth was itself a defence against libel: a landmark moment in legal history. Hamilton did not have to argue about what truth was. Interestingly, the case did not have to be made that truth rested on the Bible, or anywhere else—or not:[270] the jury simply accepted it, and Zenger went free. Thirty years after the Dissenter Defoe was exposing the crimes of grandees, and hymning his wretched pillory, American freedom came of age. No similar case needed to be brought anywhere in America again.

Freedom (meaning "freedom to publish"), together with statecraft and the stability of a public realm seemed perhaps counter-intuitively to grow together. This was driven by an overtly Puritan press. For a while it seemed to be true in other parts of the British Empire, too.

The free press in India

India got its very first newspaper—a weekly—not in the colonial administrators' English, but in the Bengali language (in 1818). Called *Samachar Darpan* (meaning "News Mirror"), it survived for more than twenty years, until December 1841.

The brainchild of John Clark Marshman, co-founder of the Baptist Missionary Society at Serampore, it was produced overtly to further Christian objectives, and the tricky business of social reform. But what made it such a must-read for so long was its coverage of government news—the appointment of judges and collectors, the publication of government circulars—as well as European news, local events, births, weddings and obituaries. There were cultural features on English and Indian history as well as book reviews. From 1829, the paper became bi-lingual: published in both Bengali and English translations.

Northamptonshire cobbler William Carey was the inspiration behind these developments. But he might never have been able to set sail. The British administrators, fearful he might upset the people with his religious fervour, had tried to prevent him from going to India at all.

Undaunted, he had sailed on a Danish ship, arriving at the Danish-held colony of Serampore in Bengal in 1793. Once there, he wasted no time in translating the Hindu sacred texts into languages spoken by the ordinary people—the first such texts ever produced in India. Sanskrit, a priestly script, was used for philosophy rather than as a mother tongue. The brahmin élite considered the scriptures much too holy for ordinary Hindus to touch, let alone read. But Carey thought otherwise.

He continued to alarm the British government who remained anxious about his work, particularly his newspaper. They recommended that "extra-ordinary precautions must be used not to give the natives cause for suspicion that the paper had been devised as an engine for undermining their religious opinions." They need not have worried. Some of India's most distinguished Bengali Hindu pundits saw its value—and wrote for it.

US missionaries, print and Chinese capitalism
We now turn to China; ironically, the leader of the non-Western world in journalistic innovation. True, it had

invented printing possibly between the fourth and seventh centuries AD, but it's remarkable invention had stalled for centuries. China's genius was to cut blocks from wood and use them to print textiles and short Buddhist texts carried as charms by believers.

Later, long scrolls and books for élite use were produced, first by wood-block printing and then, beginning in the eleventh century, by using movable wooden blocks of type. This was fully four hundred years before the awakening in the West to the potential of such an invention. However, the complexity of the Chinese alphabet hindered its widespread use, leaving it (as we have seen elsewhere) in the hands of the élites who had no incentive to democratize it. And so it was that Protestant Germany was to claim the credit for a machine flexible enough to turn print into a mass medium.

Partly because of the narrow reach of its literature, China had only limited forms of political belonging up to the present day. Despite inventing the press in around 600 AD, China shows clearly that the impulse to communicate depends on something other than technology or profit.

The brief flowering of a free press in the early nineteenth century was due to foreign interlopers, the culture carriers of their day. Western missionaries grasped, unequivocally, the connection between printing, journalism and social reform. Without their zeal this could not—and indeed, had not—happened in a thousand years of opportunity.

It says something for their self-conscious martyr complex, not unlike Luther's and Defoe's, that these tiny platoons of innovators could confront the vast and alien continents of East and South Asia with little but a single printing press. All they needed, they believed, was prayer. It was none other than the Lord of Hosts who had made their revolutionary mandate possible, under the opportune if unfriendly gaze of the imperial authorities.

Christopher Reed, the most comprehensive secular historian of the birth of Chinese print capitalism, notes the missionary motive behind this seismic change.[271] This was what he called the "Chinese phase in the Gutenberg revolution". Typically, Western printing technologies were absorbed in the treaty ports along the south-eastern littoral, first in Macao, then in Canton, Hong Kong and Shanghai, which had opened up after the Opium War. Ironically, this was the region where missionary organizations, both Protestant and Catholic, were most active. By the end of the nineteenth century, however, only one of these multiple locations—Shanghai—turned out to have the necessary combination of location and an adequately educated Chinese leadership able to combine Western printing technology with Chinese publishing culture. The result was a new Chinese industry. "Christian missionary printing appears as ... the first of several important steps in this process," says Reed, who then, it seems to me makes light of the bold enormity of their endeavour.[272]

The pattern repeats again

Scholars play it down, but it was the same pattern repeating itself: prophetic intellectual work operating under what was believed to be God's direct communication, exactly as had happened after the Sinai event in the ancient Near East, and then later in Europe and UK. Despite overwhelming odds, these prophets began translating and democratizing the message as journalism in China, in the face of frightening penalties—also laying the foundations for a capitalistic economy.

Gutenberg in the Far East

A fuller version of this story—skated over by Reed, and focusing on the religious motivation behind the development of print in China—is provided by the young scholar, Xiantao Zhang. She wrote her Ph.D. specifically on the Protestant missionary impetus behind China's press. It was published in 2007.[273]

Zhang describes how Richard Morrison of the London Missionary Society (LMS) sailed for China in 1807. He was the first missionary to set foot on mainland China after the expulsion of the Jesuits in 1773. The Jesuits had not introduced the printing press to China. Indeed, the first Jesuit missionaries who got a foothold on the island of Macau, a Portuguese colony, did not learn Chinese. Morrison it was who was tasked by the LMS with spreading the Christian gospel through the preparation of printed materials. This he undertook, under the protection of the British in Malacca for (as is the case today) the contemporary times were hostile to Christianity. Preaching was not only banned, but Christianity itself was outlawed on pain of execution. (Reed does not mention this.) Morrison was undaunted. He resolved that "the effect of books is silent, but powerful". Protected by the British navy, he proceeded to publish as much as he could.

It was Morrison who first put traditional Chinese woodblock to use in journalism. With the assistance of William Milne (in August 1815), he began the first news periodical *China Monthly Magazine*, printed with traditional tools. His intent was to serve the majority of the Chinese population—not just the palace old guard. And the subject matter was markedly *not* just to proselytize, according to Zhang. Milne wrote: "To Promote [sic] Christianity was to be its primary object, other things, though, were not to be overlooked. Knowledge and science are the handmaids of religion and may become the auxiliaries of virtue."[274]

China Monthly concentrated on Christian subjects, but included articles on Chinese customs, astronomy, geography, and much else. Ge Gongzhen, in his book *The History of Chinese Journalism* (published in 1927) claimed this as the first modern periodical, and it is widely accepted as the beginning of modern Chinese journalism.

Much of what the missionaries found they adjudged to be admirable, but they deemed some aspects of life to be sclerotic, cruel and oppressive. The Qing dynasty had ruled for a thousand years. It was beset by opium wars, debilitating defeats and humiliating treaties. Before Morrison, the only bearer of news in the country was the *Imperial Gazette*, produced and distributed, *de haut en bas*, from the royal palace. Disseminated only to courtiers, it came out irregularly and, on both of those counts, does not constitute a newspaper. For the sharing of public information, it was, however, all there was. The missionary press, on the other hand, was a daring innovation, reporting on events and Chinese culture for the masses. Indeed, the *China Monthly Magazine* abolished the élitist readership the imperial press had served for more than a millennium.[275]

The high point of the missionary press was *Wanguo Gongbao*, which literally means "The Ten Thousand Nations' Common Newspaper". It started life, very humbly, as a weekly news magazine called (uninspiringly) *Church News* in 1868, but within twenty years it was being read by the Emperor.

One of a number of hybrid evangelical/educational newspapers, it was founded and produced under the oversight of American Southern Methodist, Young John Allen (1836–1907), in cooperation with Chinese "gentry scholars". It achieved an eventual circulation of 38,400 copies, containing a mix of national and international news, and reform proposals. So impressive was *Gongbao* that later reformists produced their own version of it in August 1895, which they funded themselves, with the same title, even reproducing some of its articles. One of these reformists was Kang Yu Wei, a radical reform-oriented scholar from a strongly neo-Confucian family. He evidently embraced Western learning after living close to the hub of the missionaries' activities in Canton.[276]

Milne gave his life in the effort, dying aged just 37—but he had secured little short of the beginning of modernity in China.

The missionary press in China was not only the product of evangelical revival, but also the earliest form of social media.[277] By the end of the first Protestant century in China, the pioneering journalist and foremost intellectual and social reformer Liang Qichao (1873–1929) could opine that "free thinking, speech and press were the foundation of every civilization, from which modern world development derives. The Newspaper is the centre of people's thinking and speech."[278]

Not only did the missionaries, via the newspaper, celebrate Chinese civilization; they also introduced modern ideas of cosmology and justice for women. They are credited with achieving the end of foot-binding. Unlikely as it seems, the ultimate accolade came from none other than Sun Yat Sen, first provisional president of the incipient Republic of China. Missionary-educated, he came to power in 1911, asserting, ironically enough: "The Republican movement began on the day when Robert

Morrison set foot on the soil of China."[279]

The little Protestant platoon had in effect replicated the pattern we've seen elsewhere. This "tiny fraction" deployed a progressive intellectual approach, fired by their spirituality, creating an enormous social, political, and cultural impact for another hundred years.[280]

Missionary publications came to shape the transition of print journalism from a centuries-long monopoly by the state into a diverse, modernizing and "frequently radical public journalism".[281] The impetus was undeniably spiritual, the prophetic sensibility that fuelled it unmistakeable, even to later pioneers, reformist politicians and Chinese scholars. Writes Zhang:

> Without doubt, it was the broad agenda of social and educational concerns that sprang from deep sources in the evangelism of the missionary journalists that was the most significant element in inculcating a modern journalistic culture amongst the Chinese gentry-scholars.[282]

The missionaries' achievements proved mixed, however. They were more successful at disseminating their language, technology and a glimpse of the possibility of an autonomous public sphere, together with the habits of freedom, than inculcating their faith.

Chinese intellectuals adapted the model the missionaries set them to a distinctive secular form of cultural modernity, while retaining Confucian influences.[283] This departure set in train the demise of the free press. Confucian scholars secularized the innovations of freedom, and Communist censorship suppressed it altogether.

China now ranks fourth from bottom of 180 nations

in the World Press Freedom Index, after seventy years of atheism. It is a salutary testament to that "peculiar spiritual energy" that gives rise to journalism at all and, without which, it withers and dies.[284]

Without the ballast of long centuries of development in thought and practice about the self, public opinion and the value of oppositional government, China's free press expired. The missionaries' efforts, though productive, failed to produce an enduring Fourth Estate without the soil of a certain spiritual receptivity to root itself in. The seeds of a recovery may still exist: as I write, China is advertising for British journalists in the online *Hold the Front Page* industry gazette.

Yet, even while China was closing down the opportunities of a free press at the turn of the nineteenth century, innovations in investigative journalism by another passionate Puritan-inspired Nonconformist were opening them up back home, at exactly the same time.

This was a journalist credited extravagantly with being the very "founding father of the modern world". He was a founder who not only saw his newspaper as a "pulpit", but himself—even more remarkably with respect to today's secular lens—as "a Christ".

WT Stead—"founding father of the modern world"

"Goodbye, my dear friend. I am going to gaol with joy unspeakable ..."

With such a jarring sentiment, the world's first investigative journalist rapturously greeted his sentencing.

His crime? A daring exposé of child sex-trafficking, called archaically "The Maiden Tribute of Modern Babylon". Daring, sensational—and successful—Stead's campaign stunned London and helped to end the capital's iniquitous white slave trade.[285]

William Thomas Stead (1849–1912), founder of the British tabloid newspaper, should be a household name, yet today he is all but forgotten.

His fearless and exemplary campaigning to end the sexual exploitation of children by middle-class white men should be a by-word in our own sexually rampant, #MeToo age.

True, his forlorn little prison uniform appeared as part of the *Breaking the News* exhibition at the British Library in 2022, but he is otherwise relegated to a strange obscurity.

Strange, because Stead risked his liberty and reputation to raise the age of consent. He roused bourgeois society from its collective denial about the iniquities being visited by the city's respectable husbands upon the bodies of virgins across the city, and got the law changed.

It was an open secret that no one wanted to confront: sexually innocent girls were being consumed—to order. It was not taxi-drivers and kebab-shop owners who lured the destitute and delinquent to their doom. London's wealthiest most respectable men paid for the procuring and deflowering of virgin children. Even King Leopold of Belgium was exposed by Stead for ordering fresh young girls from London.

He showed how easy it was to procure an innocent 13-year-old for sex—by doing so himself.

He made sure he had impeccable confidantes to his plan, to avoid being misunderstood. He had discussed his scheme with the Archbishop of Canterbury and the Cardinal of Westminster; even the Salvation Army agreed to guarantee his bona fides.

He knew he was courting jail, but he took the risk anyway. A girl was identified—Eliza Armstrong—sold by her mother for £5 to an accomplice, whom women's campaigner Josephine Butler had rescued from a life of prostitution. The accomplice took the child to a brothel. Stead administered chloroform to her to demonstrate the way rape and assault were commonplace in London, but instead of violating her and then slinging her back onto the street, he placed her in the caring hands of the Salvation Army, who spirited her away to a safe house in the south of France.

Public opinion was scandalized. Society denounced Stead as a monster and a pornographer. He did not care. His reputation mattered to him not a shred compared with the injustice he felt he was exposing.

He reckoned he had no choice. He could not go to the police, for they were complicit in the trade (as he explained to the judge at his trial). Moreover, the subject was socially taboo, as it is, still. No one would even talk about it. Even to *know* about it was to be thought complicit.

Stead had to risk *proving* beyond a doubt what was going on. His series of damning articles had its effect. The Criminal Law Amendment Act, which would raise the age of consent from 13 to 16, had until that point been in danger of falling. It was debated in the House of Commons late in May 1885 and parliamentarians, having read the articles he wrote, voted overwhelmingly for Stead's reforms.

Sadly, his carefully built bastion of precautions against the risk of prosecution did not save him. He fell afoul of a jury and a judge, who deemed that purity of motive was not enough. No one could violate the law even when "persons who entertained certain ideas might carry out what they supposed to be a good object."

The judge sent him to Newgate prison for three months, with hard labour for abduction and indecent assault.

The scoop scandalized London and divided the people. It antagonized upper-class men and working-class parents alike, the latter whom Stead had accused of selling their children for sex.

Stead admitted he had been drinking heavily during the whole episode to cope with the enormity of it.

He was regarded by some as a fanatic and a hypocrite, but this was a clear case of blaming the messenger. The militant feminist Millicent Fawcett stood by him: she and Josephine Butler held a public meeting during his incarceration and raised 100,000 signatures for a petition for his release.

Stead, ill but exultant, wrote in his journal, even as he went to gaol. "It is not often that a man can look back upon his conviction and sentence as a criminal convict with pride and exultation. Such however is my case ..."

It is surely evidence—if evidence were needed—of the secularization of our national discourse and the training of journalists that the obscurity that has descended upon this "tornado of humanity" is so dense. Strange indeed, I suggest, as Stead pioneered some of the key innovations in the media that survive to this day.

Where Defoe had the idea of investigative long-form journalism, Stead turned it into a tabloid genre.

When John Morley offered him the assistant editorship of the *Pall Mall Gazette* in 1880, Stead implemented ideas that laid the foundations of newspaper design, developing the use of illustrations and introducing crossheads to break up solid, unrelieved text.

He used his newspapers to champion causes: women's rights and foreign policy, to name two. John (later Lord) Morley, an atheist, called him "the most powerful journalist in the island ... His extraordinary vigour and spirit made other people seem like wet blankets, creatures of moral défaillance".[286]

Stead took hold of the interview, an innovation pioneered by the American sensationalist James Gordon Bennett—maverick proprietor-editor of the *New York Herald*—and forged it in his own image. His interview with General Gordon resulted in Gordon being sent to the Sudan, thus changing UK foreign policy from *laissez faire* (which exacerbated the Irish Famine) to interventionism, from which it has rarely deviated to this day.

He also introduced the "scoop". His astounding investigative campaigns improved the conditions of London's poor; his *Truth about the Navy* crusade brought about a renaissance of sea power. But the main change in the *PMG* was in the tone of the paper. "When Stead saw that a thing required to be done, he campaigned for it with a vigour and urgency that no one has ever excelled", writes one. He had "the compelling ardour that springs from absolute conviction in the rightness of a cause," says another.

Although Stead's reign was a hundred and fifty years after the religious pioneers of the modern press—and much had happened in the meantime—he developed to its logical end the prophetic truth-teller role of the journalist. This is because he himself—as well as his peers—attributed his explosive practicality to one thing: his faith.

He was just 22 when he was offered the editorship of the Darlington *Northern Echo* in 1871—despite never having stepped into a newspaper office. He wrote to a friend: "what a glorious opportunity of attacking the devil." When he became assistant editor at the *Pall Mall Gazette*, he wrote in his journal that he must "combine the function of Hebrew prophet and Roman tribune with that of Greek teacher".[287]

He saw the poverty and immorality that accompanied the industrial revolution as an affront to God. The alarm needed raising about the vast scale of suffering as publicly as possible, and Stead rolled up his sleeves and wrote: "I felt the sacredness of the power placed in my hands to be used on behalf of the poor, the outcast and the oppressed."

The Baptist Christian Socialist, Dr John Clifford—who took his Memorial Service thirty years later, on 25 April 1912 in London's Westminster Chapel—called him "a journalist as Paul was an Apostle and Knox a Reformer, and woe to him if he did not preach and make potent the good news God gave him".

These are, to our modern ears, almost unbelievable words. But there was much more to follow in Clifford's eulogy: "To me, he was as a prophet who had come straight out of the Old Testament into our modern storm-swept life." Stead, he said, had sought to proclaim God's will through journalism to an increasingly secular and materialist world; for him, the newspaper was "a sword to cut down the foes of righteousness, a platform from which to hearten and inspire the armies of the Lord, a pulpit from which to preach his crusades, a desk at which he could expound his policy for making a new heaven and new earth. He was a man with a mission, and journalism was the organ through which he wrought at it." Above all, Stead "was a prophet with a prophet's insight" and "a prophet's fearlessness."[288]

Stead was, in sum, the almost complete embodiment of the claim that this book has been seeking to make: that journalism—and the most significant milestones in journalism's development—erupted out of a vigorous religious vision. This was a discomfiting force for what its practitioners regarded as truth, and that resulted (whether you agreed with it or not) in nation-building.

However, in contemporary times, there were many who disagreed. Indeed, Stead was loathed by George Bernard Shaw, who called him "a complete ignoramus", a Philistine and "unteachable", while admitting somewhat lamely that he had never met him.[289] Shaw, the Marxist aesthete who was busying himself with the justification of Siberian labour camps,[290] called the "Maiden Tribute" episode a "put-up job", typically ignoring its truth, force and success.

Matthew Arnold dubbed Stead's tabloid treatments contemptuously as "The New Journalism"—an epithet that stuck. Indeed, Stead's "uncouth enthusiasms"—and not just his subject matter—caused enormous embarrassment to an establishment that saw him as a northern interloper, an outsider and a "muckraker".

But the term muckraker is, in itself, religious—coined by John Bunyan in his *Pilgrim's Progress* for the man who was so concerned with the ordure of the world about him that he forgot to look up at the salvation on offer.

These *ad hominem* attacks were far from true of Stead, the Christian extremist. When he was in Holloway prison, for his work exposing child sex slaves, he had what he called his "third conversion", when he clearly heard a voice saying to him "Be no longer a Christian, be a Christ."[291] He noted how Christ must be "very grieved" over what Christianity had become.

While respectable Christians worshipped and praised Him in their churches, very few would follow Him into the "slums"—where overworked needlewomen slaved and starved, where dockyard labourers clamoured for work, and neglected street children grew up "like little wolves". He imagined Christ in London, walking through the loveless and joyless slums into comfortable churches, where He would find Christians "sitting there in their cushioned pews, praying their prayers and saying their creeds, and worshipping Christ". Stead was convinced that the divine call to "Be a Christ" meant sacrificing personal ambitions and respectability in order to enter the slums *as journalists*, to help the poor and suffering.[292]

He resolved to change journalism itself: to "organize a secular Church", with the journalist as preacher, readers as the congregation, and a select body of readers as lay leaders.[293] The journalist would, he believed, strive for the kingdom of God on earth by promoting the ideal of "The Citizen Christ", who would approach broken society "as a healer", and elevate the body politic with an ideal of self-sacrifice in politics, instead of selfish scrambling for place and power.[294]

Extreme this might have been, but it reflected a broader truth: newspapers were replacing churches as moral voices in late-Victorian Britain. This was neither humbug nor insanity, for Stead was widely credited with changing the country for the better. "The most creative force in English journalism between the demise of Delane and the coming of Northcliffe", writes Piers Brendon.[295] His daughter Estelle adds: "He practically moulded the England of his day to a larger degree than any man in it."

And he did it from the bottom up.

Stead overtly and publicly emulated the Puritans—particularly his hero Oliver Cromwell—and carried this mantle, realizing more powerfully than any before him the *Zeitgeist* of an era of public communication. He harked back two hundred years to the battle for souls fought out in the burgeoning Press of the Civil War and, before that, to the Protestant Reformers—for whom, as former *New Statesman* editor Paul Johnson put it, "printer's ink [was] the incense".

It is oddly fitting that as he lived, so he died—in headlines. He went down with the *Titanic* in the early hours of 15 April 1912, on his way to lecture on world peace at the Carnegie Hall in the US. His body was never found.

Conclusion

The revolution that Luther began went on reverberating across the world—in America and India—and for centuries to come. This innovation always occurred by the same means—the translation of scriptures; and the dissemination of sermons, as news that flew off the new presses—upsetting and reforming the old orders and setting alight new populations with the opportunities and access that print created. All this was underpinned by a political theology that was certainly vulnerable to opposition—and that, in China, failed altogether. When this spiritual underpinning fails, journalism—which was historically the agent of that theology—quickly reverts to being propaganda or entertainment: a tool in the hands of its publishers, as we still see today. When it succeeded, and despite personal flaws (as in Stead's case), it changed things for the better, and those changes stuck.

Why, then, are the achievements of proto-journalism around the world not more celebrated? Could it be that Stead's reformist zeal is something of an embarrassment? In the next chapter we look at secularization—the loss of religious faith—to understand its effect on authentic journalism.

But first, a story . . .

STORY—Healing the broken: the Marine Surgeon's tale

"Well, I felt a bit of a nana," chuckled the bearded 47-year-old doctor from Barnoldswick, recalling the first time he attempted a formal bow with the traditional six-foot, white, silk scarf of the Bhutanese.

A Yorkshire soldier, John was not likely to take easily to the ancient ways of deference insisted on by this hierarchical mountain kingdom bordering Tibet—but he persevered.

"There's a strict code called *Driglam namcha*—they're really emphasizing it. It used to take me ages to work out how to put the formal dress on."

The "dress" was the dashing floor-length *kho* worn by all men, and insisted on by the king, hitched up to the knee and tied behind. John cheated by fixing his with Velcro.

He wore it to speak to officials in the *dzong*—the local council—and, despite a native suspicion of authority, was impressed by the Bhutanese habits of respect. "I'd always question folk's decisions myself," he said, "but now in the West no one recognizes any authority at all, it seems to me."

Independent, with strong roots and a large extended family—he was one of seven children—John Burslem identified with the people he'd come to work alongside. Impressed by their humility—outwardly respectful but not awe-struck—and with strong social bonds, he approved of Buddhist King, Jigme Wangchuk's efforts to harness the good in Westernization, while fencing himself in against what threatened his people's ways.

Tourism, impossible before 1974, is still restricted: religious temples and shrines are mostly out of bounds ("decommercialized"), and tourists were then charged up to £110 ($200) a day for sight-seeing. Bhutan still has no official diplomatic relations with the superpowers—unless you count Belgium ...

The king, "precious ruler of the dragon people", and overlord of a land traditionally described by Tibetans as the "lotus garden of the gods", is anxious to maintain his heritage.

But development—in which John's missionary society, Interserve, was participating—will happen. "We want a balance between gross national product and gross national happiness", the king told a *Newsweek* reporter. Although the wheel was only used for the first time in 1960, when the first road was built, there are now hydro-electric power schemes and AI data-integration projects, although direct dialling arrived only in April 1990. For rich trekkers, and escapists, it was a compulsive magnet.

For John, too—a former Marine Commando, who had two first ascents in the Karakorams to his credit—it would seem an ideal posting. But it was human tragedy, not mountains, that called him. Measuring every word, much as he must have measured every toehold up Abvar Sar in the western Himalayas, he described to me the sorrow that hit him during a trek in Nepal in 1977. He had been contemplating becoming a "semi-professional mountaineer": doing locums and spending his salary on adventure. Now here he was, holed up in a tiny clinic with a sick friend whose recovery became protracted. For the rest of the trek, John stayed with him acting as the clinic doctor. A pregnant young woman was brought in with what had started as a trivial wound from a cow horn. She had been carried for three days to a clinic where the doctor was away, one day to a further clinic where they gave her a single injection, then she aborted—and then a further two days to John's clinic.

"During this horrendous journey back and forward over the mountains the abdominal wound had developed gas gangrene, and she now had peritonitis. I watched her die," he recalled.

John, the epitome of everyone's idea of "northern grit"—with service tours in Northern Ireland and the Arctic—had an emotional breakdown. He collapsed with grief in that isolated mountain clinic at so tragically unnecessary a death.

He wrote later, in *God's Doctors Abroad*: "The sorrow and anger were directed against myself; this woman's death, or at least others like it, could be laid fairly on my doorstep. As I frittered away my time, money and expertise on self-indulgent trivia, young mothers were suffering from want of a few pennyworths of care."[296]

He went straight home and joined Interserve, prepared to throw his whole life into service anywhere. A nominal faith since the age of ten had matured under the shock of grief: he felt now it had to be one hundred per cent if it is to be anything at all. Three years later he flew to Bhutan, seconded to the Leprosy Mission's fifty-bed general hospital at Mongar, responsible for the health of 30,000 people. He'd survived what he imagined would be the "suffocating piety" of mission college (All Nations), discovering to his surprise that his colleagues were not "limp poseurs"—he married one of them, Hilary—and that the course was "intellectually stretching and earthily practical."

Nine years of rigorous existence with a young family in a concrete bungalow followed. For all its picturesque splendour, Bhutan is among the poorest of the UN's least developed nations.

Ironically, the tragedy that triggered his conversion was mirrored later when his wife Hilary died having their second child. To move her after things began to go wrong was not feasible: a two-day rough drive to Thimphu, the capital, followed by a flight to Calcutta, the nearest adequate hospital. Why had they opted to have the child born in so remote a place? She'd had a series of major problems, following a dose of typhoid, and they both knew the risks. John is blunt: "There's no way she was going racing off. What sort of witness was that? Childbirth's a major cause of death among Bhutanese women. You can't have Christian folk rushing back home for every bit and piece."

The awfulness of this story forced me to reconsider the words of the fellowship's commitment, and the family's adherence to it: "Lifestyle has to be one which gives credibility to ministry." (All these years later, revising this story, I find it hard to bear.)

John Burslem denied it had been hard, or that his lot had been unjust—but he was irritated at the Western lifestyle of entitlement, and the complacency it breeds about the need elsewhere.

"If you look at the average church collection plate, it's a pittance," he says. "So many problems could be solved if every ten churchgoers tithed the salary of one church worker. Instead of buying fancy food and new carpets, they should be giving their money to the poor." He muttered something sheepish then about not meaning to pontificate, before ambling off into the garden to smoke his pipe.[297]

PART THREE
SECULARIZATION AND THE UNDOING OF THOUGHT

Chapter 10
Losing the Plot

If Christianity gave us the great religious innovators of journalism, it is logical to imagine that secularization will have an impact on journalism's inheritance. This chapter attempts to do two things, therefore, based on the foregoing discoveries. First it looks at what secularization is. Then it puts secularization in its place, as just one among many other different "narratives" or "worldviews"—options that govern the way journalists choose to construe "stuff that happens". For it is into such narratives—or "arcs"—that journalists fit the raw data of their senses, making more or less sense of the whole. Journalism faces a crisis of trust, partisanship and purpose—all of which are attributable to secularization—and all of which have contributed to the news deserts emerging everywhere.

What is secularization?
Secularization is the leeching of a sense of biblical relevance from public life. The journalistic innovators, on the other hand, up to the end of the nineteenth century were often Puritans. They were outsiders, religious dissenters who

lived by a specific narrative: a narrative of reality and of human development, discerned in the Bible.

To compound matters, secularization picks up on evolutionism, and is viewed as inevitable: an ineluctable process, against which we are powerless. It affects our appreciation both of history and of agency. It is compounded by "progressivism"—a political idea of change—to which evolutionary theory erroneously gives force.[298] As life improved for a while (through better healthcare, education and industrialization), religion—despite so often fomenting significant changes in human welfare—became identified with what was left *behind*.

Christianity remained glued in folk memory to the obscurantism it *challenged*; to poor drainage and bad teeth, someone once said. It is not thought of as the very impetus for change itself, although that was clearly the case with Luther and the Reformers—and with Daniel Defoe, William Stead and others.

The theory had it that, as we became more rational, more mobile and richer, we would inevitably become less "superstitious".

Max Weber said secularism was both brought about and characterized by rationalization, privatization of religion, and the mobility of the workforce. One of the earliest secularists, Charles Southwell named his newspaper *The Oracle of Reason* (1841), pitting reason against faith. It became not just description, but prescription—and the two became confused. Sociologists then attempted to make a "science" of the process of "becoming secular", with its own associated "theory".

Since human beings are held to have evolved from pagan religious groups, the more religious among us are viewed as the least evolved. This view has several tributaries, although France has been a great source and breeder of secularistic theorizing.

Auguste Comte (1798-1857), the French-born founder of sociology—which was to replace theology, in the early nineteenth century—viewed religion very seriously. Its replacement by science, though essential, he thought, could only be conceived religiously. He was particularly concerned about law and order; how to mobilize and control the masses. So, he founded a new religion, the atheist Church of Humanity, with Christianity being deemed to be useful, but defunct.

Sigmund Freud also played a large part in secularization and, therefore, in the undermining of the value of Christian motivation. He recast civilization itself as a system of sexual repression that damaged, in particular, the mental health of women.[299] Civilization was built on the suppression of our drives, he wrote in *Civilized Sexual Morality and Modern Nervous Illness*. "The single steps by which it has proceeded have been sanctioned by religion; any instinctual satisfaction that was renounced was offered to the deity, and the common property acquired in this way was declared to be holy." He said that "only the weaklings had acquiesced in such a gross invasion of their sexual freedom."[300] The alternatives for weak constitutions were neurosis or immorality.

This theory, he suggested, badly affected women, particularly: he attributed "the undoubted intellectual inferiority of so many women ... to the inhibition of thought that is essential for sexual suppression." Freud, the "bogus psychologist" (Roger Scruton), felt constrained to ask himself whether our civilized sexual morality was worth the sacrifices it forced on us. The inference was plain: the future was to have less religion and more sex, particularly sex before marriage. Atheism would relieve us of the religious burden of civilization, even at the cost of its fruit.

The history of an idea

The word "secularism" was first deliberately inserted into the English language by the campaigning socialist and "liberated blasphemer", George Jacob Holyoake (1817–1906), as a less antagonistic alternative to "atheism". Holyoake was the embittered son of a Birmingham blacksmith, an admirer of the socialist Robert Owen whose influence had affected his life chances as a teacher. After a lecture in Cheltenham in May 1842 he suggested that "the deity should be put on half pay"—and added that "I flee the Bible as a viper, and revolt at the touch of a Christian."

His reward was six months' imprisonment for blasphemy in Gloucester Gaol, but this only had the effect of further radicalizing him. A friend and backer, the lawyer WH Ashurst, later advised Holyoake to call himself a secularist, with the special object of "freeing himself from the imputations of atheism and infidelity".[301]

Such imputations were also affecting the propagation of socialist doctrines and the attendance at meetings.

The word needed explaining by Holyoake—and he did so in the newspaper he founded, tellingly called the *Reasoner*.

He found it necessary to describe the paper, on 25 June 1851, as a journal concerning itself with "this world"—relating to "the issues of which can be tested in this life". This was a deception, in light of the real meaning of the word "secularism", but it was a necessary one for the radicals.

The militant atheism espoused by Holyoake and

Continental Marxists found less ready adherence in England, where the working man preferred religious agnosticism.[302] It was a deliberate disguise to avoid alarming the down-to-earth British worker who, though put upon, was too influenced by Methodism to want to be part of the Marxist revolution.

All aspects of the modern economy and society today have been heavily secularized. Marxian historicism—his theory, which included that the process of religious demise is ineluctable—is a prevalent cultural undercurrent. Journalists have bought into it, too.

And, despite the demise of overt (if not covert) Marxism, the media deem it necessary still to filter religion out of almost any consideration, except where stories concern madmen, dangerous politicians or criminals. Even in these stories, the secular filter operates: the religious dimension of the ethnicity of sex-grooming gangs, for instance, was still largely being ignored twenty years after the alarm was sounded by concerned parents.[303]

Choose your worldview

A moment's recollection will assure us that secularization is not inevitable. It is just one form of narrative about the way the world stacks up. John Burslem's story, for example, is just one of many extraordinary stories I encountered in my career that can be read differently, according to the belief system you bring to it. For people who do not share John's worldview, it will probably be incomprehensible.

A tough soldier who had a breakdown may either move us or appal us, according to the way we see the world. It would appal, say, the Spartans of ancient Greece, who abhorred weakness. They destroyed those, particularly children, who showed signs of it. A British woman deciding to risk her own and her baby's life rather than to avail herself of a costly airlift to a Western hospital may provoke admiration or condemnation, depending on the way one makes sense of the world.

How we "see", how journalists shape what is there into a story, is a matter of individual perception, and that depends primarily on worldview.

Chronology is a vital part of what provides Burslem's story. His heart was broken with grief for an unknown woman who died so needlessly. This experience preceded his own otherwise incomprehensible personal sacrifice.

And his wife Hilary's fatal identification with the poorest of the earth would also be incomprehensible, even offensive, according to a Health and Safety or feminist rubric, without understanding her preceding journey of faith.

We are all involved in a competition of grand or "meta" narratives, but without spiritual conviction, we—like a trimming politician—simply oscillate between them. How does this affect journalism today?

Making sense of stuff

Being a journalist means to make sense of life—of "stuff that happens", which is also one definition of journalism itself.[304] Our minds are constantly organizing "stuff that happens" alongside other stuff that happens. Now that I was a convert from secularism to Christianity working in the mission, I was able to organize the "Burslem stuff" according to a different narrative—the narrative of Christ's sacrifice for the poor. Before that, I probably would have seen it as just crazy or awful, and therefore discounted it.

For the philosopher Paul Ricoeur, the very "narrating of stuff that happens in story form" creates order and structure. Otherwise it would be unintelligible. But this narration, which becomes history, also recounts events and deeds that disrupt the prevailing order, and so reorders it. We must inhabit some narrative or other if we are to make sense of what is in front of us. Journalism, when we read it, becomes for us (the reader), part of the immediate reordering of current trends; we relate it to some dynamic sense-making of history. That's why it's important.

But whatever we think truth is, we know in our bones that some reordering is closer to the truth than others. The Black Lives Matter movement defaced statues and, in the process, attempted to reorder—even rectify— history: the narrative we have inhabited together.[305] But without a bigger sense of common purpose, this narrative risked being merely a process of redaction, achieved by force.[306] Journalism's stories depend upon— and have to synchronize with—a larger story for reader traction. This requires choices to be made about context and chronology, from which different meanings derive, depending on the context or trajectory you bring to them. Lesslie Newbigin explains:

> Tacitus could record the fact that someone called "Christus" had been crucified but had given rise to a pestilential sect without this information changing his mind. The two disciples on the way to Emmaus knew that Jesus had been crucified but that had not changed their belief that the Messiah, when he came, would be a successful practitioner of liberation theology. The crucifixion of Jesus was just a ghastly disappointment. What changed their minds, what brought *metanoia*, was the fact that Jesus was alive. And that meant that the crucifixion

was a fact of a different kind. As Einstein used to say, what you call a fact depends on the theory you bring to it.[307]

This is of profound importance for reportage, not just in how stories are reported, but in what is selected as significant. And here's the rub. In Western thought, there has for some time been no agreement about any larger, over-arching story. Even chronology—contingency, or what follows from what—is disputed. John Burslem may attribute his sacrifice to a broken heart and to his Christian conversion, but why should anyone else? Perhaps he was just overwrought, after too much service in Northern Ireland? Perhaps he and Hilary had altitude sickness? In order to get into his version of this story, we also have to see it as he saw it, modelled on something overwhelmingly more compelling than convenience or pleasure.

We must ask of any given situation, "What really happened?" The representation of reality has changed over time, and that is because plausibility—the quality of "seeming to be true"—has changed.

Let's think about it. A big problem for storytellers who might want to debunk or discount John and Hilary's motivation is that we do all live by some story or other, whether we realize it or not. It's just that some stories make more sense of all that is, "seen" and "unseen", than others.

Human beings are born into history; we are immersed in the empirical truth that one thing happens after another—and usually, though not necessarily, *because* of another. We are therefore "historical beings".

One meaning of the multifaceted (and confusing) word "historicity" is the fundamental and radical fact that human beings make history. We do not arrive on the earth at a moment that is *ex nihilo*—a moment that is completely irrelevant to all that has gone before it; we are thrown into history, and we can make choices. We can help make up the world in which we find ourselves.

According to philosopher Martin Heidegger, and his concept of being (he uses a word *Dasein* meaning literally in German, "being there"), being is inseparable from the objective "world" in which we exist.

For René Descartes, the fact that he could think was the only indubitable fact of life—unless of course he stopped thinking. But we are not simply a disembodied mind, engaged purely in thought. There is in fact more to my being than my thinking the world into existence. According to Heidegger, and counter to Descartes, we must unavoidably play a part in the unfolding of history *because* we are thrown into it. But what part? We do have a certain amount of choice over that.

For Ricoeur, our future "field of action" involves us in a narrative with a plot—an idea that links reality with creativity. "Emplotment is the art of eliciting a pattern from a succession." [308] A novel with no plot would be meaningless, though of course such examples exist, and may even be compelling—think of James Joyce's clever and deliberately "pointless" novel, *Ulysses*.

"The plot sets up a sequence of events and characters, whether real or imaginary, in a certain directed movement under the control of a particular point of view. Emplotment is a historical or literary text's capacity to set forth a *story* that combines the *givens* of contingent historical existence with the *possibilities* of a meaningful interpretation of the whole."[309] A changed point of view of existence gave me the most meaningful possibility of making sense of the

Burslems' own motivation—and opened me up to a world of stories.

Without such an over-arching point of view, everything seems increasingly meaningless; the seeking out of "news", ever more pointless. And so it is.

Living *as if* there were no plot to our lives, as if we were random eructations of the universe and that all that happens to us is accidental—as we seem increasingly to do—makes as much sense as deciding to write a novel where nothing leads to nothing. Nothing happens. We might as well be waiting for Godot, instead of a God who acts.

However, an awful lot of people do live just like that, more or less: as if a book were just a long series of ultimately meaningless words on the page. So with journalism; why would one write it at all? If we are part of some narrative, do we—can we—still just make it up for ourselves, or are we part of something bigger than ourselves? In a sense, is there a purpose to be discovered; something real that is "telling" *us*? And if so, what? We must decide, for to get it wrong implies a nihilism that none of us actually believes or is capable of living.

Who's got a clue?

If human beings interpret and make sense of their world through story—and philosopher Alasdair MacIntyre says that all of us are "traditioned" in one way or another[310]—one way of describing what we are speaking of is "worldview". A worldview is "a commitment, an orientation of the heart".[311] It is a fundamental, comprehensive, essentially true and consistent set of assumptions about the basic constitution of reality. Often unconsciously held, it provides the foundation on which we live life, and it "lies deep in the inner recesses of the human self", or soul.[312] We cannot, in fact, live without a clue; without some framework or set of fundamental beliefs about the world and our calling and future in it.[313]

What is the average contemporary journalist's worldview? Nowadays, pretty much the same as any other non-expert's. James Sire, who wrote the book on worldview that is used in universities all over the world, offers nine basic alternatives, each of which can be expressed as a story, or set of presuppositions.[314]

One story, and perhaps the most prevalent, is "progressivism", which is the Christian view of history without the Christian bit. It begins in a past that is believed to be ever-evolving, towards our ever-increasing mastery over nature through science and technology, with no reference to transcendence or grace. Reliance on this worldview leads, for example, to existential panic about climate change because, deep down, we do not actually believe the dominant story any longer, that "we are making progress".

In fact, rather the opposite seems now to be the case. The story of progress is not working. This story should lead inevitably through some immanent dynamic to a supposed world of endlessly expanding opportunities, freedom and material prosperity. But that turns out to be just another *belief*. It is *not* actually working, and it is giving way to despair.

Here is one example at random, among many: Woodbridge—a historic, small market town in Suffolk (once identified by the *Sunday Times* as "the best place to live"), built around an iconic water mill on the Deben River, and full of "destination cafés" and artisan bakeries—now has pockets of what the local newspaper calls the "worst deprivation in Europe".[315] Three machete attacks in the space of two hours were reported by the press in April 2024.[316]

This is not supposed to happen, according to the progressivist rubric. Things are not supposed to get worse.

Or take another example: AI's robots may be cleverer than we are, able to write books for us with one click; but we would not deem them so clever if they could turn against human beings one day to destroy us. If all progress is towards the good, why are we so uneasy about apps that can mimic our writing style at the click of an button? Choices must be made about their programming, but on what ethical basis?

The trouble is that the progressivism narrative has—like all other such metanarratives—been subverted, though not destroyed, by postmodernism. "What we possess ... are the fragments of a conceptual scheme, parts which now lack those contexts from which their significance derived."[317]

There is no one, over-arching story; all stories are equally "true/untrue", or contain bits of truth from all the other worldviews. And what the heck anyway? Nothing ultimately matters, and it is predatory to seek to co-opt others into our own particular view or amalgam of views.

Except that this position does not work. Such a view leads to stasis, anomie and contradiction. A million Uyghurs languish, largely unreported, in their concentration camps in the deserts of western China, while China sets about building government-sanctioned communications and nuclear security infrastructure on the British mainland, as if these two things existed outside of any continuum of common sense, or any unity of being.[318]

John Burslem's story, on the other hand, is of a piece with the 5,000-year-old metanarrative that is the Judeo-

Christian story, known as "theism". His personal tragedy was nested within that bigger story. It was meaningful to him, and to the mission that sent him out, because he was responding not to his own instincts, but to something objective to him.

Within the vast scope of the Christian narrative, his was not just a random event to be tossed aside with a shrug; not just "his thing", or his "group thing". John Burslem believed in the resurrection of the Jew—Jesus—so, he believed in life after death. It changed totally the way he and Hilary lived—and the way she died. Newbigin puts it this way:

> The resurrection is the point at which the question "What really happened?" becomes most pressing. To believe that the crucified Jesus rose from the dead, left an empty tomb, and regrouped his scattered disciples for their world mission can only be the result of a very radical change of mind indeed. Without that change of mind, the story is too implausible to be regarded as part of real history. Indeed, the simple truth is that the resurrection cannot be accommodated in any way of understanding the world except one of which it is the starting point ... If it is true, it has to be the starting point of a wholly new way of understanding the cosmos and the human situation in the cosmos."[319]

It will seem odd to many readers that any Westerner could so live their lives today that they make the ultimate sacrifice *because of a story*.

Walter Lippmann has defined the function of news as "signalizing an event". The function of truth, however, is he says, "to bring to light the hidden facts".[320] There were hidden facts in the Burslem story that, when light was shone upon them, revealed to me a bigger truth: that death is not the end. A kind of martyrdom that honours the very least among the world's poor—people whose language they barely knew—reflects the sacrificial death of the one the Burslems' called "the Lord of the universe *who rose again*". It was a story of self-giving and integrity, in the light of a greater hope. The fact that such a sensation was not headline news everywhere tells us explicitly about our civilization's moral amnesia and about the demise of the modern self, in its capacity to bear witness in the public square.[321]

We turn now to question just how much we understand of the achievement of a public square in the political realm. Journalism through honest disclosure, as we saw in the case of the Burslems' story, is deeply implicated in its health. And how journalists "know" things is incredibly important in this equation.

The following story alerted me to different kinds of truth, some more disclosed in the public square than others.

STORY—"Truth is what we say it is"

It was 1982. I was the newly appointed Race Relations Correspondent for the Westminster Press Group—their first such assignation.

It was the very early days of political, social and legal recognition of black and minority ethnic groups.

The Toxteth and Brixton riots had just erupted. The country was in a state of shock. There had never been mainland riots on such a scale, and the burning of whole districts of what were known as the "inner cities" reminded the older generation of two World Wars that had been fought to end war. Now here were conflagrations and devastation nationwide, searing our illusions of peace and post-colonial integration.

My appointment was an attempt to milk a potentially fruitful new arena for media coverage.

I was excited by my new responsibility. I had read Indian Civilization at university. My favourite book as a child had been about an African boy who grew lettuces for a living, as did my own father at our rented smallholding in Suffolk. I was interested in cultures and welcomed having my own "beat" to nurse.

There was a lot going on, thanks in no small part to The Thamesdown and District Council for Racial Equality (TCRE). This was a council-funded quango of local worthies, including members of the local authority, a full-time professional race worker from London, and the vicar of a local church—all with a mission, albeit with different perspectives. It was serviced by a small secretariat.

I began going to West Indian social hangouts. I liked watching the domino contests that were a particular form of relaxation. I learned about the different island homes of origin of the railway workers who lived on the outer estates of Swindon—and I learned about the anxieties of the community elders for their young.

Given then recent events, white politics now surrounded the settling down of such communities of colour in Britain. Indeed, the terms "white" and "black" were new and alien to me. There were Africans living in our village, but we had never thought of ourselves in those terms.

Swindon's West Indians had no meeting place to call their own; nothing in Swindon reflected their story and heritage. As an economic migrant from a rural background, I felt empathy with their sense of strangeness. I set about campaigning against the Council's resistance to a community centre where people of Caribbean origin could meet. I used the newspaper's monopoly on council reportage successfully to shame its members into allocating the finance.

It was my first experience of campaigning journalism. It pleased The Thamesdown and District Council for Racial Equality (TCRE), for whom I was clearly a useful ally in their own longer-term and decidedly more Machiavellian objectives, of which I was largely ignorant.

I was useful, so it transpired, as long as I reported things the way they wanted. My naïve enthusiasms obviously impressed them, to my own detriment.

The first race march
Suddenly, a young black boy is stabbed to death by a white skinhead. The town erupts. It is the signal the TCRE has been waiting for. They immediately announce plans for a march through town—the first "race march" in Wiltshire's history.

The story comes via the police to the Chief Reporter, and the plans make headlines in the *Swindon Advertiser*. This is my moment. I go into action, interviewing community elders I have befriended, in pursuit of finding a new angle.

It comes in the form of a protest, but not by the black community against the indigenous population that had evidently killed one of their own. Instead, these elders were against the march, anxious that the TCRE had put them in an unwanted spotlight and exposed them to perhaps greater trouble.

Precariously settled in a very white, traditional part of the country, they were afraid of the publicity such a march might entail. They wanted to mourn privately and get on with their now blighted lives in a country that had already proven unwelcoming enough.

I reported these views for what they were—the wisdom and legitimate opinion of those in the West Indian "community" with most to lose: the parents. In turn, the TCRE blamed the messenger, twisting the story as the outcome of my white privilege. The Council identified here a perfect means to drive further a wedge between black people and the majority, and they launched a full-frontal attack on the newspaper—and me.

Unbeknown to me, a public meeting had been called (in my absence) in response to my story. I was—according to a West Indian friend who was there—slandered and condemned as a racist.

The editor of the *Advertiser* received an official complaint about my coverage a few days later, and I was reported to the Press Complaints Commission on a charge of racism. I was bemused, stunned and shocked to my core. I had stumbled into the heart of a storm of political subversion for which I had no training. I had been simply doing my job; expressing the dissent of a group of community elders to a plan with which they disagreed. They were being silenced by white, left-wing political activists bent on controlling the message.

I spent much of the next two decades unscrambling how race is used like this as a political weapon, often undermining the very people the agitators purport to support.

This is a ruse that Dr Paul Stott at the School of Oriental and African Studies, London University, helped me to unpack. Stott—a self-confessed former anarchist turned academic, who married an African woman—was "let go" from SOAS, where he was their terrorism specialist, and later joined the right-wing think tank the Henry Jackson Society. What I had reported was truth, he assured me.

Of what, then, was I being accused? Why is the truth racist? Are there different truths? Did not everyone want truth? I had learned the hard way the answer to all these questions—and it nearly cost me my future.

Politics impinges on news reporting to a degree for which my training had not prepared me. Language and the reporter's perspective are contested territories. Words are weapons, not just tools. They can build up or break down. They can fight covert or even fictitious wars, and they can create peace.[322] They can also destroy careers—and blind us to change.

Vanguard of the revolution

Nine months later, it was all over. My shorthand notebooks had been pored over by the Press Complaints Commission (later: the Independent Press Standards Organization, or IPSO), transcribed, and put through the wringer.

I had waited in an agony of suspense. My career as a fearless truth-teller could be over before it had even properly started. Fear and uncertainty—a kind of self-censoring—seeped deep into my psyche, to emerge many years later in a book and a doctoral thesis about the meaning and possibility of multiculturalism.

Meanwhile my editor, with a typical grin, seemed to find the whole episode amusing. A former sub on *The Times*, Patrick Wheare had plenty of experience of stressful moments—and this was one of them. He never wavered in backing me during the long and pointless ordeal. We celebrated with a party at my flat when it was over. The next day, the paper published a notice—as required by the PCC—exonerating me completely.

But my career had taken a new turn. Some weeks later, I confronted the Director of the TCRE, Clive Norris, the person who had filed the complaint. He merely smirked and told me: "Don't you know Jenny that black people are the vanguard of the revolution?" It had all simply been a ruse, one small step on the road to the TCRE's vision of a Marxian utopia.

It was Karl Kautsky who conceptualized the idea of the revolutionary vanguard; a concept taken up by Vladimir Lenin, who popularized the notion of small cadres of disaffected workers that would foment the critical mass of resentment against the bourgeoisie, which could then be used to generate the demise of capital.

And it was the Black Panthers who took up the idea in 1960s America.

My life had been taken up and used in this silent war as if it were merely coinage in a game of political barter I did not even know existed.

I had been the victim of theoretical posturing: an

ideological stratagem that took human beings' captive to an agenda that was not disclosed, and for which I had not been prepared.

This was not democracy in action, but undisguised intimidation; such bullying continues today in the guise of "wokery" and any cause useful to its narrow purpose.

Chapter 11
Neutrality or Truth? Knowing What to Report

At the moment of death we will not be judged by the amount of work we have done but by the weight of love we have put into our work. This love should flow from self-sacrifice, and it must be felt to the point of hurting.
Mother Teresa[323]

"Love itself is knowledge; the more one loves the more one knows."
St Gregory the Great[324]

Outsiders as watchdogs
Coming to an understanding of the motivations of the eighteenth-century pioneers of Reformist journalism is to understand the big story within which our smaller stories stay true. It is to see more clearly what has been lost in the way journalists see things now. So, here, we turn to look at some alternative ways of knowing and ask which way delivers the goods best. I start with a story, by way of

illustration, and then go on to describe what has made our current secular perspective for knowing so desolate.

My narrative example concerns an investigation of child abuse in the Catholic Church in Boston, Massachusetts, USA, which centers on the *Boston Globe's* failure to follow up on its initial story until a new editor took the helm: Marty Baron, a Jewish journalist from Florida. Priests had been "using the collar to rape kids", and the cover-up went right up to the level of the Vatican. Baron decided from his very first week in post to focus on the story. His attitude contrasted with the unintentional collusion of the *Spotlight* reporters who had lived in Boston all their lives. Why was this the case? The incumbent journalists had buried the story in the *Metro* section of the paper five years earlier. But, according to one interested stakeholder, "He [Baron] comes in and suddenly everybody's interested in the Church. You want to know why? It takes an outsider. Like me. I'm Armenian. How many Armenians do you know in Boston?" These are the words of the abuse survivors' attorney, Mitchell Garabedian, the only lawyer not working for gain or trying to shut down the victims' stories.

Epistemological therapy

What was true of Marty Baron also characterized the early journalism pioneers. They, too, were outsiders—and they cared. Baron shared this desire to know, which is what philosopher Esther Meek calls "covenant epistemology". She puts it like this: "Caring is the vector that carries us into the world. To care is to move toward the unknown in hope. Caring ... is what thrusts us or pulls us into the world."[325]

But she asks an even deeper question than the one about motive. It is the ultimate "unavoidable truth" question:

How is it that what we think we know is authentically true?

On to that we can pile other questions: Why do people see things so differently? Does truth exist? Is there more than "knowing about" something? Why does "getting to know" someone or something change the way we see them or it?

Meek sees our current epistemology in psychological terms, as "damaged". It needs therapeutic correction, because it is limited and self-deluding.[326]

Like Baron, Meek is on a mission to return us to a better, more accountable way of seeing. She believes that seeing, as a human activity, can be redeemed.

She wants to recast knowing so that it is thought of as a sort of visual touch, "one that evokes mutuality and reciprocity".

Instead, what we have all too often—especially with the big tech platforms—is consumption, which is a kind of rape. This kind of knowledge is "unchastity" or instant gratification, says the monk, Ronald Rolheiser. It is "free of all taboos and hesitations, which stem from a sense of sacredness or from a fear of violating reality's natural contours." It lacks reverence and it distorts truth, leading to a certain "darkening of the mind."[327]

This kind of knowing led to the callous phone-hacking scandal. *How* you see affects not just *what* you see, but what you *do* as a result.

There is also, says Meek, a kind of seeing that sets up distance between us and the object. There is a kind of seeing that moves beyond objectifying, allowing us to see from the inside out. She nudges us to think of the word *insight*. This term is linked to a kind of seeing that we rightly call vision. In this definition "we sense possibilities and significances hitherto overlooked."[328]

These are all forms of knowing. Some have certain usages—science, for example, is one way of knowing. There are other ways that involve more of ourselves than others. Colin Gunton calls science "disconnected seeing", which is nowadays our default way of knowing.

This alienation is the legacy of the Enlightenment—and it had obscured the *Boston Globe* journalists' empathy and reciprocity. There is an exchange required between knower and known.[329] Instead, we tend now to consume knowledge for power or financial gain. We rarely view it in terms of our full humanity through a spiritual lens. This deeply undermines journalism.

There are countless examples of what ensues as a result: journalists who hack a dead girl's voicemail, or who "doorstep" the missionary parents of a suicide victim son; other writers who believe they can remain immune from their own inhumanity because "the story" justifies it; and still others who refuse to cover some of the biggest stories of our era because they are told explicitly, "don't mention the Christians". They have—literally—ceased to be able to care enough to know rightly. This is why journalism is dying—and this type of reporting deserves to die.

The tell-tale sign of epistemological malaise—and even abuse—is reader switch-off. Boredom, indifference, cynicism, says Esther Meek, are symptomatic. Healthy knowing, on the other hand, invites in the real—and authentic reality responds to our overtures with the gift of surprising self-disclosure. Augustine's self-knowledge changed the way reality itself was represented.

Meek has the antidote for indifference—and so did Marty Baron, who got the story other journalists missed. If knowing is, at its core, caring, then caring leads to knowing fully. This, I venture, is the heart of "public-interest journalism": "To know is to love; to love will be to know."[330] Put briefly, Meek counsels us to consider what it is we long for—and use that as the basis of epistemic recovery, "blowing on the coals of our longing" and translating that into all-knowing.

The "prophets" of early journalism had such vision. These writers often worked for both political sides—or neither—but always in the interests of what they cared about and believed with Puritan zeal to be just. Pilloried or imprisoned, they kept going. Only in China, with the complete loss of the faith that spawned it, was the free press defeated.

The pioneers of journalism were largely outsiders. By the end of the eighteenth century, this fact was consolidated enough for Edmund Burke to call them the Fourth Estate. Outsiders are uncomfortable people; often happiest on the margins; often in trouble. For journalistic outsiders, their job is their compensation. Like court jesters, they are licensed with the right of free utterance, calling to account the comfortable and socially acceptable. Their access to power is for a good reason: it is not for self-aggrandizement or profit.

The man called Jesus was the ultimate outsider, the quintessential prophet and the ultimate anti-establishment voice—and he was put to death. "His isn't a private truth claim brokered in the back corridors to halls of power to maximize personal gain, but an open, public truth claim that he backed up with his own life, death and resurrection. He is there to be tested, scrutinized and investigated."[331] As Jonathan Heawood notes, "When truth and falsehood grapple, there is no guarantee that truth will win. Falsehood, by its nature, plays dirty, while the truth is tragically honourable."[332] And that will, paradoxically, always be its strength.

What went wrong?

The question confronting us nowadays is why it is that the sense of an embodied truth that is accessible to caring, tenacious reportage has suffered such attrition? What currents of thought have made it difficult for journalists? For the "deconstruction" of the way we have historically thought about the world affects us like a miasma, a gas we cannot see but from which our work is suffering. It is as if—like the chief of the *Spotlight* investigations team—we have become too "at home" in the world of postmodern philosophy to distinguish what matters most.

Deconstruction, as a form of critical analysis, whispers insidiously to us that there is no truth to be known— and we accept the premise. If there can be no consensus on what constitutes a story, what is the point of us? We stumble about in the dark. The story fragments, and so do we. We become subject to any idea or influence out there, without knowing it; opinions that are always inconsistent, undermining, deceptive and inauthentic. One BBC news item may bewail climate change and the devastation of the environment; the very next announce the "disastrous" fall in UK car sales, which is presumably good—not bad— news for the environment?

Arundhati Roy, Booker Prize winning novelist from Kerala in South India, observes that traditional stories of South India can start anywhere and end anywhere, because—in a cyclical worldview—there is no end or beginning. When there is no over-arching narrative about life's purpose, it does not matter where or when you begin to tell it.

The West's narrative tradition was different. Stories had a resolution: they went somewhere. They began in one place and ended in another—like Abraham starting up Mount Moriah with Isaac and being a changed man by the time he walked back down.

Smaller stories made sense in the context of larger ones.

Postmodernism, however, has generated what Jean-François Lyotard described as "incredulity towards all metanarratives". They cost too much. Lyotard collapses ethics in the light of the collapse of universals—you cannot have an ethic that is only particular to one over-arching story. Yet, he nonetheless does not entirely dispense with moral values: for instance, the difference between justice and injustice.

The real injustice for our culture today, he believes, is to co-opt others into our "language regimen". His new definition of injustice is to use the language rules from one "phrase regimen" and apply them to another. For instance, a new development of apartments can boast in its marketing, without a blush of being "exclusive and prestigious", even while the public culture of the UK has outlawed behaviour or attributes that may exclude certain types of consumers. The phrase regimen of these apartment marketeers exists on its own narrow terms, without reference to any bigger context.

Ethical behaviour for Lyotard now consists in remaining alert to the threat of this "injustice". It demands that we pay attention to things in their particularity, rather than enclosing them within what he calls "abstract conceptuality".

But this argument is hopeless. It leaves us in a worse mess. We have a chaotic plethora of micronarratives of lived experience that are all regarded as equally valid—despite being fragments, only—and that make no demands on us to be transformed according to an ideal.[333] It perfectly explains small-scale moral disasters—like the nightmare experience of engaging with X (Twitter)—and the wider lens of the collapse of journalism. Where the moral consensus breaks down, "the story" is unclear. Are we making progress? Is our world about to end? Does news matter as much as making money? Does it really matter if advertising can no longer be distinguished from news?[334]

For Nick Cohen, a columnist at *The Spectator*, what counts is "the f***ing story", even when there is no longer any story to which anyone will concur, and no funding for it. To him, "the story" is still oddly self-evident. He does not feel the need to define story; merely stress it emphatically enough.

The pro-Stalin Berlin correspondent in the film *Mr Jones* does not, on the other hand, at first believe in the idea that "truth is one". She believes truth, after Einstein (who gave us relativity), depends on your perspective. This is her view until Gareth Jones returns to her from Ukraine, ashen-faced and emaciated, having witnessed for himself the Holodomor—famine—and the hunger that drives the peasants to eat their children.

She then realizes, suddenly, that there cannot possibly be different perspectives regarding such a horror. "You are right. Truth is one," she finally admits.

Journalistic truth is ultimately moral truth—and moral truth is different from Einsteinian space/time truth.

Loss of collective meaning

Let's now continue with our contextual analysis, the better to "get" our journalistic crisis. Postmodernism, as

I have just tried to show, implies that the stories we tell ourselves and others have no determinate meaning and, as a result, are in the end not worth telling. Not only are they subject to normal misreading, for reasons of intelligence or background, but there is little or no sense that can be made of them that is common to audiences. And, if that is the case, why read?

Stories now mean whatever individual writers (and readers) assert them to mean. These meanings are not capable of correspondence. When different people believe substantially different stories about the world, the telling of the little stories nested within those "worldviews" begins to fall apart.[335] "A near future of cultural anarchy seems inevitable," says James Sire.[336]

Journalism works well when there is something considered worth knowing by a broad enough spectrum of people. On the other hand, postmodernism demands that we are all equally adrift in our individualism. The "ghost of an idea" may still haunt such newsrooms as remain, but we use lack of budget as an excuse not to cover real stories properly, or at all, because we are confused by the ideas that swim around our heads. The deeper questions that matter to us all do not get asked. And anyway, Google has convinced us that real news doesn't pay.[337]

It is interesting, then, how business news, which hinges on something we can all agree on—the importance of money—flourishes. The financial press in America is thriving; new business news outlets open up all the time. On the other hand, 1,800 communities across America have been left with no news outlet at all, becoming "veritable news deserts".[338]

Even more seriously, we reinterpret stories so they no longer justify coverage.[339] A real story of worldwide interest would be the relentless southward slaughter by Islamist Fulani herdsmen of the Christian settler populations in Northern Nigeria, which plenty of journalists know about following conferences held at the UK Foreign and Commonwealth Office.

However, if climate change is believed to be to blame for this situation, the authentic religious drivers of the mayhem can be conveniently lost in the global environmental agenda.

We may not even realize just how much like quicksilver this fear-based reinterpretation operates. A story like this requires moral judgement, because of the plethora of motives that can be ascribed to what's happening; these are judgements that secular journalists, following government communicators, are increasingly disinclined—or unable—to make, for the reasons I have outlined.

Climate change, land hunger, unemployment, tribalism, herder versus settler friction—all these factors are invoked by Western activists. But the native people themselves, who after all are *in situ* and bear the brunt, believe it is driven relentlessly by religious motives—which is a trigger for secular journalists to zone out.[340]

I have a Nigerian colleague who used to be CNN's West African stringer: it was his job to find leads to stories that foreign correspondents with the proper resources could then follow up. He broke the story of the Chibok girls who were abducted en masse from their school by extremists of the Islamist Boko Haram militia—and who, at the time of publication, are still missing.

He also provided first-hand evidence of the slave route to Libya of modern Nigerian girls from Edo province, desperately seeking a new life in Europe and ending up being traded to Arab merchants.

My friend was good at his job. After every atrocity in Plateau State by Fulani herders, he would dash along the unmade, storm-devastated dirt roads with his camera, and film the dead and the mutilated for posterity. I have travelled those roads myself and visited the mass graves. I have met the women and children with scars "above the neck"—a Quranic expression for punishments reserved for the infidels. I have photographed their hands with fingers missing from machete blows; as well as children with only half an arm.

And I have covered the mission of this stringer to get food and schooling into the Muslim ghetto near his home, after he met a starving child alone on the streets of Jos and followed him home.

A gentle pastor, a prince of his tribe, an Oxford-educated Canon in the Anglican Communion, he was eventually moved—probably for his own sanity—to Abuja to run the Province's Communications operation. He told me that CNN did not cover Northern Nigeria any longer. He told me that his bosses had said to him: "It's because it is religious. It's too controversial."

A wager on the transcendent
This is a counsel of despair. The possibility of hope itself has been compromised—and it is not surprising. While it was the possibility of meaning that gave the old Europe its creative energy,[341] since the Holocaust that has largely gone.

Historically, this was a civilization built on a belief in the Word of God made flesh. How can that truth be reliable if God Himself was silent when those considered his own were sent wholesale to the gas chambers in a so-called Christian country? The enormity of that is surely insurmountable.

George Steiner elucidated the horror of the silence at the heart of our contemporary world. If the Word proved so empty, so powerless against the slaughter of God's people, the possibility of meaning is mocked. Of what use are words?

The horror of the Holocaust seems to deny not only hope, but grace. How can we create stories, *respondingly*, in any relation—howsoever construed—to a spiritual prime mover who was apparently so powerless? How can the old "wager on the transcendent"—Steiner's suggestive phrase for faith—be anything other than absurd? As a result, all language fails. The world falls dumb. The whole project of life is humbled, humiliated and rendered null. All linguistic content, predicated on meaning based in love, becomes void. Everything except business journalism—business being about material gratification—becomes pointless. Deconstruction reflects civilization's despair at evil taken to its logical end. Its monstrousness has defeated us— and all we are left with is the mapping and exploitation of matter. Or is this the case?

In a necessarily almost inaudible whisper, says Steiner the Jewish journalist and writer, the fact of Good Friday offers strange hope. God allowed even Himself to be "cancelled".

What Steiner cannot acknowledge is that Christians believe God allowed this to get us to understand where human projects lead. We wanted to rule ourselves, without Him. Very well then.

Good Friday, without Easter Sunday, leaves our civilization with the fact of God's own apparent ending of Himself on the Cross. Yet for Christians—out of the crucifixion's meaninglessness, cruelty, futility and disgrace—there emerges an even deeper Truth. The awfulness of what unredeemed humanity really looks like was unmasked: something new, which points both back to the absolute evil of evil and forward to the even more powerful power of love.

Creation and recreation have no end because it is how God made it. God cannot and will not ever end himself. He puts Himself as His Son through a horrifying death in order to prove that Creation is in fact indestructible because it flows out of his very being, which is love.

A "conjuring trick with bones" or the defining fact of history: the resurrection of Jesus Christ, witnessed in real time by hundreds of people, is a fact that redeems depths of depravity we cannot plumb.

This hope is the most basic underscoring of experience attested to by those who are dying. My own father said, some days before his death, and after surviving two years imprisoned during the Covid lockdown from 2020, when all he could do was wave wanly at his family through a window: "There is always something." What he meant by that was that the cherry blossom was blooming again on the spindly tree outside his window. Or the cook's 3-year-old had unexpectedly produced a crayon drawing that said: "I love you, Peter."

Neutrality or truth?
We are all living at a time of ethical and technological revolution in which there is only the vaguest consensual viewpoint on what matters to tap into. Everyone has "their own truth". Public opinion has become public lack of opinion. The myth that was modernity—that promised once you get rid of the "wager on transcendence", and the religious metanarrative it spawned, then the universal

truth would become obvious—is completely played out.

For a secular journalist, different beliefs have replaced it. Reporters either adhere to "neutral" ground on which to stand that says truth cannot be found—only a middle position between two equally valid positions, loosely called "right and wrong". Or else to a misplaced loyalty to a biased position, deemed to be "correct" by staff who run the news desks.

But, even from the secular perspective, it is obvious there can be no neutrality about the Holocaust.[342] So, there can be no neutrality in the sense modern journalists wish.[343] George Monbiot has said that you cannot be neutral about whether it is raining or not. You simply look out the window to find out the truth. Aidan White wrongly believes that "strict neutrality" is what journalism is all about. Perhaps he means "not taking sides" in order to let the reader make up their own mind when presented with differing perspectives. But this approach does not work because a perspective is not a fact. He invites journalists and civil society to "explore the ethical consequences of how we apply strict neutrality"[344]—but this is surely not a complete answer.

Victor Navasky, former editor of *The Nation*—the oldest, continuously published magazine in the United States—writes: "No sophisticated student of the press believes that objective journalism is possible. The best one can hope for is fairness, balance, neutrality, detachment."[345] These elements do not equate, either. Martin Bell, the BBC's former War Correspondent, puts it succinctly in his autobiography: "There is a distinction to be drawn between fairness and neutrality. Fairness is the bedrock of good journalism ... But neutrality? Neutrality is a snare and a delusion. It makes no judgements. It stands aside at an equal distance between good and evil."[346]

Neutrality is also no guide as to how to report whether or not it is raining.

Unfortunately, even Bell does not define "fairness", but the point is still worth making. Aidan White concludes: "... holding a debate on these questions is almost bound to improve the quality of decision-making and ethical journalism. It is legitimate to come to different answers—so long as we address the questions." If only this were the case.

What can save journalism?
We might perhaps identify several solutions to this moral conundrum within a "generous pluralism". Marvin Olasky, using his metaphor of the biblical plumbline to identify stories, reproduces an extraordinary excerpt from a "hard-hitting" New York monthly titled *McDowell's Journal*, published in August 1834 by the eponymous clergyman.[347] His motto was "The world is our field, prevention is our aim", printed in his newspaper as a spirited justification of the biblical sensationalism he practised. He summarized its burden in one short sentence, in capitals: "IT IS OUR DUTY TO EXPOSE LICENTIOUSNESS." And a majority of US newspapers did just that—for decades. A century before Barth, they cried "Stop!" Today, more often, we simply shrug.

Olasky grasps the nettle. He identifies a regression from what he calls *Christian objectivity* in reportage through four later phases of deterioration: from "straightforward materialism"; to objectivity as a "balancing of subjectivities"; to objectivity as "disguised subjectivity"; and, finally, to "undisguised subjectivity".[348] This latter phase leaves us with either a journalism based on identity politics—the mania for all stories to be about racism, sexism, gender identity, and various other forms of "outrage"[349]—or on infotainment, where stories take no risks in a capitulation to titillation. His answer is a return to a biblical "plumbline" by which to decide what the story is and about how the elements of it should be weighed. But can one expect a return to a biblical basis for journalists to practise their craft?

The clue to truth—and how and what to report—are, I believe, implied in the epigrams that begin this chapter. Because she loved him, Mary Magdalene knew it was the Risen Christ when she saw him on Easter morning in the garden where he had been earlier entombed. She was hardly neutral about whether the man she met was the gardener or not. That was not a neutral knowing. One could argue that this loving knowledge made her the very first journalist. Certainly, she has, ever since, been called the "Apostle to the Apostles". She was the first witness to the moment in history from which all of history before and since cascades. So many of the greatest writers imply that the more you love, the more you know—and want to tell.

Lamin Sanneh, the Professor of History at Yale University—who was a convert from Islam—noted, in 1998: "What is plain now is that society cannot be content with drawing on the reserves of Christian moral capital without attention to replenishing the source."[350]

If thought leaders cannot give an account of the basis on which they pursue truth, other ethical systems will come into play. Or, just as worrying, the trivia that continues to distract us from the ferociousness of reality will continue to blind us to what is at stake, as noted by Christopher Walker, the *Times*' former Middle East correspondent, in the *British*

Journalism Review. "The move down from heavyweight to the welterweight division has arisen not only from the new emphasis on the trivial in the choice of stories, but also an aggravating habit by the home and foreign desks to demand that stories be tailored to suit the angle emerging from the morning and afternoon conferences." [351]

No one will get it all right. Sin confounds all human effort; and arises sometimes from—and gives rise to—deep psychic wounds that cause distortion in how we see. Luther was an anti-Semite. Karl Barth was an adulterer. WT Stead was a spiritualist and adulterer. But Aidan White is right, if by "raising the questions" he means allowing for a generous pluralism. This may be the best future we can hope for in journalism, which must after all—as with everything else—allow the tares to grow up with the wheat.[352] So long as the wheat is allowed to grow, too. But that is increasingly the problem. Even the Muslim former anti-terrorism tsar warns that pluralism is at risk, leading to Britain's culture of censorship endangering journalists.[353]

Truth is personal
Journalists are in a predicament.

In trying to rid their news of bias—especially what they see as religious bias—they end up avoiding reality or operating in a moral void.

The epistemologist Esther Meek, following Michael Polanyi, says that truth is "personed", so it cannot avoid being biased. We feel personally betrayed, for instance, when someone lies to us, or when truth is compromised or distorted. Objectivism is the belief that nothing can be allowed to "bias" our knowing—but, in that case, there can be no truth to know. This renders the world as composed of impersonal objects. "It treats the world as an object to be dissected and manipulated, a way of knowing that gives us power over the world," says Meek.[354]

The point is there is no commitment-free knowing—or reporting. True knowing transforms you. Unless it is allowed to do that, it leads to the most subjective of worlds: to a knowing immune from the transformative impact of others, and of the real. Ed West, son of the foreign correspondent Richard West, notes in his Substack newsletter that AI chatbots respond better if you are polite![355]

Journalism is the eternal struggle against authoritarianism, self-aggrandisement and greed. It should be a counterweight to all that threatens society, maintaining a space for human flourishing. It is to be a flag planted in enemy territory—but it remains only a flag. It fails when it arrogates to itself the same dishonest, arbitrary will to dominion that it exists to expose. And it fails when it exceeds its remit and gets involved in the story—or when it puts profit first.

Humility regarding the religious origins of the press might help sustain an honest and inclusive pluralism in the mix of mainstream news discourse in our secular times. Such knowledge alone might ensure that the watchdog of investigative journalism is not left barking up the wrong tree—or failing to bark at all.

Chapter 12
The Fourth Estate: Recovery of a Mission

"Unless we can return to the principles of public service, we will lose our claim to be the Fourth Estate. What right have we to speak in the public interest when, too often, we are motivated by personal gain?"
Rupert Murdoch—quoted with deep irony

Putting it into practice

I began this book by following a hunch that there is something spiritual about real journalism. Certainly, for my own journalism, conversion to Christianity was a game-changer.

My stories no longer arose out of a desire merely to make a deadline. I wanted instead to confront the spiritual facts in any place from which I reported.[356]

I called this "religious literacy in journalism", for it gave me a better way of seeing and getting stories.

In 2005, I founded a small internationally networked charity dedicated to helping the mainstream media do this, too.

The need for this proved irresistible after 9/11, and the bombing of the London Underground on 7 July 2005 confirmed it.

Few if any could understand these events at the time, which erupted as if from nowhere.

However, there had been many explanatory publications by Osama bin Laden (and others), stating his religious motivation.

He had issued two *fatwahs*—religious edicts, in 1996 and 1998—declaring a "holy war" on the US.

His justifications were Islamic: revenge for the ending of the Ottoman Empire; and the fragmentation of the Muslim *ummah* (world) by Turkish leader Mustafa Kemal Ataturk, who abolished the Caliphate.

Bin Laden, like all Muslims, had a long memory: a global reading of history that simply had no salience in the West any longer.

"Their most fundamental grievance, continually expressed, is the modern collapse of the Islamic world in the face of 'Christendom'", wrote US analyst Paul Marshall.[357]

Yet much of the media ignored or downplayed this explicitly religious narrative, rationale and motive.

They would instead interpret such pronouncements by means of a grid of Western concerns and preconceptions, such as third-world liberation, economics or recent events in the Middle East.[358]

What had happened over time was that the West's "life world"—the way in which language is enacted to describe a society's experience of reality—had ceased to be relevant to the new facts of globalization.

This had caused an unforeseen social and political earthquake.

One nation's secularism had become another nation's apostasy—and modern technology created the means for the two to collide spectacularly in the skies above New York.

There was almost no mutual comprehension.

A dangerous vulnerability
The West still runs its "multiculturalism" on the basic premise that all ethnic religious groups want the same things.

However, this is not the case; and the West is massively resented in its secular blindness to deeper meanings.

The "pathological results" that follow—when "human beings in community" are separated by the West from the models of meaning that have hitherto served them—proved on 9/11 to be literally "striking".

Charles Elliott, former CEO of Christian Aid, wrote in a different decade, which is nonetheless relevant to the post-9/11 world: "[w]hen the remembered, community-stored, ritually re-enacted wisdom is no longer relevant to the needs of society, society and the individuals within it are at their most vulnerable."[359]

And we are spectacular vulnerable.

Different ways of seeing and knowing
Can we recover our mission as journalists by engaging with the world with a different kind of seeing?

In order to "see" what bin Laden was saying, you needed a more adequate kind of knowledge than the knowledge that secular materialism afforded.

"We have said 'Seeing is believing' to such an extent

that we have needed to be persuaded of the point that believing is seeing", says American educationist David P Barash.[360]

Another way of saying this is to think of the two Greek words for knowing: *oidos*, knowing "about"; and *ginosko*, knowing "inwardly".

Science, or the activity of the left brain, is the former. Relational knowing, or right-brain knowing, is the knowing we have of a loved one—or the one we worship—which is the kind of "whole knowing" that religious truth implies.

Truth is personal, therefore. "As humans we have to see words made flesh to understand them," says Steven Garber.[361]

We feel betrayed when people don't tell the truth. We lose respect and interest. Truth is not a set of impersonal prescriptions, dogmas or data. Truth is embodied.

Recovering trustful knowing
There is an old European tradition to trust the messenger rather than an anonymous written report. A news report gains credibility from the reputation of the person who delivers it.[362]

In the eleventh century, there were two monasteries in rural Wales a hundred miles apart across rugged terrain. Every third year they would exchange messengers, who would live in the other house for a week to share the news from their own community.

Medieval clerics had a profound suspicion of information that came to them in written form.[363]

Veracity, or truthfulness, was incarnational: to be worth trusting (or internalizing), news had to be embodied (or "personed")—and embodied well. The very words "truth", "trust" and "troth" derive from a shared etymology.[364]

There must be an illustration of what fulness of life and fulness of truth "live like" and "look like", otherwise our stories lack contingency.

The fulness of life looks like Christ.

Christians see most fully when we see humbly *through* Christ. When we do, He comes to aid us in our frailty. He shows us what matters most. The maverick called Jesus was the ultimate outsider, the quintessential prophet and the ultimate anti-establishment voice, speaking up against anything that reduced our humanity—and he was put to death.

However, the most recent evangelical book about the impact of Artificial Intelligence on society—from medicine, to employment, to security, to the arts—had no contribution on the subject of journalism.[365]

The Church should have skin in the game. This remains the case in Nordic countries, where the State still funds mainstream journalism schools set up by the Church.[366]

Yet, among journalists in the UK, I have never met an "out" Christian in the public way that Defoe or Stead were known; even over a drink, no one was telling. It's different in the States, which has other problems. Among the British media, some might admit publicly to a Salvationist ancestor—as did the BBC's Jeremy Paxman and Andrew Norfolk of *The Times*, respectively. Otherwise, only a religious affairs correspondent seems to be allowed to assent to a faith. This is yet one more way in which faith has been "licensed" and locked away.

Philanthromedia: a new, old way of doing journalism
I undertook to run an experiment with this concept, an outfit whose story I tell as the Epilogue to this book.

Suffice to say here that the work I advocated did not

require of journalists any formal assent to a credo: I was just going to see if another kind of knowing could produce better stories.

The agency I founded—Lapido Media—had a Muslim trustee and a Sikh editor, but we were funded generously by civil society foundations with Christian roots or ethos. An early internship candidate was from Saudi Arabia. I had indigenous stringers around the world. One wrote for *Pink News*.

The truth of the validity of the universal values embodied by journalism became plain at the Global Media Freedom conference held in Docklands in July 2019, presided over by then Foreign Secretary, Jeremy Hunt, and by international human rights lawyer, Amal Clooney.

I was invited in advance to make a short speech from the floor during the "religion and the media" panel discussion.

The panellists took turns to bemoan the treatment that their respective religion was receiving from the media.

I got up and asked: "Why should you feel that the media should write sympathetically about your religion? Is this a conference on journalism or a conference on religion?"

If the panel was about journalism, then real stories of injustice, persecution, the democratic deficit and political transformation were what we should be discussing, since to see these iniquities and describe them best required religious literacy, not religious journalism.

No one can force a journalist to write about *their* religion, but we can all rightly expect them to write about oppression, poverty, corruption and hope.

The effect of what I'd said was electric. I found myself surrounded by a dozen excited journalists from every part of the world.

There were several women in hijabs, and one in particular—Lana Haroun from Sudan—who had trained the citizen journalists covering democracy protests in Tahrir Square, Khartoum against the ruling junta.[367]

This is not just abstract. It is what happened to me. My own journalistic knowing had changed from *oidos* to *ginosko*—from knowing "about" to knowing "inwardly".

This evolution in my understanding opened up better stories. Lapido Media covered some of the biggest stories of our era, which other journalists either missed or ignored: for example, the Northern Uganda war; and the emergence of political Islam in Britain. I was Melanie Phillips' initial source for her book *Londonistan*. I covered the Tablighi Jamaat megamosque development in East London, and so much more.

Stories like the Musahar ....

STORY—The people that don't exist

The Musahar are a clan whose only food is undigested grain husks, extracted from rat droppings.

This is a clan too lowly to rank even in the cruel Indian caste system. Forced to live on the margins of fields, outside any villages, they have no formal existence.

The Musahar are not even listed as a tribe—*officially*, they do not exist. They are consigned by birth to their occupation of rat-catcher.

This is because a religious myth fixes their fate.

Lord Brahma created man and gave him the horse to ride. The first Musahar had no stirrups, and so made holes in the belly of the horse to put his feet in as he rode.

This offended Lord Brahma, who cursed him and his descendants to dig holes and catch rats for ever.[368]

They believed the story themselves, and it had sealed their fate for generations.

However, the local Christians who heard about them and came to find them, despite the *tabu*, were also religious. This clan registered with them, and it broke their hearts.

They addressed the belief system of the Musahar. Then they helped them build a tiny school out of brick and bamboo outside the village, supported by a hospital that was founded two hundred years earlier by British women.[369]

They were then able to advocate for themselves with the local authorities ...

My journey towards a new journalism

I lost interest in journalism until after my conversion. I went to work in community arts in London. Then, I helped get textbooks to Bumiputera schools in Malaysia. Finally, I retrained as an English language teacher and was planning to go to China. However, a missionary encounter changed my direction, and I went to India instead.

What confronted me in India's slums was a ruthless truth so massive, I wondered how I could ever have been blind to it: that wrong religion has the power to crush whole continents and cultures.

STORY—Building out of the ruins

Mr Thanvi was an elderly kindly looking man, whose office was made of packing cases, situated under an electricity pylon in Delhi.

He introduced me to a gaunt, but smiling grey-haired man in a wheelchair who, he said, was his accountant.

This man had been pushed off a jam-packed commuter train on to which he was hanging by his fingertips, on his way to the office one morning—and left for dead.

Almost paralysed by his fall, no one came for him. Clueless as to what had befallen him, his family—now without their breadwinner—had been forced to forget about him.

With his leg broken, the bone sticking out of the flesh, he had somehow made his way to the wasteland under the pylons and to Mr Thanvi's balcony, where he was allowed to stay. Just one more beggar waiting to die.

"Suddenly I noticed that his leg was seething. The skin was moving. In fact it was full of maggots," Mr Thanvi told me. The leg had been rotting for a long time, and this poor man—a normal family man with a good job—had fallen through the cracks. It was his "karma"—the reward for something that happened in a previous life.

I was appalled at the cruelty of this story and a world without a social safety net.

I was struck even more though by the poor man's will to live, and by the kindness of a stranger.

Mr Thanvi had been a well-paid managing director of a chemical company, living in an upmarket block of flats overlooking the wasteland, who noticed one day that the ground under the electricity pylons was inhabited. People came and went down there, emerging from shanty huts made of packing cases and bits of corrugated iron. How had he never noticed them? How did they survive? What was happening to him that he noticed them now?

As had happened to me, he had had a "conversion"—literally, a change of heart. Somehow the breaking of his heart opened his eyes: there was tragedy all around him that he had never noticed.

He even told me that, as a Brahmin, he had not known there was poverty in India.

He gave up his job to work full-time for World Vision, one more "champion of the world"—as pop icon Sir Bob Geldof called them during his Africa Commission tour.[370]

I was to meet many like Mr Thanvi on my travels.

It had never occurred to me before that *nothing* "just happens". Evil destroys, and it takes many forms, but there is a goodness that combats it. I learned in my travels as a missionary journalist that all over the world people feel compelled to care, which mobilizes hope. The world is built (and rebuilt) out of the ruins of human frailty, by endless acts of redemption. This became my theme.

This discovery changed me. This alone made the point powerfully enough that knowledge is transformational. "Real journalism" *is* religious, in the sense that Meek has it.

Journalism is at its historic root "faith-based". It carries the DNA of the seeker. There is always more to know, and it is accessible to us as we go on.

More than that: there is a way of seeing, or knowing, that is available to us—and that depends entirely on a belief that reality, as Steiner says, is "responsible" or as he put it "respondable".

We love, we create, because we are loved—because we were created. We know, because we are known. Knowledge is "personed". When we see with that kind of *belief*, we see much more what is *really* there.

Chapter 13
Conclusion and a Call to Action

So, our journey is at an end. I have hoped to show that the impetus for real journalism lies deep in our common heritage—in passionately held beliefs that give rise to compassionate seeing and visionary communicating. These beliefs give us what is there in front of us; they give us the reality that counts.

Modern philosophies cannot do justice to "the whole truth". "They all stumble on something that cannot be boxed in to their 'truth'", says Kristi Mair.[371]

One example is Albert Camus' existentialism. This tragic and pervasive philosophy proffers that we are accountable to ourselves—alone—for the meaning we give to our own existence.

In our search for authenticity, we have no alternative but to journey inwards, *away* from reality.

Yet Camus cannot deny the witness of his own eyes. He said: "Beauty is unbearable, drives us to despair, offering us for a minute the glimpse of an eternity that we should like to stretch out over the whole of time."[372]

What seemed to be innate to him—his experience of beauty—pointed beyond itself to the call of eternity he so tragically had to deny.

The famous "hippy" book by Peter Matthiessen, *The Snow Leopard*, is an existentialist masterpiece. I was given it by a fellow traveller in a hostel in Leh, the capital of Ladakh.

It has the author tracking the elusive creature across the snow-laden Himalayas.

At the last, on gaining sight of his semi-mythical quarry, he gasps in wonder, longing to give thanks. But to whom? *There is no one there.*

Matthiessen's impulse to give thanks is stillborn, for he has denied the existence of respondability.[373]

For artist Eugene Delacroix, it was the same: the same sense of wonder, the same sad, abortive impulse to worship:

> Could a mere chance combination of the elements have created the virtues, reflections of an unknown grandeur! If the universe had been produced by chance, what would conscience mean, or remorse, or devotion? O! if only, with all the strength of your being, you could believe in that God who invented duty, all your doubts and hesitations would be resolved. For why not admit it? It is always questions of this life, fears for it or for your comfort, that disturb your fleeting days—days that would slip by peacefully enough, if at the end of your journey you saw your Heavenly Father waiting to receive you! I must leave this and go to bed, but it has been a happy dream.[374]

Any history of journalism that misses out the development of narrative—of ideas of the self; of the history of social protest, with its origins in Renaissance sermons and Reformation pamphleteering—is short-changed.

The past was not an accident that we can dismiss. It acts now as scaffolding for the present. We are chained to it.

The seventeenth-century paratexts schooled a generation in what news was, and how to read and make sense of it—and newspapers were subsequently able to build on that sense-making.

Charles Taylor and others have said: "Understanding modernity aright is an exercise in retrieval."[375]

Perhaps it is better in the end not to parse truth for journalists in any way except as an inchoate hunger.

Parker Palmer says that "knowledge contains its own morality, that it begins not in a neutrality but in a place of passion within the human soul."[376]

The truth is a longing we experience in the deepest, truest part of ourselves. I believe that longing still gets journalists out of bed.

It can only be mobilized by a passionate love—the passion of Savonarola, of the Reformers, of the eighteenth-century Dissenters and of Massachusetts' Puritans.

The good news, according to Polish philosopher Anna Abram, is what Aquinas taught: "Passion for truth is already in us; it is written in our human nature."[377]

A call to action

How then can journalism be saved? Perhaps we could consider the following:

- ✓ Journalists could recover their own history.
- ✓ Familiarity, at least with the Bible and other

scriptures, could qualify for the National Council Training Certificate
- ✓ Journalism schools could teach different kinds of knowing—basic epistemology
- ✓ The notion of a generous pluralism could be explored in journalism training scenarios
- ✓ The definition of "better stories" might be expanded in training schools
- ✓ The Churches could stop acquiescing in their marginalization by modelling and relentlessly advocating for proper religious literacy in culture production
- ✓ The Churches could even "own" journalism's religious antecedents in their own training apps and conferences
- ✓ The News Futures 2035 initiative might take the "dangerous" step of incorporating religious literacy in the mix—*if* it can be seen to justify better stories
- ✓ The Public Interest News Foundation could lead discussion on all the above recommendations.
- ✓ We could seek to appeal to the dissidence of the young with a recruitment call to forego big salaries and to live on the edge where change is coming.

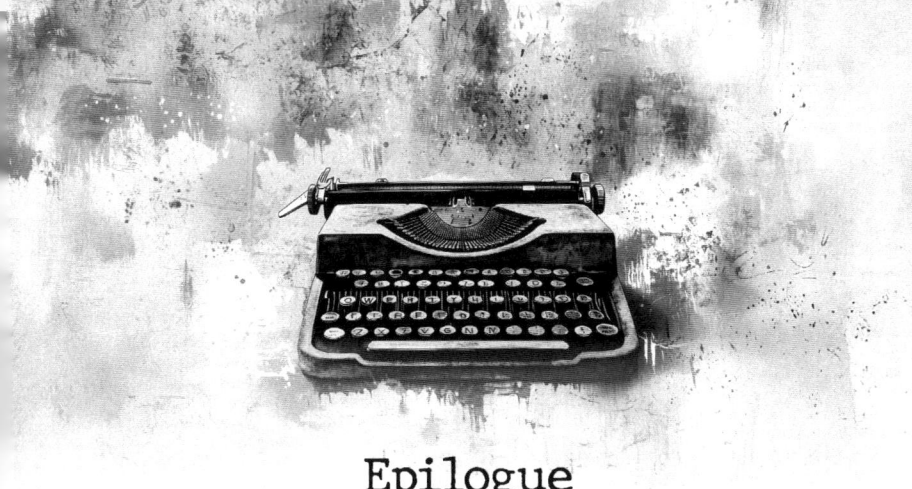

Epilogue

Lapido Media—religious literacy in world affairs
I set up Lapido Media from my dining room in 2005 with one unpaid American missionary assistant and no budget. By the time it closed down, in 2017, we had raised more than £1 million in charitable funds and individual donations, employed five staff, were read in Downing Street,[378] and were networked around the world.

Lapido means to "speak up" in Acholi, the language of Northern Uganda.

I had somehow found the nerve to make a phone call to then *Sunday Telegraph* editor—and, latterly, columnist for the *Independent*—Dominic Lawson to launch it for us.

To my surprise, I got through to him direct—and, even more surprising, he agreed to help, without a clue who I was.

Admittedly, I dropped the name of one of his recent interviewees, Bishop Michael Nazir-Ali, whom I knew well. We launched with Lawson, in conversation with Nazir-Ali, at Vaughan Smith's prestigious Frontline Club for foreign correspondents in Paddington.

This was the first time a bishop had addressed a bunch of media folk in this, their most revered watering-hole.

We called the event "Neutrality or Truth: Reporting Religion Post-7/7".

It seemed to break the dam of reserve about how to write news in the tense aftermath of the London Underground bombings. Journalists were at that moment like rabbits in the headlights, unable to digest the recent catastrophic developments in terms of religiously motivated political violence.

Multiculturalism was not supposed to be like this. Weren't we welcoming people from everywhere because they wanted to be here? The media was paralysed, unsure of which way to jump.

That terrible morning in 2005, it was four religiously motivated, Muslim suicide bombers with rucksacks full of explosives who attacked central London, killing 52 people and injuring hundreds more.

It was the worst single terrorist atrocity on British soil.[379]

But I'd given the assembled media another "good story"; and, despite being a "religion" story, it was one they could not ignore.

I had introduced to Lawson at the event a British imam's daughter who had been raped since the age of five by her own father and his whole *biraderi* (clan group), and who was still on the run from them.

I gave her the pseudonym "Hannah Shah" to protect her; and her story was ghosted by a best-selling, surprisingly tender-hearted writer of gung-ho military paperbacks, who must remain anonymous.

She had escaped thanks to a teacher who was a Methodist churchgoer. But Hannah was still being hunted by her brothers in order to avenge their "honor".

Lawson made her the subject of his column in the *Independent* on the following day—and gave Lapido Media a namecheck to boot.

Until this point, if all religions were the same, you were required to be "equal" about your coverage, which in fact meant not reporting the facts. Equality had wrongly come to mean "the same as".

"Harmonizing truth claims is the only solution society provides us with when it's faced with multiple options," says Kristi Mair.[380]

Did it mean treating the contemporary Archbishop of Canterbury, Rowan Williams, as if he were hook-clawed fundamentalist Abu Hamza? Both had beards, both preached to their throngs, both could be apocalyptic.

Ludicrously, journalists honestly seemed not to know—and, if there were a difference, wasn't it discriminatory and/or illegal to say so anyway?

The event generated three pieces in the *Times* by Ruth Gledhill that week alone; a half an hour live segment on CNN's worldwide *Correspondents* slot, with Bishop Michael Nazir-Ali and me discussing how journalism needed to change.

Lawson's column in the next day's *Independent* discussed the Christian response to Islam, based on a conversation he had held with the American evangelist he had met at the event who drove him home.

There was coverage in the *Daily Mail* and the *Sun* newspapers—and much more on the BBC and the international press.

And, at last inquiry, Hannah's story—published by Random House—has sold in excess of 40,000 copies.[381]

Taking it to the press

Just before the event I'd been given a tiny amount of funding, sourced by the Norwegian former night editor of *Aften Posten*, Dr Arne Fjeldstad, who had charitable connections in New York.

Fjeldstad had run a missionary paper on the streets of Cairo—and I'd spent two years trying to track him down. He agreed to help, and to become a Trustee (and, later, Chair).

The success of the event also triggered a grant of £40,000 from a UK trust and around £1 million pounds more over the next twelve years.

To be able to name Jesus from the platform of a club for foreign correspondents (and get away with it) vindicated my faith in journalism. To find myself a couple of years later—on page 3 of the *Daily Star*—talking about a book we had published about the Tablighi Jamaat, the group behind the so-called megamosque in East London, even more so.[382]

This short book, one of three we published, was submitted in evidence to HM Inspector of Planning when I was called as an expert witness at the Planning Inquiry into the mosque's plans in London's Docklands.

I had gone to India and visited the mosque's Headquarters in Old Delhi to ask the emir himself why he thought London needed such a massive mosque. The emir was not there. Instead, his deputy, flanked by a bearded acolyte with a broad Yorkshire accent, let me interview him—seated on the floor of the women's quarter, with my back to him.

Presumably because I was a woman—and an infidel—he had to avoid my compromising gaze.

The article I later wrote about the experience circled

the planet, in English, on the Tablighi Jamaat's own website. The piece was warm and objective: I had been treated with kindness by the emir's wife, and I stated the facts.

The plans were eventually turned down, on impeccable planning grounds—not the least of which being the lack of provision for social cohesion. It was the religious facts, sourced by good journalism, that ended this long-running saga of non-compliance and the gaming of multiculturalism.

Following this, I received an invitation to teach about religious literacy at a major National Union of Journalists event in Cardiff—and, later, to new recruits at both Reuters Foundation and the Press Association.

This was all vindication of my passionately held view that you could approach journalism from a perspective that took your own and others' spirituality seriously, *because it produced better stories.*[383]

The church's lawsuit threat

Real journalists do "get religion", and they were often far more interested and sympathetic in private to what I was doing than people generally imagine.

It was no surprise to me that I had an easier ride with journalists than with the Church, which—like any organization—tries to control the narrative when and where it involves them.

This remains justification enough for journalists to remain the Fourth Estate, the impartial outsiders of the State *and* the Church.

Twelve exhilarating years after its inception, Lapido was effectively closed down by a middle-ranking hierarch in the Church of England. I had reported his speech at a public interfaith debate about blasphemy, with Muslims and Christians present. His speech called for street preaching to be restricted to non-Muslim areas.

He did not appreciate the opening paragraphs of my online report of his statement about this — and threatened to sue if it was not withdrawn. I refused, since not to do so would betray the very thing I had set up Lapido to do: to exemplify a kind of journalism that understood religious freedom, and that without fear or favour refused to adulterate the truth under pressure. It seemed instinctively wrong that an Anglican cleric of all people should seek to suppress the Gospel – especially during a debate about blasphemy laws, when it should prove awkward.

I offered him a right of reply: a personal interview with our best journalist, but he refused.

My chairman and the new CEO who had replaced me, capitulated to his request to remove the paragraphs, without apparent demur —and without even asking me what had happened.

I had no choice but to quit. This was constructive dismissal, and I was given three months' pay to go.

My replacement stalled and then closed every one of our on-going projects and did not communicate with the staff I had appointed. Little if anything was produced during her tenure, which is why I say this incident effectively closed us down.

Two years later it was all over. No financial report was made to the Charity Commissioners during this time. The original website was taken down, and the charity's name changed. The Commission website, accessed on 17 September 2024, says to this day that Lapido Media's report is 1,510 days overdue!

Even my principal funder felt I should have taken the offending article down.

But why should my reporting have been taken down?

This same cleric was filmed at Synod —the church's parliament —not long after, moving an amendment to a motion about national evangelism, requiring that the Jews be "exempted".

In other words, this same Anglican cleric wanted to prevent the teachings of Jesus from being communicated to at least two ethnic groups.

The consequences of "cancelling" the communication of the teachings of Jesus —as he wanted to do —would be consequential. Why should those groups be hidden behind a purdah? Why not others as well? Why not everyone? And why should only the communication of the message of Jesus be prevented from reaching these groups? Why not also the messages of Islam, of Buddhism, or Hinduism, of agnosticism, of atheism?

And if these messages should be silenced, who was to stop the silencing of other free speech, whether in relation to politics or in relation to commerce? Surely, you either accept, or you do not, the principle of free speech (subject to the normal civilized restraints against calls for violence, and so on).

Clearly, this cleric did not accept free speech and free choice. As this book has tried to show, any post-Reformation Protestant cleric who can sell short the very principle on which the Reformation was fought needs to be challenged. His insistence undermined everything Lapido was set up to promote, and stand for. And yet the trustees and main donor caved instantly, without a peep. The board, with no budget for fighting defamation cases, was not strong enough to resist opposition of this kind, and without strong institutional support, journalism is useless. As Alan Rusbridger has noted, litigation weakens the press, eroding its watchdog function, enabling the rise of fake news (Alan Rusbridger, *Breaking*, 176). It was a salutary, if tragic, lesson.

Theologian Lesslie Newbigin describes the cross of Christ as "a scandal"—and many Muslims, Jews, and others will inevitably be scandalized by an overt evangelistic appeal. The Christian—and particularly Protestant—track record on anti-Semitism and Jewish persecution are baleful. But freedom of speech is, fundamentally, the freedom to communicate and to unsettle. This is ironic given, as we have seen, the Jewish basis of the West's civilization and, specifically, the roots of journalism.

But I had made the case that religious literacy helps journalism. Lapido Media's stories were used across the board. We proved just how much our culture still values journalistic freedom—and just how much the kind of stories we dug up were in the public interest.

We were early responders to the new online opportunities for journalism that drastically reduced overheads and needed no advertising revenue at all. We trialled successfully a new funding model, as a "philanthromedia charity". What we lacked was a strong-enough board, conversant with the unique pressures, opportunities and threats inherent in mainstream, as opposed to religious media, prepared and financed to tough it out.

We worked with some of the finest mainstream journalists, and I will always remain grateful for their curiosity and courage: Dominic Lawson, Melanie Phillips, Vaughan Smith, Andrew Norfolk, Dominic Lemanski, Lindsey Hilsum, Paul Vallely, Douglas Murray, Aaqil Ahmed, Caroline Wyatt, Gabriel Gatehouse, Mike Wooldridge, Jason Cowley, Tom Holland, Fraser Nelson,

Paul Bakibinga and Robin Aitken, to name just a few; and, in the United States, Paul Glader, Paul Marshall, Terry Mattingly, Melissa Harrison, Marvin Olasky and many others. An eclectic group, but all—despite different beats and political persuasions—prophetic exemplars of the subject of this book: the practice of truth-telling.

The rise of the free press and the "civil ideal" of the news is a story that needs fully retrieving for our time, but that has not been my task.

What I've tried to do is tease out those key moments when religion and the desire for freedom coalesced as a fiercer than normal passion to communicate truth—and then to show what happens when that passion loses its roots.

Those key moments act as a corrective—sometimes they even provide a radical shift in direction or method—contributing innovation, sometimes on a historic scale. In reading Larry Siedentop's *Inventing the Individual*, the *Guardian* journalist Nicholas Lezard's view was transformed. "Its basic principle—that the Christian conception of God provided the foundation for what became an unprecedented form of human society—is, when you think about it, mind-bending."[384] Journalism was its seed—and, if the seed seems to have died for a season, is it altogether foolish to work for it to bear much fruit again?

Appendix 1

Dr Jenny M Taylor, "Taking spirituality seriously: Northern Uganda and Britain's 'Break the Silence' Campaign" in *The Round Table: The Commonwealth Journal of International Affairs*, Vol. 94, 2005, Issue 382 (London: Taylor & Francis), 15 August 2006

Taking spirituality seriously: Northern Uganda and Britain's 'Break the Silence' Campaign

Abstract

The war in Northern Uganda is both rooted in religion and reinforced by spiritual power. This has resulted in an almost impenetrable wall of incomprehension surrounding what is the worst, most neglected war in Africa today. This paper describes conditions in Northern Uganda and relates the history of the "Break the Silence" Campaign, initiated and coordinated by the Church Mission Society, which significantly increased political activity as a result. International religious solidarity broke the dehumanizing and isolating circle of secular indifference to the war. The Christian churches, with their presence on the ground and unique international networks, utilized largely untapped resources for crisis resolution and peace building.

Introduction
Uganda's largely forgotten 19-year war has deep roots, as is the way of intractable conflicts. Of the fourteen insurgencies since Museveni seized power in January 1986, this is the longest. This may in part be a result of Uganda's postcolonial culture of militarism, where political disputes have been settled by the gun; the Amin, Obote II and Okello regimes were all illegitimate. It may be more a result of the peculiar Acholi legacy, whereby the British used this self-disciplined people for its police force and army, in particular the King's African Rifles, and failed to develop the region economically as it had done the Buganda and other regions. War is what Acholi men do—although there is an alternative tradition. Bishop Ochola tells a moving story of the mythic brothers Gipir and Labongo, who fell out over a mislaid clan spear. The bitterness of total separation between the clans that ensued gave birth, according to the Bishop, to a new culture of non-violence, forgiveness and *mato oput*—a ceremony unique in Africa whereby reconciliation and forgiveness are achieved through the drinking of a shared cup of bitter herbs and the symbolic "bending of spears".[385] It is Uganda's wider recent history of state murder with impunity that made resort to violence in pursuit of so-called justice seem natural after Museveni took control.

Museveni, a secularized Munyankole from southwestern Uganda, seized power in January 1986, ousting General Tito Okello Lutwa, an ethnic Acholi from the north. This was taken particularly hard by a people who saw themselves under the colonial regime as the military backbone of the nation.[386] Museveni's National Resistance Movement (NRM) unilaterally abrogated a treaty signed six months earlier by Museveni, General Okello and Kenyan President Moi in Nairobi in December 1985. As Museveni's fighters pushed north from Kampala, Okello's Ugandan National Liberation Army (UNLA) fled, slaughtering the population in revenge as they withdrew. The Red Cross believes that 300,000 died in the Luwero Triangle alone (Ofcansky, 1996). The Acholis of the UNLA retreated over the border into Sudan, where they regrouped, but their unpunished and unforgiven atrocities haunt Uganda still (Gersony, 1997, p. 8).[387] The NRA followed and behaved like an occupation force. Atrocities committed by rogue elements of the NRA around Gulu and Kitgum—in an otherwise generally disciplined campaign to stabilize Uganda as a whole—still fuel anti-Museveni feeling. The remnants of the UNLA and other dissidents formed the Holy Spirit Mobile Forces under Alice Auma, a spirit medium possessed by the *Lakwena*, or Messenger. Alice was a prophet, a warrior priestess initially bent on fomenting national unity through 'purification', who marched to within 80 miles of Kampala before being finally defeated and fleeing into Kenya. It is her cousin Joseph Kony, of whom we shall hear later, on whom the *Lakwena*—the Spirit—then fell. He took up the cause, but more as a gang leader bent on revenge than reconciliation, and still leads the cultic Lord's Resistance Army (LRA). Religion is the idiom in which the conflict has expressed itself, and by which it—and its long-suffering victims—endure. Alice's father, Severino, until recently openly ran a "church" in Gulu; Alice was governed by the "spirits" of former missionaries, priests and healers and Kony, a former Catholic altar boy, allegedly uses Old Testament discourses of war and punishment to mobilize his young fighters. The ill-learnt lessons of the missionaries have combined with an older spiritual legacy to devastating effect. To dismiss the perpetrators as merely mad, and somehow thereby to justify international political inertia, is to fail totally to reckon with a spiritual reality that pervades all African politics. It is this fact that makes international church involvement in the resolution of Uganda's conflict peculiarly salient—and with which this article deals.

In November 2003, UN Under-Secretary for Humanitarian Affairs Jan Egeland made his first visit to Kitgum in Northern Uganda. What he found there stunned him. The man who later shocked the world with his report on Darfur regarded Kitgum as "far beyond what we see in Iraq and Palestine". The international neglect he described as "a moral outrage".[388]

Twenty-five thousand children had been abducted; many tortured, mutilated, put to death for minor infractions—or simply never seen again. Perhaps 100,000 people had died often horrific deaths. Up to a million people were now in camps (Reagan, 2003, p. 4) at the mercy of Joseph Kony's LRA or, equally iniquitous, of the government troops meant to be protecting them. Some had lived in those camps for nearly a decade, starving, unschooled and without the most basic amenities. And the world had simply forgotten—or never knew.

This article provides a record of what happened after the visit of the journalist who blew the whistle.[389] Robert Gersony's "The anguish of Northern Uganda" can be referred to for the most comprehensive analysis of the politics of the Acholi war. Detailed work on the spirituality of the war has been done by Heike Behrend (2004) and Kevin Ward (2001), none of which this article seeks to repeat.[390] Instead, using the author's personal recollection of visits to and involvement in Northern Uganda, it attempts to model a type of international intervention, called "Break the Silence", that took that spirituality seriously and, according to Acholis themselves, broke the circle of fear, violence, incomprehension and isolation.[391]

Background to a campaign
The West still knows very little about the Lord's Resistance Army of Northern Uganda beyond reports of a crackpot cult peopled by "rastas who don't blink".[392] There are one or two unpublished reports produced for the US Embassy in the mid-1990s (e.g. see Gersony, 1997 and Pain, 1997); a couple of papers in learned journals and one enthnography on the Holy Spirit Movement (HSM) of Alice Lakwena, the "rebel priestess", who haunted the tabloids briefly during her mad purification march to Kampala.[393] I had been given nothing to read before my trip. All I had, perhaps rather bizarrely, were the mobile telephone numbers of two Anglican bishops still living in the north.

The situation particularly around Kitgum was far more dangerous than I had been led to believe in February 2003, when I flew to Kitgum for the first time with two Church Mission Society (CMS) personnel. Operation Iron First, the massively inappropriate US-backed military push to flush the LRA out of their Sudanese bases, had proved catastrophic. Almost at a stroke the 'internally displaced people's camps' expanded from (roughly) 500,000 to 800,000—or 70% of the population of Acholiland according to Human Rights Watch[394]—and the region felt like a graveyard. Massive human rights violations had also been committed by the "legitimate" forces, the Uganda People's Defence Force (UPDF), during and after Operation Iron

Fist.[395] The main roads were passable only in convoy—and even these were attacked, as also were World Food Programme convoys. People were deeply traumatized and starving. There were still two flights a week into Kitgum from Gulu, but that was all.

Bishop Benjamin Ojwang and his wife Margaret, who met us at the tiny airport, complained that night that all he had time for now was burying his congregations. They had lived at the Diocesan compound for less than a year. Ojwang was consecrated in February 2002 at All Saints Cathedral, Kitgum, only the second man to accept the poisoned chalice of this new diocese. That there is an Anglican church here at all, led by a gentle and humorous man who jokes in English and wears all the same rig as one's local bishop, is astonishing enough. That he is managing to hold the line for his people against terror and starvation is little short of miraculous. As we drove in, we noticed the mangled wreckage of the diocesan jeep in which his predecessor's wife had died, blown up, it is supposed, by a Sudan-supplied LRA landmine.

It was not until late at night when Ben started talking about the war and its effects on his diocese that the awful truth of our situation emerged. "They come for you at 5am. If you're still alive at 6 you know you'll be alright", he said unexpectedly, his soft voice barely audible against the night sounds. The shadows cast by lamps; the ants marching in battalions up and down a damp wall; a huge, winged bug landing on my leg and stinging me painfully: these things are etched on my mind with those words. I could not sleep that night, as I began to realize that an entire people lived with this awful tension night after night. If the rebels come, they are without mercy. They might steal food, and march the children away, roped together. Or they might kill you first. Or rape your wife in front of everyone and then hack you to death before torching your whole village. Your own people do this to you. If they took your daughter, they might return her minus lips as a warning against speaking out against her tormentors, or minus fingers as a warning against carrying weapons against them, infected with AIDS and incurable.

The two nights I spent at the compound were nights of sheer terror—and also a weird peace. From this same compound Bishop "Ben" as he has come familiarly to be known, was abducted on 17 May 2004 with six members of his household and all his goats. The mad courage he showed after his rescue—"I still love you" he told his abductors—resonates with the peculiar distortions of my own feelings that night.

It was the first time in my life I had experienced physical dread. And yet any attempt to end the sufferings of Northern Uganda, and perhaps all of Africa, must address this fear to understand its vice-like grip on people's imagination, motivation and will.[396] Fear in Africa, as in all traditional societies, is many faceted and insidious: fear of revenge and of the marauding spirits let loose by unforgiven or unavenged wickedness. Here, fear of the LRA's physical brutality is compounded by a fear of Kony's alleged supernatural powers. "This factor [spirits] cannot be ignored …. The people believe it and we cannot ignore it. It is very difficult to get information from them", Minister of State for Defence Ruth Nankabirwa was quoted by *The Monitor* as saying. Spiritual "error" can only be addressed by spiritual "truth". The courage of church leaders comes from belief in the action of a stronger spirit, not from the denial of the spiritual. The power of the Holy Spirit of Jesus Christ over the spirit world is well documented in the Bible and elsewhere (Ferdinando, 1999), and receives a ready response among those with access to it.

Acute impotence, bereavement, loss of cultural patterns and the unhallowed memories of recent history additionally contribute to the hell of life for the now 85% of the entire Acholi nation who live hugger-mugger in "protected camps". The huts, built in 1997 on the orders of Museveni's men, often at gunpoint and within 24 hours, are far too close together and prone to burning from cooking fires.[397] The people, unable to go to their fields for food, are not fed adequately, or equipped.[398] By way of illustration, in Otuboi camp, Kaberamaido District there is one borehole per 6000 people. In the same camp, with a population of 15,663 internally displaced persons (IDPs), there are just 10 pit latrines, i.e. one latrine per 1566 people.[399] One of the most overlooked humiliations is the lack of provision for menstruating women in a landscape denuded even of leaves from trees.[400] Such figures cannot do justice to the misery from hunger, victimization, degradation of children's health from ring-worm caused by lack of sanitation, and diseases like cholera and TB, which are endemic. In 2003 the local MP reported that 74% of all households in the north were without a single blanket, compared with 25% nationally (Reagan, 2003, p. 3). Ninety-one per cent of the houses were grass-thatched, compared with only 21% in western Uganda. The under-five mortality rate was 178 per 1000 live births in the north, compared with 135 per 1000 in the central region. A staggering 70% of children in Gulu, Kitgum and Pader are under-weight or 'stunted' according to the same report. Horrifically, according to the 1989 Census, there were only 236 businesses in the whole of the north, compared with 101,793 in Central Uganda. By 2004 HIV/AIDS in the Gulu area was the leading cause of death, claiming more lives than military confrontation and constituting 69% of deaths.[401] "Survival sex", where girls offer themselves in exchange for soap, food or school fees exacerbates the virtual collapse of a comprehensive health care system caused by the flight of health workers and historic underdevelopment.

Others—usually women—venture out to get water or grow cassava, believing it better to die trying to provide for themselves than die of hunger and thirst in the huts. Although some of the camps were the inevitable result of people fleeing to market centres to escape rebel attack, it is also true that Museveni was operating a scorched earth policy to punish the Acholis.[402] The accusation that these are actually concentration camps has more than a ring of truth. Kony's rebels seem to operate around the camps with near impunity, burning, raping, looting and abducting. And the army allegedly uses the camps to protect themselves, camping within the rings of huts, not on the exposed flanks (Ward, 2001, p. 203). What struck me forcibly, however, was the lack of anger; a whole people stupefied beyond rage.

Real horror can become a kind of pornography. But I will tell just one story as told to me by a 16-year-old abductee I will call John, who had been rescued by the UPDF. He had a small brother with whom he had been abducted, a child who was frightened and wanted to run away from the madness and go home to his mother and get on with his schooling. Joseph Kony got wind of the lad's misery and decided to set an example. He made the boy dig a small hole in the sandy ground and lie face down in it. Then he ordered "John" to take a club and club his little brother on the back of the head until he was dead. The twist was that, just before his little brother died in unspeakable terror and pain, he was ordered to whisper in his bloody ear who had done this to him.

Hillary Andersson, BBC East Africa correspondent, gave vent to my own feelings: "Send in a mercenary crack squad, get foreign help—do whatever it takes!" she demanded in a harrowing report.[403]

The "Break the Silence" Campaign was CMS's emergency response to this cry. CMS had had no missionaries in Gulu or Kitgum since 1985, despite bringing the Gospel there in 1904. Kevin Ward comments: "There was a sense that the North had a low priority for CMS in comparison with other parts of Uganda" (2001, p. 194).[404] And yet there was still a mutual sense of identification, the more so as the Diocese of Northern Uganda was already, remarkably, planning its centenary celebrations for November 2004. CMS's communications team resolved to try to convince the Board to back a campaign that would "highlight the humanitarian catastrophe caused by the enforced displacement of 800 000 people and seek international intervention, led by Britain, to solve the crisis, as happened in Sierra Leone".[405]

Launching the campaign

CMS flew Bishop Ojwang and his wife to Britain for a six-week tour on 20 August 2003, and to launch the campaign with a news conference at the Mothers' Union HQ, Mary Sumner House in Westminster next day. His first day began with two live interviews for the BBC, first with James Naughtie of the *Today* programme and then for *Good Morning Scotland*. Convinced that the Museveni government and its troops had failed the north, he pleaded for international help. Naughtie suggested that the LRA was a cult "controlling vast numbers of people, and they keep them in something akin to imprisonment". Ojwang attempted to correct him by saying that "over one million" of his people were being kept in "protected camps" but without protection, i.e. Ugandan government protection. "No protection is being given to them. Even the Kony people can come up to the camp, and even abduct people near the camps." Naughtie, unable quite to believe what he was hearing—he struggled with analogies of Western cults when he mentioned David Koresh, Waco and "brainwashing"—asked what the Church could do. "Because, if it is true that 20,000 children have been abducted, quite apart from what's being done to grown-up people by way of brainwashing, it's obviously a crime of gigantic proportions."[406]

He was right. The sheer magnitude of the problem beggars belief, defying normal categories of secular reportage. The enormity slithers away from Western comprehension, too awful, too inexplicable. How can it be that we gave Waco saturation coverage, but we have barely covered this—for 17 years? You could almost hear Naughtie's brain grinding.

Ojwang ploughed on: "The church role ... is a prophetic role to speak on behalf of the voiceless and appeal to you that you come and help us. We are now being defeated". Again, he added, with affecting simplicity: "It's difficult to control and that's why I am coming to an international body to intervene. *It has defeated us*" (my emphasis). Ojwang—an orphaned shepherd boy who was educated at 'bush school' then by CMS—articulated the frustration and despair of his nation.

From the studio the Bishop went with two children and David Oyelowo, the Nigerian-born Royal Shakespeare Company actor and star of BBC's *Spooks*, to present a petition that CMS had organized to No 10 Downing Street, with a letter to Tony Blair urging the government to "exert its role within the Commonwealth" to avert a humanitarian disaster. The letter, drafted in consultation with the Church in Northern Uganda and with Kacoke Madit (loosely the London-based wing of the Acholi Religious Leaders Peace Initiative (ARLPI) in Northern Uganda), urged the parties to (in summary):

1. negotiate a settlement "resolv[ing] the root causes of potential conflict in the region";
2. offer non-military support to the Ugandan government to strengthen its capacity to engage in dialogue and meet its obligations to protect the life and property of its people; and
3. "meet the immediate needs of the civilians in the 'protected camps' and redress the imbalance in infrastructure".

The symbolism of the event in Downing Street, perhaps more than the substance of the letter, was a stunning morale boost—one which may be lost on those for whom such gestures are daily media fare. But for a people who have come to consider themselves as little more than animals in the eyes of their own government, it played well in the Kampala press the next day.

One of the children carrying the petition was the daughter of an Acholi émigré, Aldo Okot, a former Catholic priest turned lawyer who received asylum in Britain after the NRA coup. The other was the son of the TV satirist Mark Thomas, whose piece about the campaign appeared in *New Statesman*. "In its "Break the Silence" campaign, the Church Mission Society has highlighted the killing of the abducted children and the appalling atrocities committed against them ... Jan Egeland, has said that 'this crisis is in many ways worse than Iraq'. So where are the human rights dossiers from Jack Straw released in a blaze of publicity?"[407]

Ojwang and Oyelowo made speeches. Ojwang said: "We cannot give up because that means throwing the Bible away ... We have to struggle even up to the end."[408] He also spoke to Lindsay Hilsum, International Editor for Channel 4 News, who had covered the NRA campaign in the 1980s; and to several BBC World Service strands later in the day. His interview for Radio Bristol was cited by Valerie Davey, then Labour MP for Bristol West, in an important 9/11 memorial speech on the UN to mark the second anniversary of the World Trade Center bombing. She commended the "campaign by churches" and asked that ministers remember Uganda as they sought to extend the UN remit to intervene in the internal conflicts of sovereign nations. Davey's former constituency coincides with the Diocese of Bristol, which is twinned with Kitgum. Churchmen often ask her to host Acholi clergy on advocacy visits. This twinning, the little-known Anglican "Companion Diocesan Links" Scheme, administered from Church House, Westminster, is an unresearched source of encouragement for beleaguered churches. Davey subsequently kept up the pressure, asking several questions of ministers in the House on Uganda, and signing several Early Day Motions.

CMS also arranged for Ojwang to meet the then Foreign Minister for Africa, Chris Mullin, on 17 September in Whitehall. The Bishop repeated his view that Uganda needed increased outside intervention. He proposed peacekeepers to protect the camps and suggested that Joseph Kony be hunted down and tried for crimes against humanity.

Other high-profile engagements included addressing 5000 evangelical leaders at NEAC—the Fourth National Evangelical Anglican Congress at the Winter Gardens, Blackpool—and meeting the new Archbishop of Canterbury Rowan Williams there—the only meeting to which the Archbishop agreed. A photograph of the two men embracing went around the world. Dr Williams told the Bishop he had raised the situation in private with Prime Minister Tony Blair. Ojwang also gave the blessing at the Communion Service for Europe's biggest Christian youth festival, Greenbelt, before 17,000 young people.

The Bishop's tour sparked two further years of activity by CMS. Four hundred and fifty congregations around Britain signed up to pray, give, and write to their MPs. One black Pentecostal congregation gave £24,000 for a night shelter to be built in Pader. Luton Borough Council gave permission for the town to host a weekend of fund-raising activities, after one young mother heard a CMS report of Northern Uganda's abductees on the local radio, and motivated six churches in the town to take an interest. Media activity in Britain was amplified by strong coverage in the Kampala press thanks to CMS church contacts on the Kampala-based *New Vision*. The Bishop's trip to England proved effective. It resulted in a "considerable increase in political activity" according to Foreign and Commonwealth Office officials.[409] In November, UN Under-Secretary for Humanitarian Affairs Jan Egeland visited Kitgum for the first time. Most VIPs only visit Gulu—reinforcing the isolation of Kitgum, Uganda's most north-easterly outpost. Egeland was stunned by what he found, describing the international neglect it implied as "a moral outrage".[410]

It is a moral outrage to see thousands of children that have been abducted going through the most horrendous torture by the rebel movement and the same groups now being neglected by the whole international community. I cannot find any other part of the world having an emergency on the scale of Uganda that has so little international attention ... *this is far beyond what we see in Iraq, or the Palestinian territories.*[411]

He told the IRIN news service it was one of the last "dark spots" for international attention in the world. "Liberia, eastern Congo, all have had significant investment in trying to relieve human suffering", he said. He intended to "more than triple" the aid budget to Northern Uganda as a result of his visit. "We told them we are massively increasing our presence in the north. My own department is set to expand from one office in Gulu to four offices in different locations in the north", Egeland said. None of the extra money would achieve anything, he added, unless "the government makes a real effort to improve security so that our aid workers can do their job".[412]

The week before Christmas the German deputy head of mission in Kampala, Holger Seubert, said that the European Union had stepped up consultations with the Ugandan government to find a solution. "The issue is being discussed in Brussels. The EU is saying there should be kind of a roadmap. From the EU, the matter will be forwarded to the Security Council in New York."[413] World Vision project coordinator Michael Oruni at the Uganda Children of War Rehabilitation Project in Gulu later expressed the general perception that it was the Break the Silence campaign that changed international apathy into action:

The difference it made cannot be [over-]estimated. It pulled down Jan Egeland which made a very big difference. The US for the first time started waking up and saying: 'Is it that bad?'

The Uganda government had, up until then, been allowed to make light of the war, Oruni said.

The government played a very big role in making the world believe this was a small issue in the backyard of Uganda. The President referred to the LRA as "a jigger in the toe". You need a safety pin to remove it. That was more than five years ago.[414]

Egeland's reaction had a ripple effect with aid agencies. Christian Aid, Tear Fund and Oxfam all increased their aid through appeals and appointed new expatriate officers to the region. Amnesty International and Oxfam incorporated Kitgum into their Small Arms Campaign, launched later that year, featuring Bishop Ojwang in their publicity film. Before Christmas 2004, when Bob Geldof's team were researching material to film for six programmes about Africa to be broadcast in the summer of 2005, the BBC World Affairs Correspondent Mike Wooldridge referred the crew to my office at CMS. After a series of difficult negotiations, Geldof finally decided not to go to Darfur, but to film in Kitgum.

A more prosaic event may ultimately prove the most strategic: a bus trip by 15 Anglican bishops from all over Uganda to an IDP camp outside Gulu. Organized and sponsored by CMS, this was the first solidarity visit to the north by the Church of Uganda hierarchy. A US government official has described as a *sine qua non* the "fundamental reordering of the north – south relationship".[415] The churches are crucial to that. Newly installed Archbishop

Henry Luke Orombi led the deputation, accompanied by Revd Dr David Zac Niringiye, CMS Africa Director, himself a Ugandan. A *New Vision* reporter was also on board. The party travelled on 27 February 2004 to Pabbo, 25 miles northwest of Gulu, the largest of the 62 camps scattered all over Acholiland. For the delegates themselves the trip both shocked and galvanized. Niringiye wrote in *New Vision*: "I could not believe what I saw—sub-human existence! The most enduring sight was children—in the thousands."[416] He concluded that Kony had no agenda, the situation could not be dignified with the name "war" or talk of "negotiations". The military solution merely resulted in the deaths of "soldiers" who had been recruited at gunpoint—every one a much-loved son or daughter. It was a human tragedy, he said, which should be "exposed and isolated", with Kony himself evacuated as Charles Taylor had been.[417] He then met all the editors of *New Vision* to change the way they were reporting the war. "I said to the editors—don't just report rebels, rebels, rebels. Tell the human story. Tell stories of these kids."

On 29 January 2004 President Museveni and Luis Moreno Ocampo, the Prosecutor of the International Criminal Court (ICC) announced at a joint press conference at the Hotel Intercontinental, Hyde Park, London that the LRA had been referred for investigation for crimes against humanity. The ICC announced that "the prosecutor has determined that there is a sufficient basis to start planning for the first investigation" into LRA crimes against humanity. This was a generally unwelcome test case. Even by April 2005—well over a year later—the Acholi leaders were still unconvinced that enough consultation had taken place to give them the assurance that such a measure would not bring more LRA terror down on everyone's heads. Churchmen, including Archbishop Odama, Chair of the Acholi Religious Leaders Peace Initiative (ARLPI) and Anglican Bishop Onono Onweng of Northern Uganda Diocese, went twice with other religious and traditional leaders to The Hague in March and April 2005 to express misgivings about the ICC process. They felt the process had been imposed on them without regard to local sensibilities, or traditional methods of reconciliation, as well as of possible retributive consequences of international interference, which had ample precedents. Camps are spread out across the countryside, incapable of real protection. When Onen Kamdulu, former chief of LRA operations, gave himself up in early 2005, fifty of Kony's forces retaliated on 21 February by attacking the Alokulum DP camp/trading centre, about six kilometres southwest of Gulu, in an attempt to kill his mother, who was known to be living there.[418] The urgent plea for peacekeepers has thus far been ignored by Museveni.

The initial furore of opposition that greeted the ICC initiative—amplified by Christian Aid who found itself on opposite sides to Amnesty International on the issue—is elucidated by a comment of the Kacoke Madit coordinator, Caesar Nyeko Poblicks in London:

Our main argument [is that] the LRA is almost like a mad person with your child on top of the roof. Whatever mechanism you have, you can pick him up with a gun, you can pick him up with whatever, but what is really important to you, this mad man ... is it killing him, or saving that child? Everyone knows he's a mad man, he's done bad things—but our argument which we are mistaken for sympathizing with the LRA, is how many of these children can we save, to rejoin their families?[419]

The world still seems powerless to rescue a child.

The Acholi Religious Leaders' Peace Initiative (ARLPI)
The Break the Silence Campaign worked in consultation with its CMS partners, the Anglican bishops of Gulu (called Diocese of Northern Uganda) Nelson Onono Onweng and Benjamin Ojwang of Kitgum, as well as with Kacoke Madit in London. Both Bishops were key members of the ARLPI which Onweng had founded in 1998, after he met LRA rebels in the bush. ARLPI describes itself as "an interfaith forum which brings together Muslim and Christian (Catholic, Orthodox & Anglican) leaders in Acholiland, Northern Uganda. ARLPI provides a proactive response to conflicts through community-based mediation services, advocacy and lobby and peace-building activities."[420] Its motto—*Kacel pi kuc*—means "together for peace" and its goal is "to create a conducive climate for sustainable peace and development in Uganda".

ARLPI is remarkable given the Anglican-Catholic rivalry that characterized the colonial-era and that was cemented during the Amin and Obote regimes (Ward, 2001). Currently chaired by the Catholic Archbishop John Baptist Odama, the calibre of its work is the more remarkable given pressure on priests to sanction the Holy Spirit Movement in the 1980s. A Catholic priest, who was later transferred to the Diocese of St Joseph in Gulu, held masses regularly in the HSM temple at Opit, while a former seminarian worked as supervisor or altar boy there (Behrend, 2004, p. 77 f/n 7). The crucifix and the tablecloth on the altar came from the Catholic mission of the Verona fathers in Kalongo in Kitgum District. The current lack of unity of purpose among traditional Acholi leaders has helped squander peace dividends, compounded by diaspora activists whose funds have paid for Sudan-supplied weaponry.

Nonetheless, ARLPI has won credibility inside and outside Uganda in its short history, although the cost is great. Founder Bishop Onweng said: "Working with everybody who is sick makes you also sick. Spiritual work with no resources is quite hard."[421] Its first Chairman, Anglican Bishop Macleord [sic] Ochola Baker, first Bishop of Kitgum, is a tall, dignified and impressive man whose own past suffering at the hands of rebels has given him considerable authority. His wife died when her jeep was mined, and his daughter committed suicide following rape by rebels. In July 2004 in Barcelona, Ochola received on behalf of the group the prestigious Chicago-based International Parliament of World Religions Paul Carus Award for Outstanding Contributions to the Interreligious Movement. He said: "I have tried to change the game from confrontation to cooperation".[422] Other peace awards followed, including one from Japan in 2004.[423] One local Oxfam worker told me of her respect for the leaders. "People trust them. They keep their promise." When Museveni was arming the Karamojong to fight the Acholi in 2000—when practically the entire Acholi herd, the staple of their economy and culture was raided—it was Ochola who refused to allow the Acholi to arm themselves in revenge.

ARLPI notably succeeded in lobbying the Ugandan parliament for an Amnesty Bill, which became law in January 2000, guaranteeing safe passage to any rebel, including the commanders.[424] They worked in a context of terror on the one hand,[425] and of government treachery on the other to promote understanding. Priests have been murdered by Kony's rebels and imprisoned by Museveni's soldiers (Ward, 2001, p. 200). And yet, on 10 January 2005, they secured an invitation for the Acholi Parliamentary

Group, religious and other leaders from Gulu to spend the day at the president's ranch in Ankole, Western Uganda. According to Bishop Ochola, Deputy Chairman of the ARLPI, this was unprecedented: "This was the first meeting in all that time. The relationship was not good. We were grateful. That improved the relationship very much."[426]

As Gersony points out, fear of the Acholis may have prevented more decisive protection by the Ugandan army. A US government official puts it more bluntly: "Museveni is still in punish mode."[427] The UPDF have in the past identified Acholis with the ousted Obote regime, with the revenge massacres against NRA supporters in the Luwero Triangle and subsequent insurgencies in the north as Museveni's NRA bedded down.

After the war ended in 1986 the International Committee of the Red Cross claimed that at least 300 000 people had died in the Luwero Triangle and that officials had failed to account for half to a third of the region's population. UNLA forces in Luwero were sometimes referred to as 'the Acholis' because of the large number of Acholis who comprised its officer and enlisted corps … NRA conduct, by comparison, was observed by international witnesses to be generally disciplined and correct.[428]

In June 2003 the ARLPI bishops organized a four-night sleepover with night commuters in Gulu bus park to draw in the international community. Night commuters are mostly children who stream into town from local villages and IDP camps for the night. There are thousands of them and, until 2004, there were no official shelters for them. They sleep under lorries, and on pathetic pieces of sacking in hospital compounds and on shop verandahs. Some even try to study in the available lamplight. Every morning they trek away again, those who can, to school. They travel accompanied only by older siblings and are vulnerable to TB, rape by UPDF soldiers and AIDS. The sleepover from 25 June 2003—the rainy season—was videoed, as was the desperate speech Bishop Ochola made on the first night, when he exploded the myth of "the pearl of Africa":

> The image of Uganda abroad is very shiny, very beautiful. Uganda is the model of leadership in Africa. Uganda is very prosperous. Uganda is very peaceful. But when you talk of Uganda, you have to realize that Uganda covers a geographical area that includes northern Uganda. Even in the missionary's or ambassador's offices, [in] diplomatic mission offices in Uganda here, it is always written: 'Don't go beyond Karuma' [Bridge on the River Nile]. In other words: We have been cut off from the rest of Uganda.

He went on:

> Let Museveni be the first person to cry out for these children away from the town here! Let Museveni be the first person to say that children in northern Uganda are not studying! They are not going to school! They are sleeping in the bushes! They are sleeping on the streets! Let the world know! Why can't we be realistic and accept our weaknesses? This is a weakness on the part of the government that your children, your wives, your mothers are sleeping in the cold! In which country can this happen! It cannot happen in London. It cannot happen in Paris. Where the Parliament of

> Uganda keeps quiet on our problem of abductions of the innocent children. What have they done to Kony? What have they done to Museveni? These children here what have they done? We are very sad. Why should they be treated like this? God gives children as a gift to parents. And they should be allowed to grow. They should be allowed to enjoy their human rights like any other children in the world. Why should they sleep in the bus park or under the verandas in Gulu here? Is that what God wants? Is that what God wants? ...Why is the world keeping quiet? Are we not part of that body? Are we not one in Christ?[429]

Bishop Niringiye of Kampala is encouraging Acholi leaders to strive to achieve a consensus. He says:

> One. The Acholis must speak with one voice about how to end this carnage. And two, we have got to be able to dialogue. Kony is a lunatic, a witch, all these evil things. He depends on evil spirits. We must isolate him. Although one can't dialogue with someone who cannot accept reason, there has to be a way out of violence. What was done to Charles Taylor—buy him out. He is a witch. We need to work at identifying one or two countries which are open to considering the possibility of taking him.[430]

With such efforts, the Church keeps a sense of shared humanity alive. It nurtures a tiny seed of hope and goes some way to filling the vacuum in social and political action. "The churches are present in the countryside, in trading locations and towns, and in the camps in ways unparalleled by any other organization. The churches have means of access to people that the government does not. Church leaders and traditional leaders in the community often overlap" (Ward, 2001, p. 201). They keep alive the cultural memory, insisting on traditional forms of redress for wrongdoing, maintaining space for alternatives to despair (Ward, 2001, p. 198). The much-documented rituals of reparation, particularly *mato oput*, where the aggrieved parties "drink a bitter herb" from a common vessel in mutual forgiveness is, says Ochola, pre-Christian evidence of God's grace to the Acholis.[431]

Sadly, the sheer scale of killing, caused by its mechanization, is beyond the scope of the old ways, while the abrupt and rationalist solutions of the West do not address the nature of the problems—and, in fact, compound them. What might be termed the "militarization of spirituality" has no resonance in the West. Armies mobilized by cult leaders or priestesses, war justified by religious texts, a cocktail of Sunday school doctrines and spirit voices—the background worldview is incomprehensible to the West. Western elites must understand the spiritual nature of power and powerlessness, and the contribution of spiritual people in healing Uganda's hurts. Ugandans understand that "politics" and "religion" are parts of the same terrain: that power flows between the visible material world and the invisible spiritual world. They understand that in their culture power is unitary and cannot be divided into separate boxes. As Stephen Ellis writes in *Worlds of Power*: "religious thought needs to be studied seriously if we are to understand politics in Africa today" (Ellis & ter Haar, 2004, p. 4).

Conclusion
The war is not over, and children are still being abducted. It is nonetheless possible to make the following observations about the Break the Silence Campaign as an appropriate model for addressing African conflict:

1. It amplified the Northern Uganda Church's call for help, dispelling some of the spiritual fear.
2. It mobilized UK churchgoers to commit to a frightening cause in prayer, letter-writing and giving. John Clark, Director of Mission and Public Affairs for the Church of England says: "Prayer generates spiritual capital in terms of morale building and encouragement".
3. It galvanized Anglican networks, and British and international agencies, more than tripling the aid budget.
4. It considerably increased international political activity.
5. It helped the middle-class in Kampala begin to acknowledge the Acholis' humanity.
6. It united the Church of Uganda in common cause, helping build a sense of nationhood.

The Ugandan Church uses religion to make new spaces for dialogue and new ways of transcending the crisis. Only the Church is simultaneously there on the ground, close enough to the people and their worldview, yet able to access international mechanisms of justice based on the unique history it shares with Anglican and Catholic missionary societies. Its historic links with the 206-year-old Church Mission Society gave wide cross-cultural access to the reality of Acholi suffering. Northern Uganda is as a result less invisible, less remote.

Caesar Poblicks Nyeko, the Project Coordinator for Kacoke Madit, summarized the effect: "When I saw Bishop Ojwang of Kitgum actually in front of Downing Street … this to me felt like humanity has the same language now".[432]

The campaign took spirituality seriously. The spiritual dimension of this conflict, such as Kony's references to establishing a government based upon the Ten Commandments, has been an excuse for lack of action by the West.[433] Foreign advisors have helped Museveni dismiss options for dialogue, and pursue the catastrophic military option.

Greater spiritual literacy in the international community would help render more operable the networks and resources of the world-wide church in future conflict. The most vulnerable of all, the children, might live to thank us.

* This essay is reprinted *in toto*, and has not been updated. Source referencing and style retained.

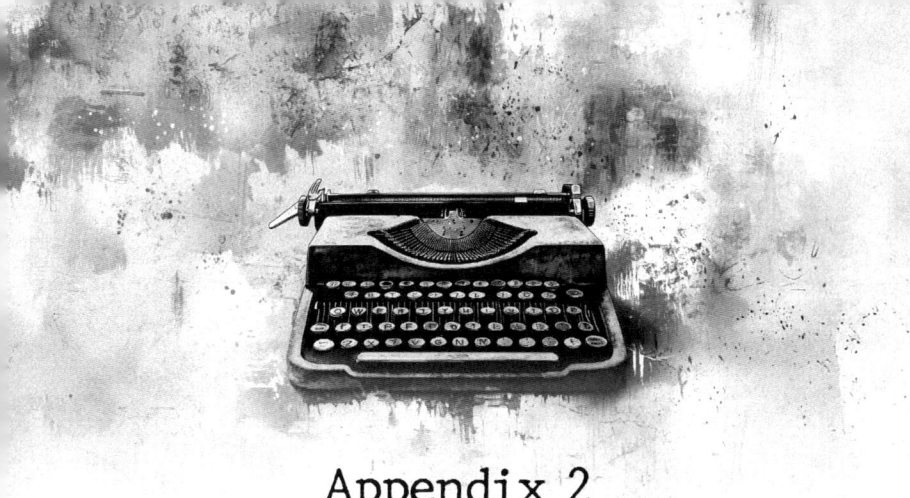

Appendix 2

"Journalism is ….": some definitions

"Information and analysis concerning recent events, published in multiple copies or disseminated beyond the immediate reach of the speaker's voice." Marvin Olasky.

"A stream of other-regarding reliable, inclusive and fact-based information providing timely intelligence for the community at large." Aidan White.

"Giv[ing] space to 'the periodical expression of the thought of the time, (and) the opportune record of the questions and answers of contemporary life." John Forster.

"The function of news is to signalise an event. The function of truth is to bring to light the hidden facts" [to facilitate democratic action]. Walter Lippmann.

"The very genius of our age." George Steiner.

[Journalism] "places matters of high importance into the public domain, so that debate and challenge could follow." Alan Rusbridger.

"To find stuff out and publish it." Alan Rusbridger.

"The Bible of democracy." Walter Lippmann.

"Important public goods, essential to the preservation of an accountable democracy." Dame Frances Cairncross.

" ... truth-telling, independence, humanity, impartiality and accountability." Aidan White.

" ... distinct from self-regarding outbursts of robust, if thoughtful, often biased, and contrarian opinion that can be assembled under the broad umbrella of free expression." Aidan White.

"A stream of other-regarding reliable, inclusive and fact-based information providing timely intelligence for the community at large." Aidan White.

" ... printing what someone, somewhere does not want printed." George Orwell

"Everything else is public relations." George Orwell.

"A mission to explain the world, to make it less obscure, to make those who live there less afraid of it and look at others with greater awareness, and also with more confidence." Pope Francis.

"... an exclusive agency for collecting, condensing, and assimilating the trivialities of ... human existence." WJ Stillman.

"News that moves you." Jenny Taylor

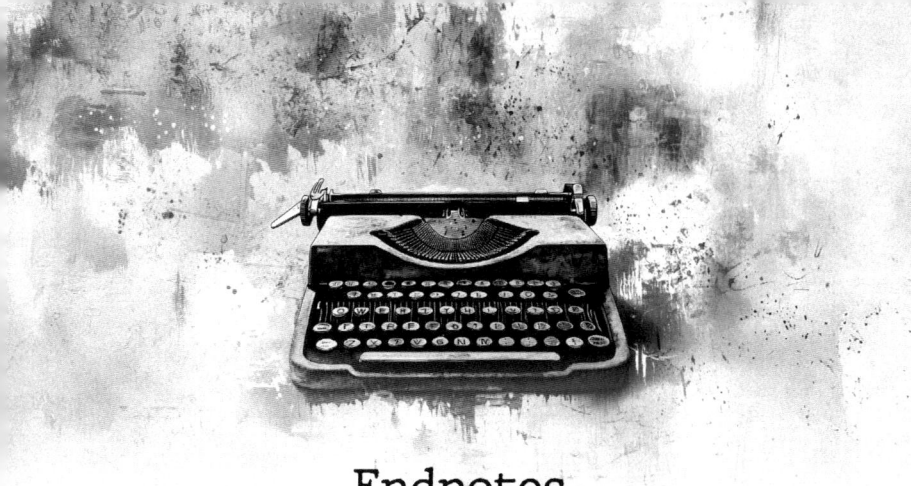

Endnotes

STORY—The children's story they could not tell: Northern Uganda's war

1   Parts of this narrative were first published as "Taking Spirituality Seriously: Northern Uganda and Britain's 'Break the Silence Campaign' in *The Round Table: The Commonwealth Journal for International Affairs* Vol. 94, Issue 382, October 2005, 559-574. Reproduced as Appendix 1.

2   Although Joseph Kony remains at large, either in Sudan or in Central African Republic, the law is catching up with his commanders. See: Nyasha Chingono, "'Justice is served': relief at ex-Kony commander's conviction in Uganda", *The Guardian,* 21 August 2024

Preface

3   *The Times,* 4 January 1993, p. 14.

4   *The Times,* op. ed., 23 March 2023.

5   As happened when a million uneducated Mirpuris were displaced to build the Mangla Dam in Azad Kashmir, and rehomed in the north of England to work in the textile factories: the idea of Lord David Alliance.

6   Roger Ballard, "Racial inequality, ethnic diversity and social policy: pre-requisites for the professional delivery of public services." Unpublished paper presented at SOAS Seminar, 1996.

7   My doctorate was called *After Secularism: Inner-city governance and the new religious discourse* (London: School of Oriental and African Studies, 2001).

8   Jill Abramson, *Merchants of Truth: Inside the News Revolution*

(London: Bodley Head, 2019), 2.

9 Cited in Jonathan Heawood, *The Press Freedom Myth* (London: Biteback, 2019), 115.

10 https://pressgazette.co.uk/publishers/nationals/evening-standard-daily-weekly-newspaper-redundacies/

11 *The Greenwich Wire* is a one-man band using freelance local democracy reporters. Mind the London news gap: The boroughs which have little coverage of council activities - Press Gazette

12 There are several works in the US that convincingly investigate this link, and I do not labour the argument, merely offer its contours. See particularly Douglas Underwood, *From Yahweh to Yahoo: The Religious Roots of the Secular Press* (Urbana and Chicago: University of Illinois Press, 2008).

13 Jenny M Taylor, "From Prophetic Press to Fake News" in Vishal Mangalwadi, *This Book Changed Everything* (Dehradun, Uttarakhand: Nivedit Good Books, 2019).

14 The collection of papers edited by Paul Frosh and Amit Pinchevski (eds) *Media Witnessing: Testimony in the Age of Mass Communication* (Basingstoke: Palgrave Macmillan, 2009), which sounds hopeful, is written in such dry, abstruse academese it would bore journalists themselves to death.

15 Heawood, *Press*, 128.

16 CEO of the *Financial Times*, John Ridding, speaking at the WAN-IFRA World News Media Congress at Copenhagen on 28 May 2024.

17 AI content deals: publishers weigh money against pressure (substack.com)

Chapter 1: A Licence to Harm

18 Davies, *Hack*, xvii.

19 Heawood, *Press*, ix.

20 Alan Rusbridger, *Breaking News: The Remaking of Journalism and why it Matters now* (London: Canongate, 2018), xxiv.

21 Davies, *Flat Earth News* (London: Vintage, 2009), 2f

22 Davies, *Flat*, ibid.

23 Rusbridger, *Breaking*, xxiv.

24 Shirkey in Rusbridger, *Breaking*, 199.

25 Shirkey in Rusbridger, *Breaking*, 134.

26 Malcolm Muggeridge, *The Green Stick: Chronicles of Wasted Time*

Vol 1 (Glasgow: Collins, 1981 [1972]), 273.

27 Muggeridge, *Green*, 220.

28 Muggeridge, *Green*, 282.

29 Muggeridge, *Green*, 285.

Chapter 2—Prophecy, Discourse and Reality

30 Biblical archaeologist Seth Sanders describes what happened in his *The Invention of Hebrew*, a ground-breaking book, received when it was published in 2009 as a revolution in scholarship.

31 Sanders, *Invention*, 37.

32 Sanders, *Invention*, 159

33 Sanders, *Invention*, 38.

34 Sanders, *Invention*, 1.

35 What is startling in Sanders' work is the evidence from stones.

One example, from Siloam in the southern Levant will have to suffice for the sake of verification. The Siloam inscription describes the vision of Balaam, son of Beor, recognized as a famous foreign prophet in Numbers 22-24. This vision is inscribed in a very public place, on the wall of a way station or shrine just across the Jordan from Israel. It represents, by the 8th century BC, the professional tradition of visionary speakers and not, as had been the case, mere scribes. The huge import of this needs to be spelled out:

"The Siloam [and Deir Alla] inscriptions show a regional southern Levantine trend: monumental writing that asserts its role as communication, not as a built object or an icon of its royal builder. The inscription designates itself with a word for 'message', rather than 'king' or object, at the beginning of the first sentence. The text now points not to the item on which it is inscribed or the king who is supposed to be speaking it, but the account it contains. And these accounts no longer assign primary responsibility to the king: their protagonists are craftsmen and prophets. This trend finds its most extensive expression in biblical narrative, which is never authored by the king and where people and prophets assume new prominence as agents ... they tell a story that is not initiated by a king or focused on military activity. Key to the drama is the speech and actions of a collective group." Sanders, *Invention*, 140.

The Siloam and Deir Alla inscriptions answer affirmatively therefore the question, "Can we understand the Bible's distinctiveness as the result of a decision to communicate in a new way?"

This argument may seem a long way from the subject of this book, but it points to it.

36 Craig Bartholomew, *The God who Acts in History* (Grand Rapids, Michigan: Eerdmans, 2020), 188.

37 Bartholomew, *God*, 194.

38 Bartholomew, *God*, 195.

39 Sheldon Pollock, "Cosmopolitan and Vernacular in History" in *Cosmopolitanism*, ed. Carol Breckenridge et al. (Durham, North Carolina: Duke University Press, 2002), 16. Cited by Sanders, *Invention*, 38.

40 Sanders, *Invention*, 38.

41 Sanders, *Invention*, 39.

42 Gottfried Herder, *1877-1913 Samtliche Werke Vol. 18:387* cited by Sanders, *Invention*, 27.

43 Benedict Anderson, *Imagined Communities: Reflections on the origin and spread of nationalism* (London and New York: Verso, 2016).

44 Sanders, *Invention*, 164.

45 Ibid.

46 Ibid., 154.

47 Anderson, *Imagined*.

48 Acts 2: 4-11. (NIV).

49 Sanders, *Invention*, 170.

50 Isaiah 1: 10, 17. (NIV).

51 Annelle G Sabanal, "Act Justly, Love Mercy, Walk Humbly with God" in Lorenzo C Bautista et al. (eds) *Faith and Bayan: Evangelical Christian Engagement in the Philippine Context* (London: Langham Global, 2022), 29-47, 30.

52 Ibid., 31.

53 Ibid., 33.

Chapter 3 - The Representation of Reality

54 Luke 24: 11. (NIV).

55 From the website About SoF (sofn.org.uk). Accessed 21 December 2022.

56 Oliver O'Donovan, *Resurrection and Moral Order: An Outline for Evangelical Ethics* (Leicester: IVP, 1986), 65.

57 *"Teleiosis exothen"*—Perfection is from without. Basil, *De Spiritu Sancti* 16.38, cited by O'Donovan in *Resurrection*, 65.

58 Erich Auerbach, *Mimesis: The Representation of Reality in Western*

Literature (New York: Doubleday, 1957), 17.

59 Auerbach, *Mimesis*, 15.

60 Gospel of Luke 22: 62. (KJV).

61 Auerbach, *Mimesis*, 45.

62 Auerbach, *Mimesis*, 46.

63 Why did people vote for Donald Trump? Voters explain | US news | The Guardian 9 November 2016.

64 Augustine, *Confessions*, (397-400). No pages. https://augustinesconfessions.com/chapter1.html#:~:text=1.%20%E2%80%9CGreat%20are%20you%20Lord%2C%20and%20greatly%20to,sin%20and%20proof%20that%20you%20resist%20the%20proud. Accessed 10 August 2022.

65 James O'Donnell, *Augustine 'Confessions'* Volumes I-III (Oxford: Oxford University Press, 1992). Cited in Garry Wills, *Augustine's Confessions: A Biography* (New York: Doubleday, 1979), 17.

66 Ovid, *The Poems from Exile: "Tristia", "Ex Ponto" and "Ibis"* (London: Penguin Classics, 1994), Kindle Edition.

67 Augustine, *Confessions*, Bk VII.18.

68 O'Donnell, *Augustine,* II, xxx.

69 Human sacrifice sadly remains endemic wherever the Gospel is not practised. I have personally heard of it from locals even in western Nepal. References to God detesting it exist throughout the Old Testament, for example Deuteronomy 12:31, 2 Kings 16:3 and many others.

70 Roland Bainton, *Christianity* (Boston and New York: Mariner, 2000), 116.

71 Bainton, *Christianity,* 116.

72 Auerbach, *Mimesis,* 70.

73 Auerbach, *Mimesis*, 31.

74 Ibid.

75 Auerbach, *Mimesis,* 72.

76 Tierney, *The Crisis of Church and State 1050-1300*, 135, cited in Siedentop, *Inventing the Individual* (London: Allen Lane, 2017), 218.

77 Siedentop, *Inventing*, 216.

78 Siedentop, Ibid.

79 Siedentop, Ibid.

80 Siedentop, *Inventing*, 220.

81 Note that when Sanders refers to the Bible he means the Old Testament/ Hebrew Bible.

82 Sanders, *Invention*, 1.

Chapter 4—Putting Down the Mighty

83 Elizabeth Warren, *Savonarola: The Florentine Martyr, A Reformer Before the Reformation* (London: SW Partridge, 1880), 13.

84 Warren, *Savonarola*, 14.

85 Warren, *Savonarola*, 14.

86 Paper made of wood pulp was not invented until the 19th century.

87 The irony of this should not be lost on us since the Reformation which printing made possible was sparked by Luther's famous protest—his 95 Theses—against the very existence of "indulgences".

88 Neil McGregor, *Germany: Memories of a Nation* (London: Penguin), Kindle edition loc 2796.

89 RN Swanson, *Indulgences in Late Medieval England: Passport to Paradise* (Cambridge: Cambridge University Press, 2007), 64, and passim.

90 2 Maccabees 12.42.

91 Swanson, *Indulgences*, 10.

92 Andrew Pettegree, *The Book in the Renaissance* (New Haven and London: Yale University Press, 2011), 28.

93 Pettegree, *Book*, 29.

94 Stephen Jones, *New Biographical Dictionary* (London, 1811), 205f., cited by Eisenstein, *Divine*, 2.

95 Colophon is the blurb that details the typesetter, place of publication and other publisher details, now commonly at the front of books, but in the period under discussion, it was placed at the back.

96 Elizabeth Eisenstein, *Divine Art, Infernal Machine* (Philadelphia: University of Pennsylvania Press, 2011), 29.

97 Eisenstein, *Divine*, 29.

98 Pettegree, *Book*, 141.

99 Warren, *Savonarola,* 15.

100 Warren, *Savonarola,* 16.

101 Pettegree, *News,* 60.

102 Desmond Seward, *The Burning of the Vanities: Savonarola and*

the Borgia Pope (Stroud: Sutton, 2006), 116.

103 Brian Richardson, *Printing, Readers and Writers in Renaissance Italy* (Cambridge: Cambridge University Press, 1999), 82.

104 Other sources insist Savonarola burnt very little art. He was not anti-art, just profanity. See Seward, *Burning*, passim.

105 Daniel Defoe, *The Storm* - Google Books, 4.

106 Pettegree, *Book*, 53.

107 Pettegree, *News*, 67.

Chapter 5—The Nightingale Sings

108 Ibid.

109 Elizabeth Eisenstein, *The Printing Revolution in Early Modern Europe* (Cambridge: Cambridge University Press, 2012), 127.

110 Erwin Panowsky, "Artist, Scientist, Genius: Notes on the 'Renaissance-Dammerung'", *The Renaissance: Six Essays* (New York, 1962), 128. Cited by Eisenstein, *Printing*, 152.

111 Eisenstein, *Printing*, 154.

112 Graham Tomlin, *Luther & his World* (Oxford: Lion Hudson, 2012), 13.

113 Tomlin, *Luther*, 58.

114 Andrew Pettegree, *Brand Luther* (New York: Penguin, 2016), 72. Pettegree definitively scotches the "somewhat contrived" debate as to whether the original document, now lost, was literally hammered to the door in the normal way or is simply part of the Luther mythology. The recent chance discovery of the original version of a printed broadsheet of Luther's earlier theses on Scholastic theology for debate at the degree ceremony of one of his students, just a month and a half earlier is, he believes conclusive. "... almost certainly the indulgences were posted up on the door of the castle church, as the accepted narrative would have it, most probably in a now lost printed edition of Johann Rhau-Grunenberg."

115 11 September 2022.

116 Michael Reeves, *Unquenchable Flame* (London: InterVarsityPress, 2009), 40.

117 Reeves, *Unquenchable*, 40, citing Oswald Bayer, "Justification: Basis and Boundary of Theology", in Joseph A Burgess and Marc Kolden (eds) *By Faith Alone: Essays in Honor of Gerhard O Forde* (Grand Rapids, Michigan and Eugene, Oregon: Eerdmans, 2004), 78.

118 Reeves, *Unquenchable*, 42.

119 This is a bit like saying if you can't get to a lecture yourself, you can join the livestream on zoom.
120 Tomlin, *Luther*, op cit. Pettegree, *Brand*, op. cit. Reeves, *Unquenchable*, op. cit. is a much shorter, highly readable introduction to the "heart of the Reformation".
121 Pettegree, *News*, 69.
122 Elizabeth Eisenstein, *The Printing Revolution in Early Modern Europe* (Cambridge: Cambridge University Press, 2005), 149.
123 G. R. Elton, "Introduction: The Age of the Reformation" in *The New Cambridge Modern History* Vol. II *The Reformation 1520-1559*, 3.
124 Eisenstein, *Printing*, 145.
125 A book is only described as an "edition" if there are substantial changes to the original set of type.
126 Owen Chadwick, *The Reformation* (London: Penguin, 1990), 73.
127 Chadwick, *Reformation*, Ibid.
128 Marshall McLuhan and Quentin Fiore, *The Medium is the Massage* (London et al: Penguin, 1996 edn), 22.
129 See Chapter 5 in Eisenstein, *Printing*, for a discussion on the connections between the development of perspective in art, and self-awareness, particularly the lurid self-promotion of the Italian Aretino, "founder of the gutter press", which she attributes to "new powers ... placed at the disposal of men of letters after the advent of printing", p. 145.
130 Arthur Geoffrey Dickens, *Reformation and Society in Sixteenth Century Europe* (New York, 1968), 51, cited by Eisenstein, *Printing*, 164.
131 Chadwick, *Reformation*, 30.
132 Chadwick, *Reformation*, 39.
133 Elton, "Introduction", 3.
134 Christopher Marsh, *Popular Religion in Sixteenth-Century England* (Basingstoke: MacMillan, 1998), 197ff.
135 Eamon Duffy, *The Stripping of the Altars: Traditional Religion in England 1400-1580* (New Haven and London: Yale University Press, 2005).
136 Duffy, *Stripping*, 4.
137 Cited by Tomlin, *Luther*, 31.
138 Steven E Ozment, *The Reformation in the Cities: The Appeal of Protestantism to Sixteenth-Century Germany and Switzerland* (New

Haven and London: Yale University Press, 1975).

139   Although, as Ozment shows later, a widespread system of "concubinage fees" whereby bishops milked the failure to "contain" clergy under their charge, puts a shocking spin on the vaunted asceticism of the Middle Ages.

140   Ozment, *Reformation*, 27f.

141   Ozment, *Reformation*, 28.

142   Ozment, *Reformation*, ibid.

143   Ozment, *Reformation*, 72.

144   Ozment, *Reformation*, 63. Ozment discusses whether this work is perhaps wrongly attributed to Joachim Vadian, reformer of St Gall, which need not detain us.

145   Ozment, *Reformation*, 49.

146   Max Weber, *The Protestant Ethic and the Spirit of Capitalism* (London and New York: Routledge, 1997 edn [1930]), 117.

147   Cited by Ozment, *Reformation*, 50.

148   Matthew 23:4f.

149   Ozment, *Reformation*, 51.

Chapter 6 - Pamphlet Revolution: Content Is King

150   Andrew Pettegree, *The Book in the Renaissance* (New Haven and London: Yale University Press, 2011), 91.

151   Pettegree, *Book*, 91.

152   Pettegree, *Book*, 95.

153   Pettegree, *Book*, 96.

154   Pettegree, *Book*, 178. Pettegree draws our attention to Ducal Wurttemberg where, at the time of the Reformation, there were fifty known schools. Twenty-five years later there were sixty-one Latin schools and 189 vernacular schools; by 1581 there were 270 schools, and 401 at the end of the century.

155   Pettegree, *News*, 2.

156   Joad Raymond, *Pamphlets and Pamphleteering in early Modern Britain* (Cambridge: Cambridge University Press, 2003).

157   Pettegree, *Book*, 149.

158   Pettegree, *News*, 141.

159   Pettegree, *News*, 6.

160   Pettegree, *Book*, 105.

161   Ibid.

162   James Raven, *The Business of Books: Booksellers and the English Book* (New Haven: Yale University Press, 2007), 14, 40.

163   Pettegree, *Book,* 106.

164   Vo Huong Nam, *Digital Media and Youth Discipleship: Pitfalls and Promise* (Unpublished Thesis, Aberdeen: Aberdeen University, 2020). See section 3.e. "Faith for exiles" in Chapter 1 "The Time of Digital Media".

165   This, despite the teaching of Scripture, and the preaching of e.g. Savonarola.

166   Max Weber, *Protestant,* 61, et al.

167   Charles Taylor, *Sources of the Self,* (Cambridge, Massachusetts: Harvard University Press, 1989), 215.

168   Contempt for, and renunciation of, the world.

169   Luke 9: 60. (NIV).

170   Published in 1521 by Pamphilus Gengenbach.

171   Ozment, *Reformation,* 113.

172   John Calvin, *The Institutes of the Christian Religion* (tr. Henry Beveridge) (Lexington, Kentucky: Pacific Publishing Studio, 2011), Ch. 17, Section 11, 118.

173   Jean Calvin, *Institutes of the Christian Religion* (tr. Henry Beveridge) (Peabody, Massachusetts: Hendrickson, [1545] 2009), 1,16,3, p. 116.

174   Calvin, *Institutes,* 1,16,4,117.

175   Calvin, *Institutes,* 117.

176   Taylor, *Sources,* 227.

177   John Milton, *Paradise Lost,* VIII, ll. 192-194.

178   Luke 1: 68. (NIV).

179   Eisenstein, *Divine,* 17.

Chapter 7—The Religious Matrix of English News

180   Esther Lightcap Meek, *Loving to Know* (Eugene, Oregon: Cascade, 2011), 63.

181   James Sutherland, "Daniel Defoe" in Ian Scott-Kilvert, (General Editor) *British Writers: Edited under the Auspices of the British Council* (New York: Charles Scribner, 1980), 2.

182   This was eleven years before the commencement of the reign of

the five Tudor monarchs (1485-1603), Henrys VII, VIII, Edward VI, Mary I and Elizabeth I.

183   Cited by Elizabeth Eisenstein, *Divine Art Infernal Machine* (Philadelphia: University of Pennsylvania Press, 2011), 48.

184   Melvyn Bragg, *William Tyndale: A Very Brief History* (London: SPCK, 2017), 3f.

185   Bragg, *Tyndale*, 4.

186   This was the so-called Coverdale version, ostensibly the work of Miles Coverdale, assistant to and shameless plagiarist of Tyndale.

187   Bragg, *Tyndale*, 86.

188   Bragg, *Tyndale*, 86.

189   Petegree, *Book*, 121.

190   Andrew Pettegree, *The Growth of a Provincial Press in Sixteenth-century Europe* The Stenton Lecture (Reading: University of Reading, 2006), 37.

191   I discuss later in the chapter why it was that a cathedral should have been the print hub of the nation.

192   Raymond, *Pamphlets*, 13.

193   Peter WM Blayney, *The Bookshops in Paul's Cross Churchyard*, Occasional Papers of the Bibliographical Society, 5 (1990); Freist, *Opinion*, ch. 3. The Stationers Company took its name from the stations set up there.

194   Margaret Willes, *In the Shadow of St Paul's Cathedral* (New Haven, London: Yale University Press, 2022), 3.

195   Willes, *Shadow*, 24.

196   Willes, *Shadow*, 22.

197   Willes, *Shadow*, 23.

198   Willes, *Shadow*, 24.

199   Mary Morrissey, *Politics and the Paul's Cross Sermons*, 1558-1642 (Oxford: Oxford University Press, 2011). Morrissey draws attention to the close nexus between pulpit and press.

200   Barbara J. Shapiro, *A Culture of Fact: England, 1550-1720* (Ithaca and London, 2000) esp. ch. 4, cited by Raymond, *Pamphlets*, 134.

201   Raymond, *Pamphlets*, 105.

202   Raymond, *Pamphlets*, 107.

203   Raymond, *Pamphlets*, 108.

204 Raymond, *Pamphlets*, 107.

205 Nicholas Brownlees, *The Language of Periodical News in Seventeenth-Century England* (Newcastle: Cambridge Scholars Publishing, 2011), xv.

206 Simon Schama, *A History of Britain* Vol. II: (London: BBC, 2002 edn), 76.

207 Brownlees, *Language*, 25.

208 Gérard Genette (tr. Jane E Lewin), *Paratexts: Thresholds of Interpretation* (Cambridge: Cambridge University Press, 1997), 2. Citing Philippe Lejeune, *Le Pacte Autobiographique* (Paris: Editions du Seuil, 1975), 45. A French literary theorist, Genette says that paratextual material "controls one's whole reading of the text".

209 DC Collins, *A Handlist of News Pamphlets 1590-1610* (London: South-West Essex Technical College, 1943) runs to a hundred pages.

210 "Black letter" served as a major typeface in Western typography for centuries. It was also known as Gothic script. And it gave its name for a while to the news sheets that used it.

211 Collins, Ibid., 40.

212 Collins, Ibid., 67f.

213 Quoted in Brownlees, *Language*, 10. Joad Raymond gives further analysis of the "soteriological concerns" of pre-Civil War occasional news pamphlets, which established both the genre of news itself and its reception among the growing readerships.

214 Brownlees, *Language*, 4.

215 Raymond, *Pamphlets*, 95.

216 Brownlees, *Language*, 10.

217 Brownlees, *Language*, 11.

218 Alain de Botton, *The News: A User's Manual* (London et al.: Penguin, 2015), 29.

219 de Botton, News, 12.

220 Heawood, *Press*, passim.

221 Ibid, 94.

222 Joad Raymond, *The Invention of the Newspaper: English Newsbooks 1641-1649* (Oxford: Clarendon Press, 1996), 186.

223 Andrew Marvell, *The Rehearsal Transpros'd*, ed. DIB Smith (Oxford, 1971), 5, cited by Raymond, *Invention*, 187.

224 Marvin Olasky, *Central Ideas in the Development of American*

Journalism (New Jersey: Lawrence Erlbaum, 1991), 26.

225 The Proclamation of King Charles III on 11 September 2022 was required by law to be published in *The Gazette*.

Chapter 8—"Mainly a Matter of Spiritual Energy"

226 Pettegree, *Invention*, 308.

227 Anthony Burgess, "Introduction", in Defoe, D. [1722] *A Journal of the Plague Year*, A Burgess and C Bristow (eds) (London: Penguin, 1966), 12.

228 Burgess, in *Journal*, 7.

229 James Sutherland, *Daniel Defoe: A Critical Study* (Cambridge, Massachusetts: Harvard University Press, 1971), 2.

230 Sutherland, *Daniel*, 2.

231 Sutherland, *Daniel*, 1f.

232 Sutherland, *Daniel*, 2.

233 Described by an earlier scribbler, Marchamont Nedham, who was incarcerated there in 1649, as the "stinking, lowsie, barbarous Gaol of Newgate", the capital's main holding place for those awaiting trial for serious crime. See a lively discussion in Anna Keay, *The Restless Republic: Britain without a Crown*, (London: William Collins, 2022), 108f.

234 Richard West, *Daniel Defoe: The Life and Strange Adventures* (Boston, Massachusetts: Da Capo Press, 1999).

235 *Who's Who in British History: Beginnings to 1901* Vol.1 A-H (London: Fitzroy Dearborn, 1998), 332f.

236 Daniel Defoe, *Journal of the Plague Year* (London: Blackie, 1905), 133.

237 Defoe, *Journal*, 7.

238 Defoe, *Journal*, 20f.

239 Defoe, *Journal*, 24.

240 WR Owens and PN Furbank, (gen. eds), *Political and Economic Writings of Daniel Defoe*, Vol. 8 "Social Reform" (London: Pickering and Chatto, 2000), 2.

241 James Sutherland, *Daniel Defoe: A Critical Study* (Cambridge, Massachusetts: Harvard University Press, 1971), 233.

242 In Abney Park Cemetery off Church Street, Stoke Newington, purchased by a charity from the eponymous family estate, are buried many famous Nonconformists: the Salvation Army founders the Booths, and Dr Isaac Watts, the hymn-writer and friend of the Abney family descendants, among them—and many others who were denied Anglican

burial.

243   Pettegree, *Invention*, 269.

244   Pettegree, *Invention*, 270.

245   Pettegree, *Invention*, 276.

246   Henry St John Viscount Bolingbroke, *On the Idea of a Patriot King*, 117.

247   Jurgen Habermas, (tr. Thomas Burger), *The Structural Transformation of the Public Sphere: An Inquiry into a Category of Bourgeois Society* (Cambridge, Massachusetts: MIT Press, 1989), 60, citing K Kluxen, *Das Problem der politischen Opposition* (Freiburg im Breisgau, Munich and Verlag Karl Alber, Baden-Baden, 1956), 187.

248   Ibid., 60.

249   Thomas Carlyle, *On Heroes, Hero-Worship and the Heroic in History*. "Lecture V: The Hero as Man of Letters: Johnson, Rousseau, Burns" (London: Dent, 1908), 392.

250   Habermas, *Transformation*, 62.

251   Julianne, *Reviving the Fourth Estate: Democracy, Accountability and the Media* (Cambridge: Cambridge University Press, 1998), 232. Schultz reached this conclusion after helping design the 1992 Media and Democracy Project survey. This six-nation survey, which included Britain and the United States, was one of the "most ambitious cross-national studies of journalists ever undertaken", with 35 questions specifically investigating the news media's Fourth Estate role.

252   Habermas, *Transformation*, 61f.

253   Pettegree, *News*, 268.

254   Sutherland, *Daniel*, 4. Sutherland notes how Defoe later went over to the service of the triumphant Whigs from 1714, but as something of a double agent, posing as a Tory on the most virulent of all Tory papers *Mist's Weekly Journal* but paid by the Whigs. "... he appears to have used his position to tone down its asperities, or, as he put it himself, to 'disable' and 'enervate' it, 'so as to do no mischief, or give any offence to the government.'" He remained faithful therefore to his principle of moderation.

255   Jurgen Habermas, "A Conversation about God and the World" from Part VII "Jerusalem, Athens, and Rome" in *Time of Transitions* (London: Polity, 1999), 151.

256   See for instance Os Guinness. Passim.

Chapter 9—First Newspapers in New England, India and China

257 My main source for this section is Marvin Olasky's detailed research in *Central Ideas in the Development of American Journalism*, op cit.

258 Harry S Stout, *The New England Soul: Preaching and Religious Culture in Colonial New England* (New York: Oxford University Press, 1986), 3, cited by Olasky, *Central*, 29.

259 Olasky, *Central*, 31.

260 Olasky, *Central*, 32.

261 Olasky, *Central,* 32.

262 Olasky, *Central,* 32.

263 For this and other details, I refer to Mark Knight's essay in the *Oxford Dictionary of National Biography* Vol. 25, 2004.

264 Knight, *ODNB*, 409.

265 Olasky*, Central*, 39, citing *Boston News-Letter*, April 30, 1704.

266 Olasky, *Central*, 39, citing *Boston News-Letter*, August 6, 1705.

267 Olasky, *Central*, 41, citing *Boston News-Letter*, January 21, 1723.

268 Olasky, *Central*, 42.

269 Olasky, *Central,* 43.

270 Olasky, *Central*, 44.

271 Christopher A Reed, *Gutenberg in Shanghai: Chinese Print Capitalism, 1876-1937* (Honolulu: University of Hawai'i Press, 2004). This "unique work of scholarship" (Francesca Bray and Timothy Brook) argues that China won back its prestige as pioneer producers of print via the European print shop process, "the world's first capitalist enterprise".

272 Reed, *Gutenberg*, 26.

273 Xiantao Zhang, *The Origins of the Modern Chinese Press: The Influence of the Protestant Missionary Press in Late Qing China* (London: Routledge, 2007).

274 Quoted by Zhang, *Origins,* 37

275 Zhang, *Origins*, 38.

276 Zhang, *Origins*, 65.

277 Zhang, *Origins*, 8.

278 Ibid.

279 Zhang, *Origins*, 35. This reference is obscure: Zhang cites "Article in File Box 3, China Personal, CWM/LMS, library of the School of

Oriental and African Studies". But given the then missionaries' obsession with probity and detail, it is highly likely to be recorded correctly. Zhang notes also (p. 35) that Sun Yat Sen was "influenced by the Taiping Rebellion in his youth and educated in a medical college set up by the LMS in Hong Kong."

280 Zhang, *Origins*, 8.

281 Zhang, *Origins*, 5.

282 Zhang, *Origins*, 8.

283 Zhang, *Origins*, 144.

284 2020 World Press Freedom Index | RSF Accessed 8 April 2022.

285 Report of a Secret Commission, published by *The Pall Mall Gazette*, July 6, 1885. W.T. Stead, "The Maiden Tribute of Modern Babylon - I" (The Pall Mall Gazette, July 6, 1885) | The W.T. Stead Resource Site (attackingthedevil.co.uk) Accessed 2 February 2023.

286 John Morley, *Recollections*, 2 vols (London, Macmillan: 1917).

287 22 October 1880, cited in Robertson Scott, *Life and Death of a Newspaper* (London, Methuen: 1952), 117.

288 All references are to Stewart J Brown's *WT Stead: Nonconformist and Newspaper Prophet* (Oxford, Oxford University Press: 2019), viif.

289 The website WT Stead Resource Site (or WTSR) is packed with information. For GB Shaw on Stead https://attackingthedevil.co.uk/w-t-stead-by-his-peers/w-t-stead-by-george-bernard-shaw-2/ Accessed 15 December 2022.

290 See Giles Udy, *Labour and the Gulag: Russia and the Seduction of the British Left* (London: Biteback, 2017).

291 Brown, *Stead*, 73.

292 Ibid.

293 Ibid., 74.

294 Ibid.

295 Ibid., 72.

STORY—Healing the broken: the Marine Surgeon's tale

296 John Burslem, "'Unless God Builds the House'" in John Mayberry and Richard Mann (eds) *God's Doctors Abroad* (East Wittering: Gooday Publishers, 1989), 70.

297 This story first appeared in *GO* magazine, the international in-house magazine of Interserve, formerly, the Bible and Medical Missionary Fellowship. July/September 1990, 5-6. It is used with

permission.

Chapter 10—Losing the Plot

298 Bryan Wilson, one of the two acknowledged masters of "secularization theory", made this point in *Religion in Secular Society* (London: Penguin, 1969). "Christianity militated strongly against all other religious beliefs, and in particular against magical ideas, but in doing so probably eventually ... made acceptance of Christian ideas more difficult" (p. 44). Cf. David Martin, *A General Theory of Secularization* (Aldershot: Ashgate, 1978) and *On Secularization: Towards a Revised General Theory* (place of publication not identified: Routledge, 2017).

299 Sigmund Freud, *Civilized Sexual Morality and Modern Nervous Illness* (London, Penguin: 2002 [1908]).

300 Freud, *Civilized*, 40.

301 Owen Chadwick, *The Secularization of the European Mind in the Nineteenth Century* (Cambridge: Cambridge University Press, 1975), 90.

302 Chadwick in this book argues that it is the association of atheism with social reform that rendered Marx's own Christian philosophical debt unpaid by the intelligentsia he influenced. It is now a commonplace idea that Marx would not have recognized himself as a "Marxist".

303 "Ethnicity of grooming gangs cannot be ignored, police told." *Daily Telegraph* lead story, 3 April 2023. See early research on this published by the Coalition for the Removal of Pimping, 2005.

304 See Appendix 2 for a list of definitions.

305 "We didn't change history, we rectified it." Comment by Sage Willoughby, one of the "Colston Four" who were acquitted of criminal damage after toppling the statue of slave trader and philanthropist Edward Colston at Bristol docks during a Black Lives Matter protest in June 2020.

306 Richard W Fonte, Peter W Wood and Ashley Thorne, *Recasting History: Are Race, Class, and Gender Dominating American History?* (New York: National Association of Scholars, 2013).

307 Lesslie Newbigin *Truth to Tell: The Gospel as Public Truth* (London: SPCK, 1991), 10.

308 Paul Ricoeur, "Narrative and Hermeneutics," in *Essays on Aesthetics: Perspectives on the Work of Monroe C Beardsley*, ed. John Fisher (Philadelphia: Temple Univ. Press, 1983), 153.

309 Mark I Wallace, "Introduction", in Paul Ricoeur, *Figuring the*

Sacred (Minneapolis, Minnesota: Fortress Press, 1995), 12.

310   Alasdair MacIntyre, *After Virtue* (London: Duckworth, 1987 edn), Ch. 15.

311   James W Sire, *The Universe Next Door* (Downers Grove, Il: IVP, 2009 edn), 20.

312   Sire, *Universe*, 20.

313   See James H Olthuis, "On Worldview" in *Stained Glass: Worldviews and Social Science*, (Lanham, Maryland: University Press of America, 1989), 26-40.

314   The nine alternatives are: Christian Theism, Deism, Naturalism, Nihilism, Existentialism, Eastern Pantheistic Monism, New Age (or Spirituality without Religion), Postmodernism and Islamic Theism. If you find yourself thinking that all are valid, you are a Postmodernist.

315   Areas of Suffolk struggling with cost of living as winter approaches | East Anglian Daily Times (eadt.co.uk) Accessed 24 November 2022.

316   Teens arrested after machete threats in town (msn.com).

317   MacIntyre, *Virtue*, 2.

318   Sir Bernard Jenkin said on the BBC *World at One* programme on Radio 4 of the Cameron/Osborne deal with China—known as the "Golden Era"—"What this is about is a complete strategic blindness about the nature of the Chinese Regime ... All we saw was the pound notes." Yet the *Daily Telegraph* had no sense of the significance of this in terms of any bigger picture of freedom from tyranny, or national safety, or even national strategy, when—on 16 July—the day after these comments were made, it carried no news or any analysis until the 67th page of its online edition, of the British government's final reneging on the Huawei telecommunications deal.

319   Newbigin, *Truth*, 10f.

320   See Appendix 2 for definitions of journalism.

321   We are, unawares, inheritors of the thinking of yet another philosopher, David Hume, who searched inside himself and "could not find a self".

STORY—"Truth is what we say it is"

322   Putin's justification of war to "liberate" Ukraine from Nazis was fictitious.

Chapter 11—Neutrality or Truth? Knowing What to Report

323 Mother Teresa, *Heart of Joy: The Transfiguring Power of Self-Giving* (Glasgow: Collins, 1987), 57.

324 Cited by Parker Palmer, *To Know as We are Known: Education as a Spiritual Journey* (San Francisco: HarperSanFrancisco, 1966), 57.

325 Esther Lightcap Meek, *Loving to Know: Covenant Epistemology* (Eugene, Oregon: Cascade, 2011), 32.

326 Cf. Iain McGilchrist, *The Matter with Things: Our Brains, Our Delusions and the Unmasking of the World* (London: Perspectival Press, 2022).

327 Ronald Rolheiser OMI, *The Shattered Lantern* (London: Hodder & Stoughton, 1994), 46.

328 Meek, *Loving*, 26.

329 Colin Gunton, *Enlightenment and Alienation: An Essay towards a Trinitarian Theology* (Grand Rapids, Michigan: Eerdmans, 1985), 38. Cited by Meek, *Loving*, 25f.

330 Meek, *Loving*, 33.

331 Kristi Mair, *More Truth: Searching for certainty in an uncertain world* (London: InterVarsity Press, 2019), 52.

332 Heawood, *Myth*, 96.

333 Jean-François Lyotard, *The Postmodern Condition: A Report on Knowledge* (tr. Geoff Bennington and Brian Massumi) (Minneapolis, Minnesota: University of Minnesota Press, c1984), 7.

334 Jill Abramson traces the gradual and thorough breaching of the almost sacrosanct "wall" between business and news in her brilliant book *Merchants of Truth: Inside the News Revolution* (London: Penguin Random House, 2019), 69ff.

335 Sire, *Universe*, particularly Chapter 9, "The Vanished Horizon".

336 Sire, *Universe*, 215.

337 Comprehensively covered by Ricky Sutton's Substack newsletter, *Future News*.

338 "Outlets such as *The Wall Street Journal*, *The Economist*, *Financial Times*, Bloomberg, CNBC and *Forbes* continue serving massive audiences in the millions and employing journalists by the thousands. Several new players have emerged." Paul Glader, "Wisdom Journalism Flourishes While Other Journalism Languishes" (kirbylaingcentre.co.uk) Accessed 13 December 2022.

339 See Bell, *Death*, passim.

340   David Landrum, "Persecution of Christians in Nigeria is driven by Islamism not climate change" *Premier Christianity*, 2 August 2022. Accessed 3 August 2022.

341   George Steiner, *Real Presences* (Chicago: University of Chicago Press, 1989), 225.

342   Gertrude Himmelfarb has a good discussion on this in her *On Looking into the Abyss: Untimely Thoughts on Culture and Society* (New York: Knopf, 1994).

343   Switzerland's neutrality as a nation during World War II was not based on a stand for "truth" but for pacifism.

344   Aidan White, *To Tell You the Truth*. Manuscript draft, p. 17.

345   Barbie Zelizer and Stuart Allen (eds) *Journalism After September 11*, (New York and London: Routledge, 2002).

346   Bell, *Death*, 94.

347   Marvin Olasky and Warren Cole Smith, *Prodigal Press: Confronting the Anti-Christian Bias of the American News Media* (Phillipsburg, New Jersey: P&R Publishing, 2013), Appendix D, 148-153.

348   Olasky and Cole Smith, *Prodigal,* Chapter 4.

349   For a good analysis of public discourse as "hegemonic struggle" see Ben Obley's "Is Surging Hate Crime in the UK a Progressive Hoax?" in *Quillette*, 18 July 2019. https://quillette.com/2019/07/18/is-surging-hate-crime-in-the-uk-a-progressive-hoax/

350   Lamin Sanneh, in L Newbigin, J Taylor and L Sanneh, *Faith and Power: Christianity and Islam in "Secular" Britain*, (London: SPCK, 1998), 71.

351   Christopher Walker, "Small Times, Bad Times", *British Journalism Review,* Vol. 16 No. 2, (2005), 26-30. My emphasis.

352   Matthew 13: 24-30.

353   "Free speech threat from 'climate of censorship'", *The Telegraph* 25 March 2024, p. 4.

354   Parker Palmer, *To Know as We are Known* (San Francisco: HarperSanFrancisco, 1966), 2, cited by Meek, *Loving*, 23.

355   Ed West Substack, *Wrong Side of History*, April 15, 2024.

Chapter 12—The Fourth Estate: Recovery of a Mission

356   The story in Appendix 1 is a particularly graphic account of the spiritual underpinning of a forgotten war: the war in Northern Uganda which resulted in the deaths, disappearance and mutilation of thousands

of children.

357 Paul Marshall et al., *Blind Spot: When Journalists don't get Religion* (New York: Oxford University Press, 2009), 32.

358 Marshall, *Blind*, 32f.

359 Charles Elliott, *Memory and Salvation* (London: DLT, 1995), 183.

360 David P Barash, "Believing is Seeing", *The Chronicle of Higher Education* (June 27, 2003). No pages. Online: http://chronicle.com/article/Believing-is-Seeingf/11865. Cited by Meek, *Loving*, 21.

361 *Visions of Vocation: Common Grace for the Common Good* (Downers Grove, Illinois.: InterVarsity Press, 2014). Cited by Mair, *More*, 43.

362 Pettegree, *News*, 2.

363 Pettegree, *News*, 2.

364 troth - Wiktionary. Accessed 26 October 2022.

365 John Wyatt and Stephen N Williams (eds) *The Robot Will See You Now* (London: SPCK, 2021) with a foreword by Justin Welby.

366 NLA Media University College Gimlekollen in Kristiansand, Norway is one important one.

367 citizen journalist tahrir square khartoum - Bing images. Accessed 12 May 2022.

368 Shailvee Sharda (2 March 2017). "Plagued by 'divine curse', Musahars see no redemption in new politicians". *The Times of India*. Accessed 28 August 2019.

369 Kachhwa Christian Hospital was a work of the London Missionary Society, founded in the 1880s and run—when I visited—by Indian former North Middlesex Hospital neurologist Raju Abraham and his wife Catherine.

370 Geldof visited Africa ten years after the Live Aid concert that raised £150 million for famine relief there. He was distressed by the fact that things seemed to be even worse. Blair invited him to set up the Commission for Africa to research poverty on the continent for a year and report back. The report formed the substance of the G8 Gleneagles African debt and aid package in 2005.

371 Mair, *More*, Chapter 2.

Chapter 13—Conclusion and a Call to Action

372 Albert Camus, unreferenced, cited by Mair, *More*, 17.

373 Peter Matthiessen, *The Snow Leopard* (New York: Viking Press,

1978).

374 Eugene Delacroix, *The Journal of Eugene Delacroix* (London: Phaidon Press, 2001). Cited by Mair, *More*, 19.

375 Charles Taylor, *Sources of the Self* (Cambridge, Ms: Harvard University Press, 1989), xi.

376 Palmer, *Know*, 7.

377 Anna Abram, "Educating for Truth in a Climate of Fake News: Conversation with Thomas Aquinas, Bernard Williams, Wolfgang Kuhne and Pope Francis" in *Louvain Studies 42* (2019): 3-25.

378 A surprising amount of subscriber detail was provided by Mailchimp Newsletter analytics.

Epilogue

379 7 July London bombings: What happened that day? - BBC News

380 Mair, *More*, 58.

381 Hannah Shah, *The Imam's Daughter: the remarkable true story of a young girl's escape from her harrowing past* (London: Rider, 2010).

382 Zacharias Pieri, *Tablighi Jamaat* (London: Lapido Media Publishing, 2012).

383 Jenny Taylor (2005) "Taking spirituality seriously: Northern Uganda and Britain's 'Break the Silence' Campaign", *The Round Table*, 94:382, 559-574, DOI: 10.1080/00358530500303668

384 Ibid.

Appendix 1

385 Conversation with author, Boma Hotel, Kitgum, 15 February 2005.

386 For particularly sensitive material on the military and spiritual legacies of the Acholi, see Ruddy Doom and Koen Vlassenroot, "Kony's message: a new Koine? The Lord's Resistance Army in Northern Uganda", African Affairs , 98 (390): pp. 5-36, 1 January 1999

387 It is the barbarity of these atrocities that are attributed by many Acholis to the peculiarly religious nature of Alice Lakwena's original mission to cleanse the land of its sins. Both Kevin Ward (2001) and Heike Behrend (2004) tell the horrific story of the killing of a pregnant woman from an area just before the Karuma bridge over the Nile. Soldiers fleeing north in 1986 not only killed the woman, but mutilated her pregnant body, tying it to a tree and leaving the dead foetus underneath (Ward, 2001, p. 198). Kony's evils are either attributed to 'vengeful spirits' unleashed on society as a result (Ward, 2001, p. 199) or, according to Msgr Cipriano Kihangire in an Easter address in 1987,

believed to exist because "We can now see that these present sufferings are the result of our own sin" (Gersony, 1997, p. 9). Either way, the discourse is religious.

388 BBC World Service, *Focus on Africa*, 10 November 2003.

389 The author, a journalist and writer, was Head of Media at CMS at the time of her first visit to Kitgum and of the subsequent campaign.

390 Behrend's work studies sympathetically the Holy Spirit Mobile Forces, headed from 1986 by Alice Auma and later by her father Severino, then by her 'cousin' Joseph Kony, allegedly a former Catholic altar boy, who renamed the movement several times. All three were possessed in turn by the Spirit Lakwena—which means 'Messenger' in Acholi. Behrend makes the case that both leaders were initially attempting to purify the Acholi people—and, in Kony's case, Uganda itself (Behrend, 2004, p. 179)—from the repercussions of murder and rape after the Amin and Obote regimes, in which Acholis played a prominent part as officers and footsoldiers. However, she is clear that the movement degenerated "into ever more brutal bands of brigands" caught up "in the logic of violence and counter-violence" (p. 189). Ward examines the role of the Anglican and Catholic churches in fostering the factionalism that produced violence (Ward, 2001, p. 190)—and more latterly in articulating the suffering of the Acholis and preserving a cultural identity and public morale.

391 I refer to the *Abingdon Dictionary of Living Religions* (Crim, 1981) for a working definition of spirituality as "that which gives life to any animate thing; the inner, essential or non-corporeal dimension of any animate thing; a non-corporeal but animate substance or entity". Belief systems affect definitions in English. Only the belief system of Western secularism renders all such definitions invalid.

392 Betty Bigombe's description, in conversation with the author, Acholi Inn, 14 February 2005. Bigombe, the government peace negotiator and former Minister for Pacification in the North, has had nine meetings in the bush with Kony and his commanders, at one of which she was forced to strip to her pants and be 'purified' with shea oil.

393 Most of these are listed in the References.

394 See Human Rights Watch, *Abducted and Abused: Renewed Conflict in Northern Uganda*, 15 (12A), New York: Human Rights Watch, July 2002, p. 4. At the time of writing, this figure had expanded to 1.6 million, cited by Hillary Benn, Secretary of State, Department for International Development, in answer to Written Question 204703, 15 December 2004. Benn was probably referring to the World Food

Programme figure, as of May 2004, of a total of 1 609 744 people in camps throughout northern and eastern Uganda. World Vision reported that over 10 000 children were abducted between June 2002 and December 2003 alone.

395 Human Rights Watch, *Abducted and Abused*, Section V, pp. 41-63. My host, the Bishop's wife, Margaret Ojwang, had lost close members of her family. According to eyewitnesses, they had been shot at point blank range by government forces who accused them of failing to warn them of an LRA ambush, when they had gone back to their fields to harvest cassava. See *Church Times*, August 2003, p. 3.

396 Acholiland has a phenomenal love of education and there are, anecdotally, 1000 Acholi PhDs—nearly all of whom live abroad. Those educated Acholis who remain, and are capable of leadership, are deeply traumatized.

397 For instance, 800 huts had burnt down in a single fire in Parabongo Camp, six kilometres northeast of Gulu, two months before my visit there in February 2005.

398 "The government had made no advance arrangements for health, sanitation, food or other assistance, aggravating the increased infant mortality which predictably arose in these locations" (Gersony, 1997, p.49)

399 Parliament of Uganda (2004, p. 19, para. 3.2.4).

400 Ibid., p. 13, para. 3.

401 Government of Uganda statistic, cited in World Vision (2004, p. 28)

402 Conversation with Ugandan church leader whose brother was in the UPDF.

403 BBC World Service News, "Uganda's Lost Innocents", 5 July 2003, at http://news.bbc.co.uk/1/hi/world/africa/3046426.stm

404 CMS also founded girls' education in Acholiland. For lively accounts of the CMS's somewhat inauspicious beginnings, see John Keith Russell (1966), Heike Behrend (2004, especially the section "Evangelization in Acholi and the 'invention' of witchcraft", pp. 113-119) and Kevin Ward, "The armies of the Lord: Christianity, rebels and the state in Northern Uganda 1986-1999", *Journal of Religion in Africa*, 31 (2): 187-221, 1 January 2001

405 "Advocacy for Kitgum", Report to Events Officer, 2 April 2003.

406 BBC *Today* programme website at http://www.bbc.co.uk/radio4/today/listenagain/zthursday_20030821.shtml

407 Mark Thomas, column in *The New Statesman*, 1 December 2003,

p. 13.

408 Mothers' Union website report at http://www.muwinchester.org.uk/bishop_ojwang.htm.

409 Note of meeting with Lord Brentford and FCO officials, 4 November 2004.

410 BBC World Service, *Focus on Africa*, 10 November 2003.

411 Emphasis added. The comparison with Palestine was not picked up anywhere.

412 http://www.up.ligi.ubc.ca/news_feature_story.htm.

413 "Donors propose plan for peace", *The Monitor*, 17 December 2003.

414 Conversation with author at World Vision project offices, Nakasero Road, Gulu, 15 February 2005.

415 Email to author 20 April 2005.

416 *New Vision*, 8 March 2004.

417 Niringiye, an international missionary statesman and theologian was consecrated Assistant Bishop of Kampala on 22 August 2004.

418 "Army kills six rebels in Gulu", *New Vision*, 26 February 2005.

419 Interview with author, Kacoke Madit offices, London, 11 March 2005.

420 ARLPI publicity flyer.

421 Conversation with author at Diocesan Compound, Gulu, 14 February 2005.

422 http://www.cpwr.org/2004parliament/parliament/carus.htm.

423 ARLPI was the first African organization to receive the Niwano Peace Prize, after 21 years.

424 Surrender is not the appropriate word, since it implies military success where this was plainly absent. Kony condemned the Amnesty and returnees testify that one of his techniques to continue holding abductees hostage is to tell them they will not be accepted by their community if they try to return home. So far the Act has handled more than 12 000 cases around the country, 42.5% are ex-LRA (World Vision, 2004).

425 BBC, 'Church fears Uganda rebel threat', 17 June 2003, at http://news.bbc.co.uk/2/hi/africa/2996824.stm.

426 Conversation with author, Hotel Boma, Kitgum, 14 February 2005.

427 Email to author, 20 April 2005.

428 Gersony (1997, p. 9), citing Ofcansky (1996).

429 Text supplied in email by Kacoke Madit, London, 26 June 2003.

430 Telephone conversation, 26 April 2005.

431 A good eye-witness account of the *mato oput* ritual is given by Fr Carlos Rodriguez in a report, *Whose Justice? Perceptions of Uganda's Amnesty Act 2000: The Potential for Conflict Resolution and Long-term Reconciliation*, published by the Gulu-based Refugee Law Project. He writes: "Homicide, in Acholi cultural belief…asks for revenge and, as a consequence, it provokes fear".

432 Interview with author, Kacoke Madit offices, London, 11 March 2005

433 World Vision (2004), p. 15

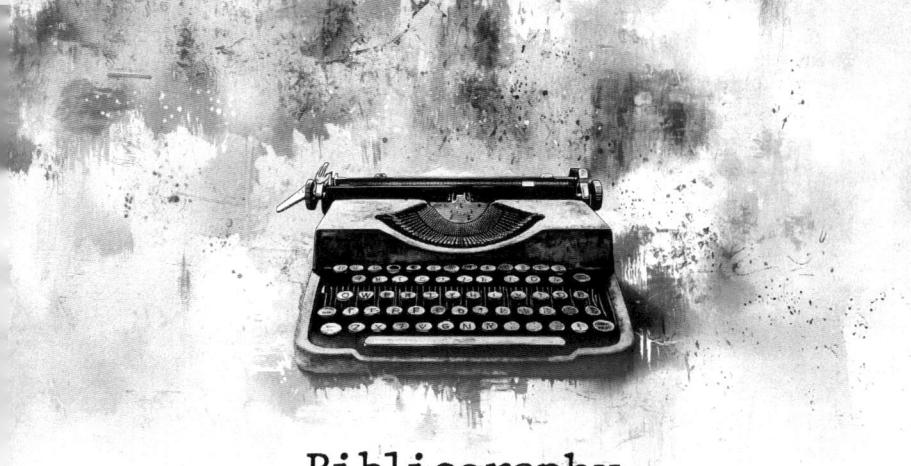

Bibliography

1. Benedict Anderson, *Imagined Communities: Reflections on the Origin and Spread of Nationalism* (London: Verso, 1991).
2. Jan Assman, *Of God and Gods: Egypt, Israel, and the Rise of Monotheism* (Madison: University of Wisconsin Press, 2008).
3. Erich Auerbach, *Mimesis: The Representation of Reality in Western Literature* (New York: Doubleday, 1957).
4. Saint Augustine, *Confessions* (London: Penguin, 1961).
5. David L D'Avray, "Method in the Study of Medieval Sermons" in Nicole Beriou and David L D'Avray (eds) *Modern Questions about Medieval Sermons and Essays on Marriage, Death, History and Sanctity* (Spoleto: Centro Italiano di Studi sull'Alto medioevo, 1994).
6. Roland Bainton, *Christianity* (Boston, New York: Mariner, 2000).
7. Karl Barth, *The Epistle to the Romans* (tr. Edwyn C. Hoskyns) (Oxford: Oxford University Press, 1933).
8. Craig G Bartholomew, *Introducing Biblical Hermeneutics: A Comprehensive Framework for Hearing God in Scripture* (Ada, MI: Baker Publishing Group. Kindle Edition, 2015).
9. ----, *God and the Old Testament* (London: Society for Promoting Christian Knowledge, 2022).
10. ----, *The God Who Acts in History* (Grand Rapids, Michigan: Eerdmans, 2020).
11. Lorenzo C Bautista, et al. (eds) *Faith and Bayan: Evangelical Christian Engagement in the Philippine Context* (London: Langham Global, 2022).

12. Heike Behrend, *Alice Lakwena & the Holy Spirits: War in Northern Uganda 1986-97* (Oxford: James Currey and Kampala: Fountain, 2004).
13. Martin Bell, *War and the Death of News: Reflections of a Grade B Reporter* (London: One World, 2017).
14. Peter WM Blayney, *The Bookshops in Paul's Cross Churchyard*, Occasional Papers of the Bibliographical Society, 5 (1990).
15. Alain de Botton, *The News: A User's Manual* (London: Penguin, 2020).
16. Henry Fox Bourne, *English Newspapers* 2 volumes. 1887.
17. Melvyn Bragg, *William Tyndale: A Very Brief History* (London: SPCK, 2017).
18. Stewart J Brown, *WT Stead: Non-Conformist and Newspaper Prophet* (Oxford: Oxford University Press, 2019).
19. Nicholas Brownlees, *The Language of Periodical News in Seventeenth-Century England* (Newcastle upon Tyne: Cambridge Scholars Publishing, 2011).
20. Anthony Burgess, "Introduction", in Defoe, D [1722] *A Journal of the Plague Year*, A Burgess and C Bristow (eds), (London: Penguin, 1966).
21. John Burslem, "'Unless God Builds the House'". In John Mayberry and Richard Mann (eds) *God's Doctors Abroad* (East Wittering, Gooday Publishers: 1989), pp. 69-83.
22. Jean Calvin, *Institutes of the Christian Religion* (tr. Henry Beveridge) (Peabody, Massachusetts: Hendrickson, [1545] 2009).
23. Thomas Carlyle, *On Heroes, Hero-Worship and the Heroic in History*. "Lecture V: The Hero as Man of Letters: Johnson, Rousseau, Burns" (London: Dent, 1908).
24. Owen Chadwick, *The Secularization of the European Mind in the Nineteenth Century* (Cambridge: Cambridge University Press, 1975).
25. ----, *The Reformation* (London: Penguin, 1990).
26. DC Collins, *A Handlist of News Pamphlets 1590-1610* (London: South-West Essex Technical College, 1943).
27. Martin Conboy and John Steel (eds) *The Routledge Companion to British Media History* (London: Routledge, 2015).
28. Keith Crim, *Abingdon Dictionary of Living Religions*, (Nashville, Tennessee: Abingdon, 1981).
29. Folke Dahl, *A Bibliography of English Corantos and Periodical Newsbooks, 1620-1642* (London: Bibliographical Society, 1952).
30. Nick Davies, *Flat Earth News: An Award-Winning Reporter*

Exposes Falsehood, Distortion and Propaganda in the Global Media (London: Vintage, 2009).
31. ----, *Hack Attack: How the Truth Caught up with Rupert Murdoch* (London: Vintage Books, 2015).
32. Eamon Duffy, *The Stripping of the Altars: Traditional Religion in England 1400-1580* (New Haven and London: Yale University Press, 2005).
33. Elizabeth Eisenstein, *The Printing Press as an Agent of Change: Communications and Cultural Transformations in Early-Modern Europe*, 2 Vols (Cambridge: Cambridge University Press, 1979).
34. ----, *The Printing Revolution in Early Modern Europe* (Cambridge: Cambridge University Press, 2005).
35. ----, *Divine Art, Infernal Machine* (Philadelphia: University of Pennsylvania Press, 2011).
36. George Eliot, *Romola* (London: Dent, and New York: Dutton, 1912).
37. Charles Elliott, *Memory and Salvation* (London: Darton, Longman & Todd, 1995).
38. Stephen Ellis and Gerrie ter Haar, *Worlds of Power: Religious Thought and Political Practice in Africa* (London: Hurst, 2004).
39. Keith Ferdinando, *The Triumph of Christ in African Perspective: A Study of Demonology and Redemption in the African Context* (Carlisle: Paternoster Press, 1999).
40. Richard W Fonte, Peter W Wood and Ashley Thorne, *Recasting History: Are Race, Class, and Gender Dominating American History?* (New York, NY: National Association of Scholars, 2013).
41. Michel Foucault, *Discipline and Punish: The Birth of the Prison* (tr. Alan Sheridan) (New York: Pantheon, 1977).
42. Joseph Frank, *The Beginnings of the English Newspaper 1620-1660* (Cambridge, Mass.: Harvard University Press, 1961).
43. Sigmund Freud, "Civilized Sexual Morality and Modern Nervous Illness" in *Civilization and its Discontents* (London: Penguin, 2002 [1908]).
44. ----, *Civilization and its Discontents* (London: Penguin, 2002 [1908]).
45. Paul Frosh and Amit Pinchevski (eds) *Media Witnessing: Testimony in the Age of Mass Communication* (Basingstoke: Palgrave Macmillan, 2009).
46. Gérard Genette (tr. Jane E Lewin), *Paratexts: Thresholds of Interpretation* (Cambridge: Cambridge University Press, 1997).
47. Robert Gersony, *The anguish of Northern Uganda: results of a*

field-based assessment of the civil conflicts in Northern Uganda, report submitted to US Embassy Kampala and USAID Mission, Kampala, August 1997.
48. Gordon Graham, *The Shape of the Past: A Philosophical Approach to History* (Oxford: Oxford University Press, 1997).
49. ----, "A Conversation about God and the World" from Part VII "Jerusalem, Athens, and Rome" in *Time of Transitions* (London: Polity, 1999).
50. Jurgen Habermas (tr. Thomas Burger), *The Structural Transformation of the Public Sphere: An Inquiry into a Category of Bourgeois Society* (Cambridge, Mass: MIT Press, 1989).
51. Jackie Harrison, *The Civil Power of the News* (Palgrave Macmillan ebook, 2019).
52. Jonathan Heawood, *The Press Freedom Myth* (London: Biteback, 2019).
53. Gertrude Himmelfarb, *On Looking into the Abyss: Untimely Thoughts on Culture and Society* (New York: Knopf, 1994).
54. Tom Holland, *Dominion: The Making of the Western Mind* (London: Little, Brown, 2019).
55. Walter Lippmann, *Liberty and the News* (New York: Harcourt Brace and Howe, 1920).
56. ----, *The Phantom Public* (New York: Macmillan, 1930).
57. ----, *Public Opinion* (New York: MacMillan, 1949 edn).
58. Jean-François Lyotard, *The Postmodern Condition: A Report on Knowledge* (tr. Geoff Bennington and Brian Massumi) (Minneapolis : University of Minnesota Press, c1984).
59. Alasdair MacIntyre, *After Virtue: A Study in Moral Theory* (London: Duckworth, 1981).
60. ----, *Whose Justice, Which Rationality* (London: Duckworth, 1988).
61. Kristi Mair, *More Truth: Searching for certainty in an uncertain world* (London: InterVarsity Press, 2019).
62. Scott M Manetsch, *Calvin's Company of Pastors: Pastoral Care and the Emerging Reformed Church 1536-1609* (Oxford: Oxford University Press, 2013).
63. Vishal Mangalwadi, *This Book Changed Everything* (Nivedit Good Books, 2019).
64. Andrew Marr, *My Trade: A Short History of British Journalism* (London: Macmillan, 2004).
65. Christopher Marsh, *Popular Religion in Sixteenth-Century England*

(Basingstoke: MacMillan, 1998).
66. Paul Marshall, Lela Gilbert and Roberta Green Ahmanson (eds) *Blind Spot: When Journalists don't Get Religion* (New York: Oxford University Press, 2009).
67. David Martin, *A General Theory of Secularization* (Aldershot: Ashgate, 1978).
68. ----, *On Secularization: Towards a Revised General Theory* (place of publication not given: Routledge, 2017).
69. Peter Matthiessen, *The Snow Leopard* (New York: Viking Press, 1978).
70. Marshall McLuhan and Quentin Fiore, *The Medium is the Massage* (London et al: Penguin, 1996).
71. ----, (Eric McLuhan and Jacek Szklarek, eds), *The Medium and the Light: Reflections on Religion* (Toronto: Stoddart, 1999).
72. Esther Lightcap Meek, *Loving to Know: Covenant Epistemology* (Eugene, Oregon: Cascade, 2011).
73. James Mill, "Liberty of the Press", in his *Essays on Government, Jurisprudence, Liberty of the Press and Law of Nations* (New York: Kelly, 1967).
74. John Milton, *Paradise Lost* (London: Methuen & Co, 1962 edn).
75. ----, *Areopagitica* (ed. John W Hales) (Oxford: Clarendon Press, 1904).
76. Mary Morrissey, *Politics and the Paul's Cross Sermons, 1558-1642* (Oxford: Oxford University Press, 2011).
77. Malcolm Muggeridge, *The Green Stick: Chronicles of Wasted Time Vol. 1* (Glasgow: Collins, 1981 [1972]).
78. Lewis Mumford, *The City in History: Its Origins, Its Transformations and Its Prospects* (Harmondsworth: Penguin, 1973).
79. Jeremy Musson, *The Development of Reformation Thought and Devotion in England, with Particular Reference to the Works of, and Those Associated With, Fra Girolamo Savonarola* (Unpublished thesis, London: Warburg Institute, 1989).
80. Vo Huong Nam, *Digital Media and Youth Discipleship: Pitfalls and Promise* (Unpublished Thesis, Aberdeen: Aberdeen University, 2020).
81. Lesslie Newbigin, *Truth to Tell: The Gospel as Public Truth* (London: SPCK, 1991).
82. ----, *A Walk Through the Bible* (Louisville: Westminster John Knox, 1999).
83. James O'Donnell, *Augustine 'Confessions' Volumes I-III* (Oxford: Oxford University Press, 1992).

84. Oliver O'Donovan, *Resurrection and Moral Order: An Outline for Evangelical Ethics* (Leicester: IVP, 1986).
85. ----, *The Desire of the Nations: Rediscovering the Roots of Political Theology* (Cambridge: Cambridge University Press, 1999).
86. Thomas P Ofcansky, *Uganda: Tarnished Pearl of Africa* (Oxford: Westview Press, 1996).
87. Hon. Ronald Reagan Okumu, *It's for You to Give a Hand: Analytical Proposal for Peace in Northern Uganda* (Gulu: Office of MP for Aswa County, Gulu, 2003).
88. Marvin Olasky, *Central Ideas in the Development of American Journalism: A Narrative History* (New Jersey and London: Lawrence Erlbaum Associates, 1991).
89. WR Owens and PN Furbank (eds) *Political and Economic Writings of Daniel Defoe*, Vol. 8 "Social Reform" (London: Pickering & Chatto, 2000).
90. Steven E Ozment, *The Reformation in the Cities: The Appeal of Protestantism to Sixteenth-Century Germany and Switzerland* (New Haven and London: Yale University Press, 1975).
91. Dennis Pain, *The Bending of Spears: Producing Consensus for Peace and Development in Northern Uganda* (London: International Alert and Kacoke Madit, 1997).
92. Parker Palmer, *To Know as We are Known: Education as a Spiritual Journey* (San Francisco: HarperSanFrancisco, 1966).
93. Parliament of Uganda, *Report of the Select Committee on Humanitarian and Security Situation in the Acholi, Teso and Lango Subregions* (Kampala: Parliament of Uganda, 2004).
94. Andrew Pettegree, *The Growth of a Provincial Press in Sixteenth-century Europe* The Stenton Lecture (Reading: University of Reading, 2006).
95. ----, *The Book in the Renaissance* (New Haven and London: Yale University Press, 2011).
96. ----, *The Invention of News: How the World Came to Know about itself* (New Haven and London: Yale University Press, 2015).
97. ----, *Brand Luther* (New York: Penguin, 2016).
98. Michael Pickering, 'Devaluation of History in Media Studies' in Martin Conboy and John Steel (eds) *The Routledge Companion to British Media History* (London: Routledge, 2015).
99. Melanie Phillips, *Londonistan* (New York: Encounter, 2006).
100. James Raven, *The Business of Books: Booksellers and the English Book* (New Haven: Yale University Press, 2007).
101. Joad Raymond, *The Invention of the Newspaper: English Newsbooks*

1641-1649 (Oxford: Clarendon Press, 1996).
102. ----, *Pamphlets and Pamphleteering in Early Modern Britain* (Cambridge: Cambridge University Press, 2003).
103. T Wemyss Reid, *Memoirs of Sir Wemyss Reid 1842-1885*, ed. Stuart J Reid (London: Cassell, 1905).
104. Christopher Reed, *Gutenberg in Shanghai: Chinese Print Capitalism, 1876-1937* (Honolulu: University of Hawai'i Press, 2004).
105. Michael Reeves, *Unquenchable Flame* (London: InterVarsityPress, 2009).
106. Brian Richardson, *Printing, Readers and Writers in Renaissance Italy* (Cambridge: Cambridge University Press, 1999).
107. Paul Ricoeur, "Narrative and Hermeneutics," in John Fisher (ed.) *Essays on Aesthetics: Perspectives on the Work of Monroe C Beardsley* (Philadelphia: Temple Univ. Press, 1983).
108. ----, *Figuring the Sacred* (Minneapolis: Fortress, 1995).
109. Ronald Rolheiser OMI, *The Shattered Lantern* (London: Hodder & Stoughton, 1994).
110. Alan Rusbridger, *Breaking News: The Remaking of Journalism and Why It Matters Now* (Edinburgh: Canongate, 2018).
111. John Keith Russell, *Men without God? A Study of the Impact of the Christian Message in the North of Uganda* (London: The Highway Press, 1966).
112. Seth L Sanders, *The Invention of Hebrew* (Urbana: University of Illinois, 2009).
113. Lamin Sanneh, *Translating the Message: The Missionary Impact on Culture* (Mary Knoll, NY: Orbis Books, 1992).
114. Lamin Sanneh, "Islam, Christianity and Public Policy" in Lesslie Newbigin, Lamin Sanneh and Jenny Taylor, *Faith and Power: Christianity and Islam in "Secular" Britain* (Eugene, ON: Wipf & Stock, 2005 edn).
115. Julianne Schultz, *Reviving the Fourth Estate: Democracy, Accountability and the Media* (Cambridge: Cambridge University Press, 1998).
116. Antonin Sertillanges OP, *The Intellectual Life: Its Spirit, Conditions, Methods* (tr. Mary Ryan) (Westminster, MD: Newman Press, 1960).
117. Desmond Seward, *The Burning of the Vanities: Savonarola and the Borgia Pope* (Stroud: Sutton, 2006).
118. Hannah Shah, *The Imam's Daughter: The remarkable true story of a young girl's escape from her harrowing past* (London: Rider, 2010).

119. Larry Siedentop, *Inventing the Individual* (London: Allen Lane, 2017).
120. R Silverstone, *Media and Morality: On the Rise of the Mediapolis* (London: Wiley, 2007).
121. James W Sire, *The Universe Next Door* (Downers Grove, Il: IVP, 2009 edn).
122. George Steiner, *Real Presences* (Chicago: University of Chicago Press, 1989).
123. John RW Stott, *The Lausanne Covenant: An Exposition and Commentary* (London: Scripture Union [for the] Lausanne Committee for World Evangelization, 1979).
124. ----, (updated Christopher JH Wright) *Christian Mission in the Modern World* (Downers Grove: InterVarsity Press, 2016).
125. James Sutherland, *Defoe* (London: Methuen, 1937; revd. 1950).
126. ----, *Daniel Defoe: A Critical Study* (Cambridge, Mass: Harvard University Press, 1971).
127. RN Swanson, *Indulgences in Late Medieval England: Passport to Paradise* (Cambridge: Cambridge University Press, 2007).
128. Richard Tarnas, *The Passion of the Western Mind: Understanding the Ideas that have Shaped our Worldview* (London: Pimlico, 1996).
129. Charles Taylor, *Sources of the Self* (Cambridge, Ms: Harvard University Press, 1989).
130. Jenny M Taylor, "The Multicultural Myth" in L Newbigin, L Sanneh and J Taylor *Faith and Power: Christianity and Islam in "Secular" Britain* (London: SPCK, 1998), 75-13
131. ----, *After Secularism: Inner City Governance and the New Religious Discourse* [Ph.D. Thesis] (London: University of London, 2001).
132. Mother Teresa, *Heart of Joy: The Transfiguring Power of Self-Giving* (Glasgow: Collins, 1987).
133. Graham Tomlin, *Luther & his World* (Oxford: Lion Hudson, 2012).
134. Giles Udy, *Labour and the Gulag: Russia and the Seduction of the British Left* (London: Biteback, 2017).
135. Douglas Underwood, *From Yahweh to Yahoo: The Religious Roots of the Secular Press* (Urbana and Chicago: University of Illinois Press, 2008).
136. Elizabeth Warren, *Savonarola: The Florentine Martyr, A Reformer Before the Reformation* (London: SW Partridge, 1880).
137. Max Weber, *The Protestant Ethic and the Spirit of Capitalism* (London and New York, Routledge: 1997 edn [1930]).
138. Richard West, *Daniel Defoe: The Life and Strange Adventures* (United States: Da Capo Press, 1999).

139. Joel Wiener, *The Americanization of the British Press, 1830s-1914: Speed in the Age of Transatlantic Journalism* (Basingstoke, Hampshire: Palgrave Macmillan, 2011).
140. Garry Wills, *Augustine's Confessions: A Biography* (New York: Doubleday, 1979).
141. Bryan Wilson, *Religion in Secular Society* (London: Penguin, 1969).
142. World Vision, *Pawns of Politics: Children, Conflict and Peace in Northern Uganda* (Gulu: World Vision International, 2004).
143. Barbie Zelizer and Stuart Allen (eds) *Journalism After September 11* (New York and London: Routledge, 2002).

Reports

Frances Cairncross, *The Cairncross Review: A Sustainable Future for Journalism* (London: Department for Culture, Media and Sport, 12 February 2019).

Index

abduction, of children, 14, 15-18, 283, 286, 290, 293, 297
Acholi Religious Leaders Peace Initiative (ARLPI), 284, 291-292, 295
Acholiland, 277, 280, 288, 292, 294, 324
Africa, 14-18, 20, 273, 287-288, 296, 320-321
AIDS, 20, 281, 293
Albrecht of Brandenburg, Archbishop, 102
Allen, Young John, 192
Amnesty International, 16, 288
Andersson, Hilary, 14-15, 282
Animal Farm (Orwell), 34
apostasy, 23
Areopagitica (Milton), 156, 158
Aristotle, 82
Arnold of Brescia, 80, 110
Auerbach, Erich, 59-60, 61, 62, 65, 69, 71
Augustine of Hippo, 65-67, 69-71, 74, 102, 108
Auma, Alice, see Lakwena, Alice

Badby, John, 147
Barash, David P, 250
Barlaam, 81
Bartholomew, Craig, 47
Basil, St, 58-59
Baylor University, 1
BBC, 14-15, 26, 39, 264-266, 282-283, 285, 292, 302, 318
Bede, 144
Behrend, Heike, 276, 323, 324
Bell, Martin, 242-243
Bennett, James Gordon, 198
Benzing, Josef, 108
Bigombe, Betty, 323
Bill of Rights, The, 158
Black Lives Matter, 215
Blair, Tony, 16, 284, 286, 321
Blandford, Revd Dr Walter, 160
Boccaccio, 81
Boleyn, Anne, 141
Bolingbroke, Henry St John Viscount, 172-173
Botticelli, 97
Bragg, Melvyn, 139, 140

Break the Silence Campaign, The, 15-18, 11, 273, 277, 282, 286-287, 297, 301
British Library, The, 195
Brown, Stewart J, 316
Brownlees, Nicholas, 149, 153, 154
Burke, Edmund, 173-174
Burslem, Hilary, 203, 205-206, 214, 216, 222
Burslem, John, 203-206, 213-214, 216, 220, 222

Cairncross, Dame Frances, 300
Caldwell, Elizabeth, 151
Calvin, Jean, 126-130, 133-135, 150, 154, 156, 177, 197, 202
camps, for internally displaced people, 14, 16, 17, 276, 280-281, 283, 286-287, 290, 292, 293, 297, 323-324
Campbell, John, 184-185
Camus, Albert, 259-260
Carlyle, Thomas, 145, 174
Caxton, William, 125
Chadwick, Owen, 112, 317
Channel 4 News, 285
Charles University, Prague, 86
Charles V, Emperor, 108, 125, 141
Charles VIII, King of France, 96
Chibok girls, 238
China, 11, 19, 188-190, 191-193, 220, 233, 238, 244, 251, 255, 271-272, 318
China Monthly Magazine, 190, 191
Christian Aid, 16, 288, 289, 324
Christianity, 24-26, 82-83, 111, 151, 200, 239, 249, 260, 271, 289, 317, 320

Church Mission Society (CMS), 14-16, 273-288, 297, 323-324
Church of England, 143, 267-269, 271, 316
Clifford, Dr John, 199
Clifford, Jeremy, 19
CNN, 239, 265, 266
Cochlaeus, 109
Cohen, Nick, 236
Collins, Tony, 11
Columbus, Christopher, 110
Commandments, The Ten, 15, 290, 326
Confessions (Augustine), 65, 66, 67, 68, 130
Cop, Nicolas, 127
Coranto, 149
Cosby, William, 185
Coverdale, Miles, 140, 311
Craftsman, The, 172-173
Cromwell, Oliver, 156, 161, 201

Daily Courant, The, 149
Daily Mail, The, 266
Daily Star, The, 266
Damon, Dan, 11
Dante Alighieri, 94, 83
Davies, Nick, 34, 35, 36, 39
De Imitatione Christi (à Kempis), 130
Defoe, Daniel, 98, 121, 163-166, 167-170, 172, 176, 177, 186, 210, 247, 251
Delacroix, Eugene, 260
de Villiers, Fleur, 7, 12
Dibaj, Mehdi, 23
Dickens, Arthur Geoffrey, 308
Dickinson, Jonathan, 186
discourse, 43-44, 46, 48-49, 50, 52, 54, 155, 172, 210, 226, 303, 304

Dominion (Holland), 1
Doom, Ruddy, 323
Downing Street, 18, 251, 253, 263, 284, 298
Duffy, Eamon, 112
Duranty, Walter, 37, 39-40
Dynasty (Holland), 1

Early Day Motions, 285
Ecclesiastes, 130
editing software, 38
Egeland, Jan, 16, 17, 276, 284, 286, 287, 288, 302
Eisenstein, Elizabeth, 92, 99
Elector of Saxony, 101, 108, 110
Eliot, Revd Professor Charles, 12, 249
Ellis, Stephen, 296
Elton, G. R., 308
Emmaus, disciples on road to, 215-216
Erasmus, Desiderius, 94, 111, 112-113
Essay upon Projects (Defoe), 169
European Union, 17, 287
Evening Standard, The, 27

Fawcett, Millicent, 197
Ferdinand and Isabella, 110
Fjeldstad, Revd Dr Arne, 11, 266
Flat Earth News (Davies), 36
Flodden, Battle of, 141
Flugschriften, 120, 123
FOMO, 127
Fonte, Richard W, 317
Forster, John, 299
Francis, Pope, 82, 300
Frank, Joseph, 148
Frederick the Wise, Elector of Saxony, 96, 101, 108, 109, 120
Freud, Sigmund, 211

Frosh, Paul, 302
Fust, Johann, 91, 92, 93

Gaius, 72
Garabedian, Mitchell, 230
Garber, Steven, 250
Gatehouse, Gabriel, 271
Geldof, Bob, 16, 17, 257, 321
Genette, Gérard, 312
Gentleman›s Magazine, The, 173
George I, 172
George III, 175
Gersony, Robert, 274, 276, 292, 323, 325
Gipir and Labongo, 274
Gledhill, Ruth, 266
Global Media Freedom conference, 252
God, 45-54, 65-68, 104-106, 133-135, 151-154, 180-184, 296, 303-308, 312-319
Gongbao, Wanguo, 191, 192
Good Friday, 240, 241, 270
Good Morning Scotland, 282
Gordon, General, 198
Graham, Billy, 27
Gratian, 73
Green, Bartholomew, 184-185
Green Stick, The (Muggeridge), 302
Greenbelt, 286
Gregory the Great, St, 229
Gulu, 16-18, 275, 277, 278, 280, 282, 286-288, 290, 293, 294, 323-325
Gunton, Colin, 232
Guptara, Prabhu, 12
Gutenberg, Johannes, 87-94, 119, 123, 189, 190

Habermas, Jurgen, 173, 176

340 INDEX

Hack Attack (Davies), 34, 302
Hamilton, 185, 186
Hammurabi, 48
Hannah Shah, 264, 265, 266
Haroun, Lana, 253
Harris, Benjamin, 182-184
Harvard College, 181
Heawood, Jonathan, 30, 35-36, 157, 233-234, 302
Heidegger, Martin, 217
Henworth, Thomas, 153
Herder, Gottfried, 49
Hilsum, Lindsey, 271, 285
Hitler, 37
Holland, Tom, 1, 11, 271
Holodomor, 37, 236
Holy Spirit, The, 52, 275, 279, 283, 291, 323, 325
Holyoake, George Jacob, 212
Houses of Parliament, 174
Hunt, Jeremy, 252
Hus, Jan, 85, 86, 110

Illustrious Providences (Mather), 181, 182
Independent, The, 263, 265, 266
India 187-188, 223-234, 254-256, 321-322
Inner Cities Religious Council, The, 25
Innocent III, Pope, 72
Institutes of the Christian Religion (Calvin), 127, 133
International Criminal Court (ICC), 289-290
International Parliament of World Religions, 292
Iraq, 14, 276, 287, 302, 325
Isbister, Dr Nick, 11
Isaiah, 54
Islam, 23, 24, 89, 188, 194, 239, 251, 255-270, 296, 319-320, 326

Jesus, the Christ, of Nazareth, 52, 61-62, 215-216, 269-270, 294, 305, 311, 317
John, St., 57, 72, 133, 250
Jones, Dylan, 27
Jones, Gareth, 37-38, 236
Journal of the Plague Year (Defoe), 167, 168
Joyce, James, 217
Junius, Letters of, 175

Kampala, 16, 17, 277, 284, 287, 289, 297, 323
Kang Yu Wei, 192
Kautsky, Karl, 227
Keay, Anna, 313
Khartoum, 253
Kihangire, Msgr Cipriano, 323
King James Version of the Bible, The, 140
King's African Rifles, 274
Kirby Laing Centre for Theology in Public Life, 1, 11
Kitgum, 14-18, 276-278, 282, 286-288, 291, 297, 323-325
Knight, Mark, 315
Kony, Joseph, 14-18, 275-276, 289-291, 295, 297, 323, 325-326
Koresh, David, 16, 283

Lakwena, Alice, 275, 277, 323
language, 18, 44-52, 139-140, 188, 212, 241, 273, 298-299, 303-304, 308, 315, 317
Lapido Media, 10, 11, 251-253, 263, 265-271
Lawson, Dominic, 263-266, 270

Lebedev, 27
Lejeune, Philippe, 312
Lemanski, Dominic, 271
Lenin, Vladimir, 227
Levine, Bernard, 22, 23
Lezard, Nicholas, 271
Lippmann, Walter, 222, 299, 300
London, 11, 25-27, 195-201, 313-317, 325
London Gazette, The, 160, 161
Londonistan (Phillips), 253
London Post, The, 183-184
Lord's Resistance Army (LRA), 14-18, 273-277, 286-290, 292, 301, 323-325
Lucius III, Pope, 81
Luther, Martin, 86-88, 90, 97-109, 111-115
Lyotard, Jean-François, 235

MacIntyre, Alasdair, 218
Maiden Tribute of Modern Babylon, The (Stead), 194-196, 200
Mainz, 87, 90, 92
Mair, Kristi, 259, 265
Mangalwadi, Vishal, 11, 302
Marprelate, Martin, 143
Marshall, Paul, 1, 248, 271, 321
Martin, David, 26, 317
Mary Magdalene, 57-58, 244
Mattey, Jenny, 11
McDowell's Journal, 243
McGregor, Neil, 88
McLuhan, Marshall, 109
Meek, Esther, 230-233, 245-246, 257, 299, 319
Milton, John, 82, 134, 156-158, 177, 220
Minto, William, 169
Moi, President (Kenya), 275

Monbiot, George, 242
Mongar, 205
Montgomerie, Tim, 36
Moreno Ocampo, Luis, 289
Morley, John, 197-198
Morrison, Richard, 190-193
Morton, Charles, 164
Mother Teresa, 40, 229
Mothers' Union, 282, 325
Mr Jones, 38, 236
Muddiman, Henry, 160
Muggeridge, Malcolm, 38-41, 43
Mullin, Chris, 285
Murray, Douglas, 271
musahar, 254
Museveni, 274-277, 280, 283, 289-297, 326

Nankabirwa, Ruth, 279
Nation, The, 242
Naughtie, James, 16, 282-283
Navasky, Victor, 242
Nazir-Ali, Bishop Michael, 263, 265
Nedham, Marchamont, 161, 313
Nelson, Fraser, 271
Neutrality or Truth: Reporting Religion Post-7/7, 264
Newbigin, Lesslie, 215-216, 221, 270
New England, 9, 137, 179, 181, 185, 315
News Corps, The, 34
News Futures 2035, 19, 262
News of the World, The, 35
Newspapers, 9, 12, 37-40, 148-149, 159-161, 172-176, 183-187, 237-238, 243-244, 266-267, 299-302, 312-313, 315-316
New York, 211, 243, 249-250, 301-

302, 315-316, 319, 321
New York Herald, The, 198
New York Journal, The, 38
New York Times, The, 37, 39
New York Weekly Journal, The, 185
Nineteen Eighty-Four (Orwell), 39
Niringiye, Revd Dr David Zac, 289, 295
Norris, Clive, 227
Northern Echo, The, 198
Northern Uganda, 14-18, 273-278, 282-283, 286-289, 291-302, 321-326
Novum Organon (Bacon), 131
Nyeko, Caesar Poblicks, 18, 290, 298

Obote, 274, 292, 323
Ochola Baker, Bishop Macleord, 292
Odysseus, 59-60
Ojwang, Benjamin, 15, 17-18, 282-285, 288, 291, 298, 302
Ojwang, Margaret, 278
Okello Lutwa, General Tito, 274
Okot, Aldo, 284
Olasky, Marvin, 1, 159, 161, 181, 184-186, 243, 271, 299, 315, 319
Onono Onweng, Bishop Nelson, 290
Operation Infinite Reach, 15
Operation Iron First, 277-278
Oracle of Reason, The (Southwell), 210
Orombi, Archbishop Henry Luke, 288, 290
Orwell, George, 33-34, 39, 300
Ovid, 65-66, 69, 74

Owen, Robert, 212
Oyelowo, David, 283, 285
Ozment, Steven, 113, 309

Pabbo, 289
Pain, Dennis, 323
Palestine, 92, 195, 276, 287, 325
Pall Mall Gazette, The, 197-198, 316
Palmer, Parker, 261, 319-320
Pamphilus seu de Amora, 123
pamphlets as precursors to newspapers, 119-124; definition and format of, 122-123; foundational role in journalism, 122-125; religious content of early, 123-124
Paradise Lost (Milton), 135, 310
paratexts, 150-154, 179-180, 261, 312
Parliament, 145-146, 158-159, 173-176, 268, 285, 294, 313-314
Paxman, Jeremy, 251
Penfold, Peter, 11
Penry, John, 143
Pentecost, 51-52, 111, 136
Pepys, Samuel, 160
Persian Fire (Holland), 1
Petrarch, 81, 83
Pettegree, Andrew, 90, 121, 142, 176, 306-307, 309, 311, 313-314, 316
Phillips, Melanie, 253, 271
Photography, 38
Pinchevski, Amit, 302
pillorying, 165-166
Pius II, Pope, 93
Plato, 82, 130
Plumbline, 243

Pollock, Sheldon, 48, 304
Porritt, Richard, 11
Press Association, The, 267
Press Complaints Commission, The, 225-226
Printing, 50, 87-99, 107-113, 119-126, 136-148, 150, 155-163, 188-193, 209-210, 261-262, 315-317, 321-322
printing press, arrival in England, 137-138; invention of, 84-92; religious uses of, 87-92
Prodigal Press (Olasky and Cole Smith), 320
prophecy, definition and origins of, 43-55; connection to journalism, 43-44, 46, 47-48, 50-51, 54-55, 176-177
prophets as creators of Hebrew language, 46-47; role in early journalism, 177
public opinion, formation of, 172-175
public sphere, emergence of, 172-176
Puritanism, influence on early journalists, 163-170, 177

Reformation, impact on journalism, 111-117, 137-144; *See also* Luther, Martin; Protestantism
religious literacy in journalism, 247-253
Renaissance, 82-83
royal control of printing, 141-142

Savonarola, Girolamo, 95-98
secularization, definition of, 209-213; impact on journalism, 209-215

sermons as precursors to newspapers, 179-185; in New England, 180-185
Siedentop, Larry, 72-73
spirituality, importance in journalism, 247-253
St. Paul's Cathedral, role in early English news, 144-147
Stead, W.T., 194-202
Steiner, George, 239-241

Taylor, Charles, 261
Thamesdown Council for Racial Equality (TCRE), 223-227
truth in journalism, 241-246; versus neutrality, 241-246
Tyndale, William, 138-140

Uganda, Northern "Break the Silence" campaign, 14-18, 273-298

vernacular languages, development of, 44-48; impact on journalism, 44-48, 139-140

Waldenses, 80-82
Weber, Max, 128, 210
Wycliffe, John, 85-86

Zenger, John Peter, 185-186

Pippa Rann Books
and
Global Resilience Publishing
(imprints of **Salt Desert Media Group Ltd., U.K.)**

SALT DESERT MEDIA GROUP LTD., U.K., was established in 2019, and currently publishes under the imprints, Pippa Rann Books and Media and Global Resilience Publishing.

Pippa Rann Books and Media publishes books about India and the Indian diaspora, for everyone who has an interest in the sub-Continent, it's peoples and cultures. At a time of political challenge, Pippa Rann books aim to nurture the values of democracy, liberty, equality and fraternity that inspired the founders of the modern state of India.

Titles on the Global Resilience Publishing list explore how global challenges can be addressed and resolved with an inter-disciplinary and transnational approach. The imprint focuses on subjects such as Climate Change, the Global Financial System, Multilateral and Corporate Governance, etc. In addition to its own publications, Salt Desert Media provides distribution services in English-speaking territories for several authors and publishers.

Sales and Distribution:
- India and SE Asia: Penguin Random House India
- Canada and the USA: Trafalgar Square Press (https://www.ipgbook.com/)
- UK: LSS (Sales) Contact: Andrew Wormleighton (andrew@lionsalesservices.com)
- Rest of World/Rights: Prologue Sales
  Contact: Rob Wendover (rob@prologuesales.com)
  Distribution: Marston Book Services above